STOCK CARS!

AMERICA'S MOST POPULAR MOTORSPORT

JOHN CAROLLO & BILL HOLDER

HPBooks

HPBooks
are published by
The Berkley Publishing Group
A division of Penguin Putnam Inc.
375 Hudson Street
New York, New York 10014

First Edition: June 1999

Library of Congress Cataloging-in-Publication Data

Carollo, John A., 1950-
    Stock cars! : America's most popular motorsport /
John Carollo & Bill Holder. — 1st ed.
        p. cm.
    Includes index.
    ISBN 1-55788-308-4
    1. Stock car racing—United States. I. Holder, William G., 1937 – II.
Title.
    GV1029.9.S74 H65   1999
    796.72' 0973—dc21   99-11884
                                                                                            CIP

Cover design by Bird Studios
Book design and production by Michael Lutfy
Interior photos by the authors unless otherwise noted
Cover photo by Bob Fairman

CONTENTS

ABOUT THE AUTHORS

BILL HOLDER

Bill Holder is a retired Aerospace Engineer from the Foreign Technology Division at Wright Patterson Air Force Base in Dayton, Ohio. Over the past three decades, he has been an active freelance aviation and motorsports writer. He is the author of hundreds of articles for dozens of magazines. Bill also has written nearly four dozen aviation and automotive books. Some of his book efforts have been used to generate funds for injured drivers as well as auto racing museum preservation. His real love is stock car racing, where he is a contributing writer to *Stock Car Racing* magazine.

Bill also loves to own old race cars. To date, he has personally restored three historic sprint cars driven by Jeff Gordon in his younger days. He lives with his wife Ruthanne in Riverside, Ohio.

JOHN CAROLLO

John Carollo is an internationally published automotive writer and photographer whose work has been seen in over 75 different auto-related publications. John has over three decades of racing involvement and lists his best asset as being a race fan first and foremost. He started out as a stock car driver and owner before going on to positions in racing organizations such as flagman, announcer and PR duties. From there, he started his own automotive communications business helping corporations gain exposure using racing as a marketing tool. He has written regular columns on racing for newspapers as well as magazines. His racing journalism won the prestigious Automobile Racing Club of America National Motorsports Media Award.

John's love for stock cars is joined by his interest and writing in the areas of street rods, customs, and modern, off road and classic trucks. He resides in Willoughby, Ohio where his non-auto interest is old house restoration.

Both authors would like to express their gratitude to the Daytona Racing Archives and the Charlotte Motor Speedway Media Department for their support.

FOREWORD

There aren't many people in this world who get to do what I do, which is drive stock cars for a living. Not only do I race a top Winston Cup stock car, but I also race many other types of stock cars every chance I get. I do this not only for the sheer enjoyment of it, but also because it keeps me in touch with what is happening at the grassroots level of our sport. In this way, I can keep an eye out for any up and coming talent who may end up racing against me some day on the Winston Cup tour!

Another reason I race whenever I can is to look for new racing technology. Just because the Winston Cup series is at the top of the sport, it doesn't mean that we invent all the new ideas. Many come from innovative amateurs who have the time to test new parts and setups at a local track, something we don't always have the luxury of doing. These guys, like all of us in Winston Cup, are constantly seeking that one small advantage that will make them more competitive, no matter what class or division they race. Many great ideas have been developed in this way and been implemented in our series. That's what racing is all about.

The world of stock car racing has become so vast and exists on so many levels, that it is difficult to cover every aspect of it. It seems like there's a class of stock car for any driver, no matter their age, experience, skill or budget. Stock car racing, while hardly organized under any one official sanctioning body, still provides many opportunities for someone to start out and work their way up. There isn't a single driver on the Winston Cup tour today who started out there. All of us have had to pay our dues on small, local tracks—dirt, pavement or usually both. Most of us have driven all types of stock cars, from Late Models to Modifieds on these 1/4 to 1/2 mile "bullrings." And each week, millions of fans travel to these local tracks to witness these little battles. Sometimes the names are different for the same type of car, which can get confusing, but the racing is always exciting, interesting and intensely competitive.

That's the way it has been for the first 50 years of NASCAR, and now, as the organization enters its second 50 years, there's more interest in our sport than ever before. It has grown beyond anyone's wildest dreams

since those first days on the dusty and gritty fairgrounds of the early '40s. Today races are battled on superspeedways like Daytona and Talladega, with more than 100,000 fans in attendance, and millions more watching on TV. The more fans our sport attracts, the more they want to know how all of this began, which is the purpose of this book.

Stock Cars! is not necessarily a race-by-race account of "who won what where in what kind of car." Instead, it is an overview, illustrated with hundreds of rare and historical photographs, that offers some of the many highlights that have helped this sport to grow and evolve.

These highlights include a look at the early days, before NASCAR was born, when "jalopies" stormed local tracks and fairgrounds, driven like they were never intended to be. The results were often unpredictable and hair-raising to say the least. Then there is a look at the very first days of NASCAR, at some of the technical details of the most significant cars and engines as they evolved over the years to the 200 mph Winston Cup cars of today.

In another section, you'll get a rundown on the many forms stock car racing takes other than the Winston Cup. There are many grassroots, entry level series with just as many types of cars and rules. After reading this section, you'll soon have a sense of what I'm talking about, and perhaps a better understanding of the support races and series where many of us professional drivers got our start.

The tracks throughout the years have played a large role in shaping our sport. Many have their own personality, and have become legends in themselves. There's hardly a person in this country who, upon hearing the word "Daytona," doesn't think of the 500 and the superspeedway.

Then there are the people behind this sport who have made it what it is today. Many of the people profiled in the following pages are ones I have known personally, raced against, or wish I had. All of them are legendary figures in this sport who have contributed to its rich heritage in their own special way.

Stock car racing offers so much to its fans. It is not only fun to watch, but it is also fun to participate in. The drivers and stars of NASCAR are very accessible to their fans, more so than any other sport in the world. We make a big effort to show our appreciation, because without you, we simply wouldn't be able to do what we do. For over 50 years stock car racing has served up thrills, spills and chills that have delighted millions of people, and its growth and popularity show no sign of slowing down—it is definitely here to stay. I'm just glad to be a part of it.

Ken Schrader
June 1999

THE WORLD OF STOCK CAR RACING 1

There have been several sports of the 20th century that have been nurtured and developed to the point of national obsession. Baseball, football and basketball top the list. However, along with these "stick and ball" sports, you'd have to consider the sport of stock car racing, which has experienced phenomenal growth in the last several decades that is truly unbelievable. From the first dirt track jalopy races to the million dollar races of today, it has been a wild, crazy, action-packed ride to the top. Today, stock car racing is considered to be the world's most popular form of motor-sport, and one of the fastest growing sports of all types in the United States.

Unlike some other American sports, stock car racing didn't always enjoy the respect of the public at large. This was partly due to the perception, somewhat founded in truth, that stock car drivers honed their skills by running bootlegged moonshine during the years of Prohibition, and across state lines throughout the '30s and '40s to avoid state-to-state taxes, especially in the Southeast. This ill-fated reputation persisted for years, becoming ever more distorted with each retelling, until the legend outgrew the truth.

Then there was the opinion that race car

Stock car racing has been around for almost as long as the automobile. But the top of the sport is the NASCAR Winston Cup. It's one of the most popular sports in the U.S., and is now a multi-billion dollar a year industry, with races and TV coverage all over the world.

"To be a stock car driver, you had to be a little 'off,' or so the thinking went."

Early stock cars were nothing more than stripped-down used jalopies with a few modifications to toughen them up, such as this bumper guard and side rub rails.

drivers were somewhat crazy, that they had a death wish. After all, who in their right mind would take a perfectly good automobile, put hours of work into it and race it as fast as they could go around a circle at great risk, without getting much in return? In those days, crashes were quite common, and safety was not even considered, so injuries were severe and deaths were more common. To be a stock car driver, you had to be a little "off," or so the thinking went.

Stock car drivers need nerves of steel to sling a car around high banking, inches apart, at nearly 200 mph. Shown above in the #12 AMC Matador is one of the best, Bobby Allison. This is at Charlotte Motor Speedway in 1979. Photo by Mike Slade.

Although it exists in several forms, stock car racing has flourished under the direction of the France family since 1947, when family patriarch Bill Sr. formed the National Association for Stock Car Auto Racing, known commonly as NASCAR. By keeping a close rein on rules to make sure the cars remained equal, France ensured that the competition would always be close, right up until the final laps. Few will argue that the NASCAR Winston Cup is perhaps the most competitive series in the world.

The Sanctioning Bodies

Much of the credit for the state of stock car racing today goes to Bill France Sr. and his son, Bill Jr. The elder France was the first to organize the sport by forming NASCAR, the National Association for Stock Car Auto Racing, in 1947. He created a racing formula, a series and strict rules to keep competition tight. Although NASCAR remains the dominant sanctioning body of the sport,

Economy Modifieds are just one level of the vast world of stock car racing. These racers are relatively easy to construct and a great way to start out circle track racing. Many top drivers have.

The Automobile Racing Club of America (ARCA) is another stock car association that is also responsible for the growth of this sport. As you can see, the cars are very similar to their Winston Cup cousins.

with many different regions and levels, there are many others as well.

Following the NASCAR formula in the early 1950s, several organizations in other parts of the country were created and utilized race car specs very similar to NASCAR. That allowed drivers to run many of the races under different sanctioning bodies with the same cars. Organizations such as the Automobile Racing Club of America (ARCA) and the International

Motor Contest Association (IMCA) joined the already established United States Auto Club (USAC) and raced similarly equipped cars. At that time, USAC was already very successful at open wheel cars with the Indianapolis 500 and the USAC Champ car circuits. It was easy for USAC to create a stock car division because many of the Indycar drivers and teams had experience with stock cars. This also allowed USAC to run companion events, offering fans more variety at the track. With similar rules, drivers were now available to compete in races in various parts of the country, focusing on the races that paid the most money. Today, however, ARCA is the only organization offering racing for stock cars similar to NASCAR. IMCA and USAC are still around, but they race Modified and other open wheel cars only.

It's interesting to note that stock car racing was first contested mainly on dirt, using horse tracks and county fairgrounds. These eventually gave way to multi-million-dollar facilities with 2 1/2 mile ovals, condos, private boxes, and seating for over 100,000 fans. A few organizations, notably ARCA, hold races on both pavement and dirt tracks,

Stock car racing has crossed the border into Canada. The Canadian Association of Stock Car Auto Racing (CASCAR) is the sanctioning body, and closely follows NASCAR in rules, format and races. Shown here are some of CASCAR's top competitors.

ranging in size from 1/4 mile "bull rings" to the awesome 2 1/2 mile superspeedways like Talladega and Daytona.

The International Scene—While stock car racing has its roots firmly planted in American soil, it has migrated to other parts of the world. Race-crazy Australia has long raced stock cars, both dirt and pavement, and regularly runs major stock car events on their Thunderdome NASCAR-type superspeedway. Japan also has a huge interest in stock car racing, and has hosted an exhibition stock car race, featuring top Winston Cup teams, for a number of years. What started out as an exhibition event on an already existing road course in Japan ended up going on to the creation of a dedicated oval track and the first NASCAR oval race ever in the Pacific in 1998. Someday, NASCAR racing in foreign countries may even become commonplace.

Canada has a surprising number of stock car tracks, and stages competitive races under a number of Canadian and U.S. stock

car sanctioning bodies. However, the commercial growth of the sport in Canada is being severely hampered by legislation regulating alcohol and tobacco sponsorship.

Grassroots Racing

One main reason for the rapid growth and success of stock car racing is its accessibility to just about anyone. Unlike Indycars or Formula One, where there really is only one very expensive level to race, stock car racing

Stock car racing offers grassroots racing on so many levels, that there's a class to suit just about any budget. That's one reason for its growth and success. These are Dirt Late Models at Cherokee Speedway in Gaffney, South Carolina, one of over 800 short tracks in the U.S. Tony Hammett photo.

Truck racing is the fastest growing segment of NASCAR racing. Aside from the Craftsman Truck series, which features full-race-prepped full-size trucks, there are other mini-truck classes that have been cropping up in various regions.

The Northeast Modified Division, most popular in New England, is the oldest of NASCAR's classes. It is just one more example of the different levels of stock car racing. Courtesy Flemington Speed-way.

has many different classes, designed to accommodate just about any budget or skill level. There are over 800 short tracks in the United States that run local, Saturday night "run whatcha brung" races for fun, glory and perhaps a T-shirt, trophy or a refund on the entry fee. The classes that run vary greatly from track to track, but there is always a beginner class or two to encourage new drivers into the sport. Many of these local stock car tracks have been in place for many decades. They vary from modern facilities with all the amenities, to not much more than ovals carved from dirt back in the boonies. Such is the nature of this sport!

One thing about modern stock car racing is the huge number of different types of race cars that fall under that umbrella. There are a number of classes that use economical

four-cylinder engines. Then, there are classes where the V6 engine has been used, and of course, the popular V8. Although the V8 engine has nearly disappeared on America's highways, it is the dominant engine used in stock car racing. There's nothing like cubic inches when it comes to power.

Although stock cars have been just that—cars—NASCAR officials were wise enough to see that more people were buying trucks than cars, and therefore devised the NASCAR Craftsman Truck series, which debuted in 1995. There are now several other racing truck series sanctioned by the NAMARS (North American Midget Auto Racing Series) and ARCA organizations that are becoming popular. Truck racing is the fastest growing segment of stock car racing. And with good reason. Truck sales account for slightly over half of all new vehicle sales today.

But there are other series as well. One of the more popular are the Legends and Dwarf cars, which resemble scaled down versions of Ford and Chevy coupes from the '30s and '40s. These miniature racers, which often run as supporting races to major Busch and Winston Cup events, are priced at a very affordable $10,000 to $12,000 range. The Legend cars are the tip of the iceberg when

Where there's a will, there's a way. To go stock car racing, all you need is some good duct tape and something with four wheels and an engine.

"Although the V8 engine has nearly disappeared on America's highways, it is the dominant engine used in stock car racing. There's nothing like cubic inches when it comes to power."

it comes to smaller-than-street-size race cars. There are quite a variety of cars with both national and regional sanctioning bodies, again allowing a number of opportunities for racers of all ages and economic backgrounds. It's grassroots racing at its best.

Legends cars were created by Bruton Smith and Humpy Wheeler at Charlotte, but the series has taken off and is now national. The cost is minimal, and the fun factor is very high. It's also great training.

7

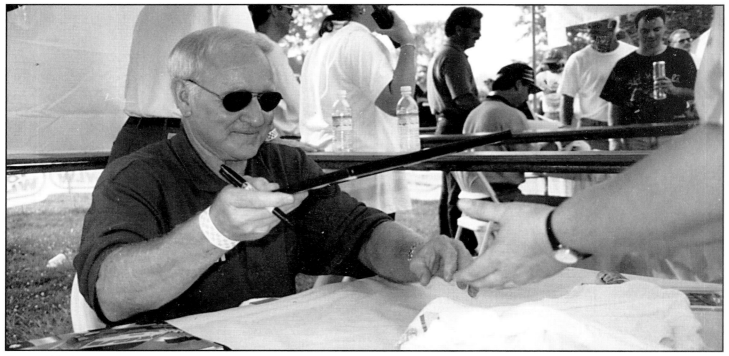

Former NASCAR champ Cale Yarborough retired from driving in 1988, and now owns his own team. All that matters little to his legions of loyal fans, and Cale takes time to sign autographs whenever he can. NASCAR is one of the most fan-friendly sports in the world. The "stars" are very accessible to their fans, and hold frequent autograph sessions like this one at every race.

It takes more to be a top driver on the Winston Cup circuit today than just being fast. Drivers must be articulate and representative of their corporate sponsors. Often, they must give speeches and make numerous public appearances. They are also often interviewed on TV. Drivers like Dale Earnhardt have turned their racing success into multi-million dollar enterprises that include licensing, merchandising, other racing teams and a many other types of business.

The Stars

Today's top Winston Cup drivers are revered by their fans much the same as top basketball, baseball and football stars are by theirs. That same recognition and respect has been a long time coming for racers. And because of this stardom, the professional stock car driver has had to evolve over the years. It used to be okay if you were a "good ol' boy," and lived hard to drive hard. But today's driver must be as comfortable in the latest Armani suit as he is in Nomex. He is much more than a driver; he just may be the public representative of a Fortune 500 company. Today's top drivers must be presentable and articulate, able to speak at public functions and corporate meetings with ease. They are often called upon to act in commercials and public service announcements. It no longer is just a matter of showing up on Friday and driving all-out all weekend.

But like all big stars, the drivers must answer to their fans first. Most of the top drivers have national fan clubs and websites.

Although today's stock car drivers don't make near the salary that their peers do in football, basketball or baseball, they still do pretty well. Salary, bonuses, contingency prize money and endorsements can add up quickly into the millions per year. One incentive is the "No Bull 5," which used to be called the Winston Million. It guarantees a $1 million dollar bonus to the winner of certain events, two of which were won by Jeff Gordon in 1998.

Avid fans will wait many hours for a ten second meeting and a personal autograph. Stock car drivers are the most fan-friendly and accessible athletes of any sport. Many drivers have been noted for their accessibility and charitable efforts. The tracks are designed so that fans can wander in the garage area after a race to get close to their drivers, unlike other sports. When is the last time you were allowed to walk onto a football field?

Big-name drivers are definitely compensated well with salary, but nowhere near what some of today's top athletes in other sports are paid. Drivers are often paid with a combination of salary and a percentage of their prize money, which means they have to perform well to earn big money. This is definitely unlike other sports. If Michael Jordan goes scoreless for 10 games, he still gets his full pay. If a driver crashes 10 races in a row, he loses a significant part of his income, not

to mention maybe his ride for the next year. Many top driving contracts are negotiated on a year-by-year basis, with renewal and bonuses largely based on performance.

But that doesn't mean drivers don't do well. For example, consider the special promotional races and bonuses devised by Winston and NASCAR to keep fan and driver interest high. In 1985, RJ Reynolds, the biggest sponsor of NASCAR, introduced the Winston Million. If a driver won three of four races in a single season—the Daytona 500, the Winston 500 at Talladega, the Coca Cola World 600 at Charlotte and the Mountain Dew Southern 500 at Darlington—Winston paid a $1 million dollar bonus on top of all the other prize money. Bill Elliott won it the first year, but no one else would until Jeff Gordon in 1997, the program's last year.

In 1998, a new promotion replaced the Winston Million and has proved to be even

Stock car racing is definitely big business. Increased TV coverage and fan attendance has made racing a cost-effective marketing tool, even though primary sponsorship, where one company is prominently displayed like these above, can cost in excess of $10 million per year.

the fans. Not only do they get to watch the added competition, but they too could win a million dollars by entering a national sweepstakes program based on the results. For 1999, that fifth No Bull 5 race was moved to Las Vegas and the West Coast market.

Then there is the Winston Cup points fund, awarded at the annual banquet, that pays a bonus to the top 25 teams. It was set up in 1971 with a then-unheard-of sum of $100,000, and has since grown to total over $5 million dollars. Typically, the Winston Cup Champion receives $2 million in addition to the prize money. To contrast just how far the sport has gone, consider this: In 1997, while earning his second Winston Cup title, Jeff Gordon took home over $6 million, a new record. By comparison, the "Golden Boy," Fred Lorenzen, set a record in 1963 when he won a whopping $113,000. Hardly enough to cover the cost of tires, fuel and basic expenses for a typical race weekend today.

Stock Car Racing as Big Business

Although corporate America has long recognized the value of racing as an effective marketing tool, the amount of involvement is much, much higher than it has ever been. When R.J. Reynolds signed on as the series sponsor in 1971, they started a corporate marriage that would develop into a self-contained industry. Stock car racing is now "big business," with an economic impact that reaches the lives of every community that hosts a Winston Cup event. When the NASCAR circus rolls into town, tens of millions of dollars are spent in the community.

As a result, many communities are building race tracks just as they do baseball or football stadiums to lure the circuit to their area. In the 1990s, there was an explosion of new superspeedways. Tracks have recently been constructed in California, Colorado, Florida, Nevada and Texas. Granted, there will be other types of race cars besides stock cars running on these new ovals, but few

more popular with fans and teams alike. It's called the "No Bull 5," a $10 million plan where qualified drivers in five races will each have a chance for an additional $1 million dollar bonus. The races involved are the same as the Winston Million with another event added, the Brickyard 400 at the Indianapolis Motor Speedway. Five drivers are qualified for each event and if one wins the race the $1 million dollar prize is awarded. But there's more involved that includes

Women account for over 40% of NASCAR's fans, which is one reason why there are more sponsors for household goods, like Cheerios and Hot Wheels toys. Fans are very loyal to the product that sponsors their favorite driver, a fact not lost on corporations. Bob Fairman photo.

"It wasn't too long ago that top teams had to go begging each year to get the minimal funds to compete just one car for one season. How things have changed."

(except perhaps Indycars) can draw crowds like the stock cars.

TV race coverage has increased to the point where every Winston Cup race, and most Busch Grand National and Craftsman Truck races are televised nationally on network or cable. Ratings have continued to increase significantly in the '90s, by as much as 30% each year.

ARCA and the Midwestern-based short track series, the American Speed Association (ASA), are also seen on national cable channels, and many local cable stations will air their hometown dirt or pave-

ment short track event. Also, many of the bigger races are repeated later in the day on certain stations after initially being carried live. But race coverage isn't the only TV exposure that stock car racing gets. There are a number of stock car-related talk shows that cover the sport inside and out. And the TV race fan can always tune in for plenty of results of the races missed.

Such increased TV exposure, along with the demographic profile of the typical NASCAR fan (over 40% are women), has attracted the attention of just about every major corporation in America. It wasn't too

Model cars, both plastic and die-cast, are also extremely popular, including those other than Winston Cup, like these dirt track cars.

How big has sponsorship money become? Just ask this man. Bill Broderick had one job, and that was to make sure the winning driver was wearing the appropriate hat in the winner's circle after the race, a job he did for more than 28 years. Sometimes, he had to change hats several times during the interview. According to Bill, there was a list of hats to be worn in specific order, for a specific amount of time. "Ten years ago, I thought corporate involvement had reached its peak," he says. "But boy, was I ever wrong."

long ago that top teams had to go begging each year to get the necessary funds to compete one car for one season.

How things have changed. Today, stock car racing is a multi-billion dollar industry, and there is a long waiting list of companies dying to sponsor a car. A top team can pretty much pick and choose if they need a new sponsor.

When a non-auto-related business gets involved with racing, they usually have increased sales in mind for their investment. Once they are familiar with racing, they quickly learn about the intense loyalty race fans have about their sport. This fierce, almost fanatical brand and product loyalty carries over to their consumer shopping. Drivers are often identified strongly with certain brands: Richard Petty is STP, Terry Labonte is Kellogg's Corn Flakes or Budweiser, Rusty Wallace is Miller Lite, and so on. Any serious fan can tell you this, a fact not lost on the sponsors.

When Bill Elliott fans buy fast food, they might be inclined to choose his sponsor McDonald's over the others, because they want to support the company that supports their favorite driver.

The other side of the coin is the reverse buying trend. Some race fans go so far as to avoid buying the products of a competitors sponsor. With several like products on the race circuit, the off-track buying is often as intense as the on-track racing. And race fans will often choose a product that is involved in racing over one that is not. Such long-standing racing partnerships have very noticeable results in the marketplace.

The relationship between automotive brand and a particular driver is also very strong. It is well-known that Jeff Gordon and Terry Labonte both drive Chevrolets, while Bill Elliott has long fielded Fords. Chances are, their most loyal fans wouldn't think about driving, much less cheering, anything else. Both Ford and GM slug it out every Sunday, following the old adage "Win

Like other sports, there is a vast merchandising side to the business of stock car racing. Drivers license their name, image, car, car number—and put it on anything and everything. Many of the top drivers have their own mobile store, like John Andretti, shown above. Also, to stretch their marketing dollar, sponsors pay to have a "show car" built, which is a mocked-up version of the actual race car. Many of these cars lack expensive racing equipment, and some don't even have engines. These show cars travel the country making appearances at car shows and other events. At left is Andretti's show car owned by Cale Yarborough.

on Sunday, sell on Monday!"

Then there is the merchandising side of the sport. Every car, driver, number and logo is licensed. The NASCAR emblem appears on clothing, books, model cars, trading cards, coolers, and a variety of games and toys. There is even a growing chain of NASCAR-themed restaurants, similar to the Hard Rock Cafe and Planet Hollywood chains. Some of the biggest drivers have trademarked themselves, and license their names and likeness on a variety of products.

Future Winston Cup Champion? Maybe. But he's definitely a lifelong fan.

"It all adds up to over 50 years of thrills, spills and chills."

Many have full-time business managers, publicists and marketing staffs to manage their fame.

No matter what the actual cost (a good estimate is at least $10 million per single car team per season for primary sponsoship), it is quickly justified. Companies are fully aware of the value of having their name on TV for a three-hour race. A 30-second TV spot on a NASCAR event may cost as much as $250,000. But if you're leading the race for three hours, with the camera on your car for most of that time, how much is that worth? It's easy to figure out.

It all adds up to over 50 years of thrills, spills and chills. There have been many times when racing looked certain to be legislated out of existence, such as during the oil crisis of '73. At the time, some government entity did a study on all the gas that could be saved if the fans no longer drove to the races, a ludicrous idea. Even now, there is talk of forbidding tobacco companies to sponsor motorsports because of all the air time they receive. But if the tobacco companies can't advertise, there are scores of companies waiting in line to step up. Racing has become too big to stop, and it will most certainly survive well into the next century. No one knows what they will be racing then, but one thing is for sure, the racing will be close.

THE BIRTH OF STOCK CAR RACING 2

Many fans believe that stock car racing began with moonshine running during the Prohibition era of the 1920s. But in actuality, stock car racing goes back to the very first automobile race, which took place in November of 1895. The race length covered 52.4 miles and started near the present-day Midway Airport in Chicago, Illinois, and ended north in Evanston, Illinois. The race was won by J. Frank Duryea in a car he had designed and built himself. The average speed for the distance was a then-blistering 5.05 miles per hour, which means it took him nearly 10 hours to cover that distance. The car that he drove, of course, was completely stock, so it isn't much of a stretch to say that this was indeed the first stock car race.

But from that point on, things get a bit scattered. There was no organized racing series anywhere in the country, and cars were still slower than horses. But it wasn't long before the competitive spirit took hold. Soon, mechanics (a new trade) were tinkering with cars to make them go faster. Early race cars evolved as open wheeled, without fenders, and dominated in races like the Indy 500. They became known as "true" racers.

Early stock car racing was exciting, to say the least. This coupe is on its way to a series of barrel rolls down the track, an unfortunate, yet common occurrence in the earliest days of stock car racing. Courtesy the Harvey Collection.

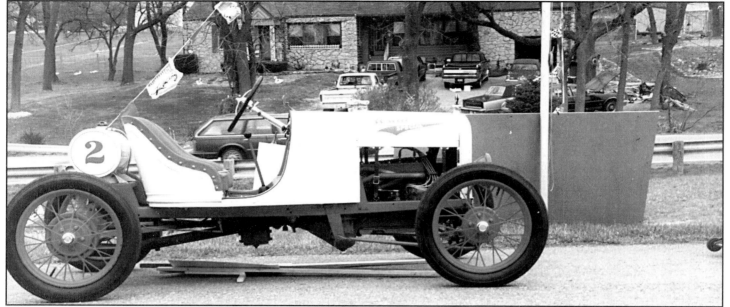

Speedsters were one of the earliest types of stock cars. These cars used parts from the 1920s and '30s with a typical engine being a modified stock Model A engine that could produce as much as 120 horsepower, quite a bit for the day. A close-up of the fuel tank is shown below.

However, although lacking the glamour and fame of Indy, stock cars did do some racing in regional events around the country. One of the first organized stock car events took place 14 years after the first car race, in 1909, on Long Island, New York. The 23-mile race, coined the "Long Island Stock Car Classic," was run on the city streets.

On August 7, 1915, Ralph DePalma, of Indianapolis 500 fame, won a stock car race at the Chicago Speedway, a track constructed entirely of wood. Many early raceways in those days were made of wood primarily because lumber and labor were cheap and abundant, and pavement was still something not yet widely developed. These high bank, wood tracks usually ran the more popular open wheel race cars with truly spectacular and often dangerous results. At this particular event, the promoters added stock cars as a supporting event.

Racing was slowly evolving, albeit loosely and in many different forms, until World War I. At that time, many sports, and in particular racing, either were slowed or were stopped altogether. In fact, the effects of this war on organized racing would be felt all through the 1920s. It wouldn't be until the 1930s before racing really began to grow and evolve once again.

The Speedsters

One of the earliest types of stock cars were called *Speedsters,* which were basically modified Ford Model As from the late 1920s. Just a few modifications were required to convert these classic machines to

Top photo: Early coupe action before a sell-out crowd is typical of early stock car racing. Most often, the track was located at the local fairgrounds. At left: Early race cars had no fenders, and when the tires touched, this was often the result. Photos courtesy Harvey Collection.

run on a dirt track. The engines were usually modified stock units that could produce as much as 120 horsepower, which was quite a bit for that Model A chassis to handle. Most of the chassis was usually stock, and the factory body parts were retained.

Running Moonshine

In those days of Prohibition, many people still wanted their liquor despite the nationwide ban. This created a new industry of making illegal alcoholic beverages. The North had the big cities and a trucking industry already in place so the distribution of illegal drink was more cloaked and harder to detect. In the Southeastern part of the country, there was less overall industry so the routes for the distribution were more pronounced. Any of this illegal drink was usually called *moonshine* in the South and as this substance was produced, it became necessary to find a way to deliver it without getting caught. The Federal forces that monitored such activities were kept quite busy

This '37 Ford Coupe was wheeled to numerous stock car victories by Curtis "Crawfish" Crider, one of the sport's early stars. Cars of this type often raced on the sands of Daytona during the late '30s and '40s.

Most of the racing in the early days was on dirt, so screens needed to be installed over the radiator and in front of the driver to stop flying debris, rocks, etc.

chasing the speedy delivery men in their "hopped up" cars, often reaching dangerous speeds on both heavily used and quiet back roads. As the business of moonshine grew more profitable, more people attempted to cash in. When stock car racing appeared at the local fairgrounds, the moonshine runners were easily talked into entering the races because the idea of a more legitimate endeavor for their performance vehicles was appealing. And the Feds were cracking down and catching more of the moonshiners. Racing a stock car at the track didn't mean jail time for those who lost.

It was a natural fit. When promoters wanted to stage a race, the moonshine runners and other daring drivers made for a great local angle and people came from miles around to see their neighbors race. There were reputations at stake, and the local bragging rights as to who beat whom to the finish line in front of so many witnesses were equally as important as the trophy and prize money. Even when Prohibition ended, the

John Rutherford, #29, leads the way in his supercharged Auburn boattail speedster on the Daytona Beach course. Note how close specatators are to the racing action, a far cry from the tall barriers of today. Many stock car purists insist this is where stock car racing really began. Courtesy Daytona Racing Archives.

moonshine industry still flourished—for one reason, to avoid taxation across state lines. What had started as a small cottage industry was now big business in many of the rural areas of the South. When stock car racing was later organized under the umbrella of NASCAR, the sport of racing was legitimized, and the money to be made was more attractive.

The Sands of Daytona Beach

Passenger cars had certainly evolved during this time, and the desire to go racing was stronger than ever. The problem was, there was a shortage of race tracks and facilities,

especially those suited for heavy, stock-bodied cars. And, as cars developed, there became a legitimate need to see just how fast they could actually run. But this required a long, flat, smooth surface, something not exactly common in the days before paved highway systems.

One solution was found on the sands of Daytona Beach, Florida, a place where many purists believe the sport of stock car racing really began. Someone got the idea that the vast expanse of flat beach would be perfect for timed runs. But when speeds became too great for the drivers to run safely on the sands of Daytona, the timed runs

Early stock cars were just stripped of dead weight, like padding, and run as stock for the most part. The original instruments are still in place on this dash.

This '30s Ford coupe still has the original sheet metal. A bit dinged up, but still the same as it rolled off the assembly line. Note fenders are cut off for tire clearance.

Is that front square bar for protection, or for battering someone out of the way? More than likely, it's there for both reasons. Such was the racing in those days, although there are some who say that nothing has changed on today's Winston Cup circuit.

were moved to the salt flats of Bonneville, Utah. This happened in 1936.

But Daytona Beach was already "hooked" on racing. Although timed land speed record runs could not be safely conducted on the beach, it was thought that slower cars could run safely there, especially if part of the highway was used as a closed course. After the timed runs moved to Bonneville, the American Automobile Association (AAA) decided to sanction a race at Daytona in 1936.

The original beach was the straightaway with the cars heading north along the smooth, hard-packed sand, dodging the tides and seagulls of the Atlantic Ocean. At the end of the straight, the cars would make a long sweeping turn in the sand, and exit the beach onto a paved road, Highway A1A, which was just over 20 feet wide. The cars would then head south on the pavement, and re-enter the beach with a long, sweeping turn onto the sand. The oval therefore was three parts sand, one part pavement. The overall distance for one lap was just a hair over four miles!

Louis Meyer, already an accomplished driver, won that first event in a '34 Ford. The event had to be shortened due to the huge ruts that soon developed in the turns. The drivers began sliding the cars around, and it wasn't long before cars were flipping, or oil pans and suspension components were being torn off. Despite the tough track, or maybe because of it, attendance was great at the beach races, which became more and more popular every year. Soon more cars and more spectators headed for Daytona making it the unofficial home of big track stock car racing.

Although most popular in the South, stock car racing did spread a bit to California in those days. A 500-mile stock car race, thought to be the first race of such a length, was held in Oakland, California, in 1938. In the east, the famous Langhorne Speedway in Pennsylvania was also active in early stock

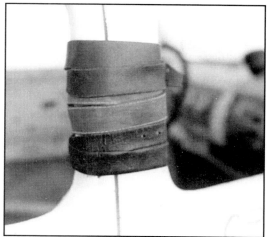

Innovation, rather than technology, was the theme for Jalopy racing. To keep his doors fastened securely, this driver used his belt.

car racing.

It seemed that racing was poised to take off, but once again, it would be stopped nearly altogether by the outbreak of World War II. But after the war, a combination of factors would help propel the concept of stock car racing forward.

One factor was simple economics. Open-wheeled race cars, like those running at the Indy 500, continued to develop with new technology, much of it learned during the war. But technology comes at a premium, just as it does today. The cost of a competitive Indycar, with its turbocharged engine and carbon fiber chassis, is far more than a Winston Cup car with a production-based

V8 engine. So racing in these classes soon became priced out of reach for all but the wealthy elite or well-sponsored.

JALOPY RACING

Another reason stock car racing took off was the fact that during the war, auto manufacturers had to devote much of their resources to building military machines, so few new model cars were built. Americans, flush with cash from the post-war economic boom, rushed to dealers to buy new cars as they rolled off the assembly line. In the process, they literally discarded their old '30s and early '40s coupes, which made them plentiful and cheap—just the right combination for grassroots racing.

These cars, which were stripped and mod-

Top Photo: A pair of '36 Fords duke it out in early "Jalopy-style" racing action. After World War II, there was a huge new car boom, creating an abundance of used '30s coupes and sedans available cheap—a perfect combination for low-budget stock car racing.

Bottom Photo: Racing on dirt could be pretty hairy—deep ruts and a high center of gravity made these cars prone to rolling over. This Jalopy, a '38 Ford coupe, is about to roll over—or did the driver catch it in time? Only those in attendance know the answer to that question. Photos courtesy the Harvey Collection.

21

Here's a typical sedan racer: fenders have been stripped, the front end is narrowed, and there are custom bumpers all the way around. Usually, they were topless, but occasionally, full-bodied sedans were raced.

Shocks and steering linkage were basic by today's standards, yet effective and surprisingly sturdy despite the rough, rutted dirt tracks these cars ran on.

ified in all sorts of ways, formed a grassroots level of racing called "Jalopy Racing." This loosely organized racing took place at fairgrounds, farm fields and anywhere else a dirt track could be formed, and would continue into the '50s. At one point, it is estimated that nearly two thousand tracks existed for local, nightly Jalopy competition. Some of these tracks survived and evolved with the sport to become established racing facilities, but most faded with time and the development of housing tracts and suburbs.

The cars that ran in Jalopy racing consisted of a wide variety of styles and models.

They had different names, too—Coupes, Modifieds, Roadsters, Roaring Roadsters, and Speedsters—depending on the part of the country they were running in and the year. These cars were very popular until the mid-'50s, when modern technology and the availability of newer used cars prevailed.

To understand the technology differences of these early stock cars, it might be meaningful to look at a number of these machines and see what made them run.

Roadsters/Modifieds

Somewhat similar to the Speedsters were the "Roadsters" that came along in the early

Early Roadsters had no front fenders, and homemade bumpers and screens for protection.

These cars had a tendency to run hot, mainly because they were running much faster speeds for longer durations than they were originally designed for. To help with cooling, extra louvers like these were punched into the front end body panels.

1930s, based on the Ford and Chevy coupes of the era. Sometimes they were known as Roaring Roadsters, Modifieds, or Sportsman cars. In 1933, a stock car race was held in Elgin, Illinois, and the first seven places were won by Ford V8 roadsters that had been stripped of fenders and windshields. The winner was Fred Frame, who averaged 80.22 mph for 203 miles. On the main straightaway, running slightly downhill, Frame consistently hit 4900 rpm—100 mph—and then had to double-clutch into 2nd gear to slow for a 30 mph corner!

Many Roadsters were narrowed, and resembled open-wheel race cars, something that was intentional. Open-wheel racers were considered the elite class, and some racers wanted to imitate them, at least cosmetically. The problem was, many of the Roadsters were based on a stock production chassis, which didn't have much rollover protection built in. Roll bars and cages were still several decades away, and because the

Some early roadsters resembled their open-wheel cousins, Indy cars. The chassis was stock, production based, but the rest of the body was heavily modified. Photo by John Farquhar.

Taking off the fenders, however, left the wheels exposed. When they touched together, this is often the result—air time. These two Modifieds were wheel-to-wheel moments before they touched and off they went. Courtesy Harvey Collection.

Early Modifieds could take so many forms. This example is a home-built unit reminiscent of a street rod.

For the first few years of NASCAR, the "mighty mods" were the top division and ran their races on newly sanctioned tracks in the Southeast. Modifieds are still run today and are NASCAR's oldest division. Courtesy Harvey Collection

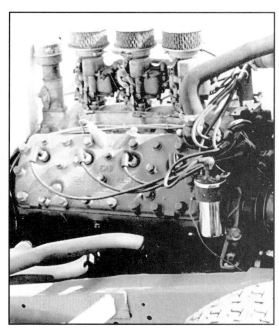

The flathead Ford V8 ruled the Roadster/Modified era of the '30s, '40s and early '50s. In full race tune, over 200 horsepower could be coaxed out of this engine, especially with a triple carb setup as shown here.

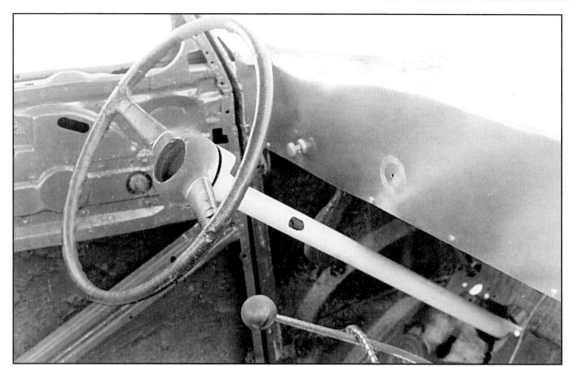

Some Roadsters were a conglomeration of various truck and car parts cobbled together. Some featured stripped down interiors, while others were completely stock. These cars also ran street tires, simply because no other type was available. Race tires would evolve later as speeds exceeded their safety limits.

Roadsters had been modified without fenders, the probability of having the wheels touch increased dramatically. Consequently, these cars were pretty unsafe.

Some Roadsters, especially those in California, were cobbled together with chassis components and parts taken from a variety of different makes and models.

Sometimes truck differentials and axles were used because their sturdier construction was better suited for racing. Some Roadsters used just the portion of a '20s coupe up to the firewall, then custom-made a front end or used one from a later model coupe. Because there was a lot of banging and bumping with these cars, it was com-

This nearly stock sedan powers through one of Daytona's sandy turns in January 1948 at NASCAR's first official race. Courtesy Daytona Racing Archives.

mon to see a grid of steel bars on the front end to serve as a bumper of sorts. And it was often used to bump other cars, as well as add some measure of protection. With these Roadsters, it was pretty much anything goes.

Even though NASCAR officially discontinued the Roadster class in favor of Modifieds, it continued to run elsewhere for many years. One organization, the California Racing Association (CRA), sanctioned Roadster events through 1956.

When NASCAR came along later, the Modified Division was the very first class they sanctioned and today, it is the oldest, eclipsing the Winston Cup Series by two years. The simple act of setting up a uniform collection of rules for the Modifieds started what would become sadly commonplace for NASCAR. Other groups in the U.S. outright copied or at least adapted the basic Modified rules for their own sanctioning body, and for the first time, rules were at least close to

each other in various parts of the country. For the first few years of NASCAR, the "mighty mods" were the top division and ran their races on newly sanctioned tracks in the Southeast.

However, Modifieds did run at tracks such as Daytona Beach. One of the best on the beach was Gober Sosbee and his famous Cherokee Garage '39 Ford coupe. Sosbee's machine was powered by a 59A Ford engine equipped with Jahns pistons, a Winfield camshaft, and Offenhauser heads and intake. Most of the many other pieces were either handmade or modified stock parts.

The car was a rocket on the super-smooth beach, reaching speeds as high as 140 mph, an amazing speed for the time. Unfortunately, according to Sosbee, the brakes were not quite up to this speed, a real problem when those long, sweeping turns on the sand came up. To get the car through the corner, Sosbee would slide the car side-

Fonty Flock (#2) and Red Byron (#22), both in Ford Coupes, lead the pack through the north turn in a 1949 race on the beach course. Byron had won the race and championship the year before. Courtesy Daytona Racing Archives.

ways to scrub off speed, rev the motor, and drop it into first gear at about 70 miles per hour, then crank the wheel and power out of the slide onto the pavement of Florida Highway A1A. A hair-raising maneuver to say the least, but such was the nature of Modified racing at the time.

Getting Organized

Bill France, a stock car driver, decided that the sport needed a little direction and organization. To that end, France held a meeting in a little motel in Daytona Beach, Florida, in December of 1947 with other drivers and car owners to try and bring order to a sport that effectively had no rules, rhyme or reason, and tended to be on the wild and reckless side. He called his new organization the National Association for Stock Car Auto Racing (NASCAR). Over half a century later, that acronym remains intact and is a household word to race fans all over the world.

NASCAR sanctioned its first race in January 1948 on the Daytona Beach course. Over 14,000 fans showed up, which was an astounding number for those days. Robert "Red" Byron, of Virginia, won with his Ford coupe by a margin of 15 seconds over Marshall Teague. They raced in the newly created Modified class which basically consisted of coupes from the '30s and early '40s with tweaked engines and with some of the sheet metal removed. Because things were so new, the rules were pretty general and open to a wide variety of interpretation. However, that didn't stop NASCAR from putting on a great season. In that first season, Red Byron would go on to win the inaugural NASCAR Championship, which consisted of an exhaustive 52 races.

"The new series was dubbed 'the Grand National' division, and the first official race was held in Charlotte, North Carolina, on June 19, 1949."

The Grand National Division

With the Modified division established and already very popular with fans, Bill France had the idea to race nearly new cars that were exactly the same as the ones the fans drove to the track. As mentioned, the interest in new cars was higher than ever before, and France thought that he could tap into this popularity by racing cars that were "strictly stock." He believed that if fans could personally identify with the car racing on the track, they would become much more interested in the sport, and he was right.

But not only were the fans interested, so were the factories in Detroit and other cities where the cars were manufactured. Even though the stock car sport was at that time centered in the Southeast, it was quickly branching off and gaining popularity in the other parts of the country, too. The factories watched intently as France started his new division.

This philosophy still guides NASCAR today, as they continue to make every effort to keep brand identity intact with all cars and trucks in their racing divisions by changing the rules when needed.

The new series was dubbed the Grand National Division, and the first official race was held in Charlotte, North Carolina, on June 19, 1949. Only American cars built from 1947 to 1949 that were strictly stock, could participate. Racers responded by showing up with all makes of cars, including Lincolns, Buicks, Hudsons, Oldsmobiles, Fords, Cadillacs, Kaisers and Mercurys. Most drove the their cars to the track, taped the headlights, raced, then drove the cars home. The fans loved every minute of it, just as France had predicted.

And what a show they put on in that first race! The track itself was dirt, and visibility was a serious problem. Some drivers counted trees or telephone poles as braking and acceleration points. Attrition played a major role in these early races, because it was not unusual for large rocks thrown from the tires to puncture the radiators of cars.

When the race was over, the apparent winner was Glen Dunaway, but he was disqualified for using the wrong rear springs in his Ford. The win then went to Jim Roper, who split the $2000 prize money with his car's owner, Millard Clothier. Roper spent his share on a new refrigerator while Clothier kept the trophy.

By 1950, the Grand National Division had become more popular than the Modified division, which was eventually broken up into regions instead of a national series, which is how it is run today. The strictly stock cars, as will be discussed in the next chapter, did not actually remain stock for very long, in large part due to safety concerns. By the time the Grand National cars were renamed Winston Cup cars in 1986, they had evolved to purpose-built racing machines with very few stock parts left.

With names all so similar, it certainly presented confusion to the fans, and was one of the motivating factors for Bill France Sr. to attempt to bring the racing together under the NASCAR banner.

While the racing organizations started in the '30s and '40s were not great in number, what they unknowingly did was to lay a great foundation for racing in the future. A foretelling of that future was seen in 1950 on Labor Day weekend, at Darlington, South Carolina. This was the very first superspeedway event, on a brand-new facility just for stock car racing. The event, called the Southern 500, signified the beginning of a new era in stock car racing. A whopping 75-car field took the inaugural green flag, and fans showed up in large numbers as well. With the success of this superspeedway, new tracks were built in a sort of mini-boom, springing up all over the Southeast to host stock car events.

The popularity of stock car racing began to attracted the attention of Detroit. They quickly realized the value of this new form of motorsport, and began supporting it in

Bill France Sr. stands next to the Ford Coupe he drove in the 1936 Beach Road race near Daytona Beach. Twelve years later, he would form NASCAR, and start one of the most successful organizations in sports history. Courtesy Daytona Racing Archives.

earnest, sometimes openly, and sometimes not. There were quite a few teams that benefited from factory "covert" assistance. As the number of dedicated stock car tracks grew, the level of competition did as well.

As the '40s came to an end, stock car racing was well on its way with the help of NASCAR, but it still had a long way to go before it was widely accepted by the public. The cars began to change with each year,

deviating from the "strictly stock" rules, mainly out of respect for safety. As speeds increased, so did the need for roll bars, driver helmets, seat belts and such. The cars began to evolve into true race cars, factories became more involved, engines and speeds increased, which translated into more fans. Thus began the next era of stock car racing.

A ROARING ROADSTER

Old number 32 was one of the most famous "Roaring Roadsters" to take to the track. It was the ride of superstar driver Dick Frazier, who drove the car to 21 consecutive victories in 1948.

This accomplishment is more meaningful when you consider that many of the victories were against the best drivers of the period, such as Jack McGrath, Troy Ruttman and the Rathman brothers. But by the early 1950s, the roadster was "retired." Three decades later, it reappeared as a pile of tattered parts at a racing flea market.

Car restorer Don Anderson of Dayton, Ohio, an avid racing buff, knew what this pile of parts represented. After making the purchase, he spent years researching and painstakingly restoring the roadster back to prime condition. It is now an excellent example of the type of hybrid technology employed by these early stock cars.

The body actually combines two different brands of bodies, the rear being a 1927 Model T Ford which was skillfully integrated with a '35 Pontiac for the front. That Pontiac grille is still in position. Underneath the modified Ford frame is a complete sheet metal belly pan, which was an early attempt at ground effects.

Suspension was the cross-spring, I-beam front axle, and matching cross-spring rear end—a standard configuration for the time period. The brakes are from a '33 Ford, while the shocks are from a '48 Ford.

The engine is a 296 cubic inch Mercury flathead with Evans aluminum heads, Stromberg carburetors, aluminum pistons, and a stroker crank with stock Ford rods. Anderson ventured that the horsepower number "is close to 225," which is certainly impressive for 1948. This magnificent roadster is currently on loan to the Smithsonian Institution, certainly an honor that it deserves.

Bob Fairman photo

BIRO'S ROADSTER

Race car restorer Mark Biro found his old Roaring Roadster in the sorriest of conditions. "The car had been driven to an old garage, and parked, still dirty from its last race, where it sat for 26 years. The trailer had sunk eight inches in the ground and a tree had grown in front of the garage, which had to be cut down to get out the car," Biro explained.

The Roadster started out as a '30 Model A Ford which had been narrowed 12 inches down the middle. The frame rails came from a 1928 Chevy and the radiator shell originally sat in a 1937 Cord. The rest of the front end is from a 1940 Plymouth and the steering is from Franklin.

Power for the classic black and white machine was supplied by a 239 cid flathead Ford that had been bored out to 273 cubic inches. It carried all the period performance parts and pieces, including an Isky cam, Jahns pistons, and an Offenhauser intake. The car weighs 1650 pounds and has a cross-spring front suspension.

The roadster was raced from 1949 and 1955. A versatile machine, it ran both dirt and pavement during its racing days. Biro, who has raced the car, says he was able to average more than 80 miles per hour on high-banked half-mile tracks.

John Farquhar photo

1938 FORD COUPE

This 1938 Ford stock car, powered by a '48 flathead Ford engine, still looks like it could still be competitive. Interestingly enough, the current owner is still the original one—driver Tom Young. He recalls that he only paid $3.00 for the car, "but I found $8.00 under the floor mat, so I came out ahead in the long run."

Tom drove the car to more than 130 feature wins, and all the guys figured that he was doing something illegal. Street tires were used, but Young used a Volkswagen tire on the left front. "When things were set up right, that tire never touched the ground," he said with a smile.

The rear end was a stock Ford unit with one modification. "I welded the gears together so that there would be a direct drive with both rear wheels driving. It worked very well for me."

The little coupe sat rather high, but Young felt the shape gave the car a little more grip in the turns. He also made it as light as possible by completely gutting the interior. About the only things inside were a homemade driver's seat and a complete roll cage, which he fabricated himself.

On the outside, Young removed the running boards and replaced them with nerf bars or "rub rails." Finally, he added some heavy steel bumpers for banging purposes. There weren't any floorboards to speak of, so when he used to pull up in front of the stands after taking a checkered flag, he would put his feet down to the ground to show off his red leather boots. That must have been something to see.

David Tucker photo

RALPH MOODY'S STOCK CAR

Ralph Moody would is best known as 1/2 of one of the most successful car building franchises in motorsports. Along with his partner John Holman, Moody turned out some of the finest stock cars to ever run in NASCAR.

This 1940 Ford coupe was one of his first efforts, back when he was a driver. When Bob Prendergast found the car, it still had the original sheet metal in place. About the only non-stock aspects were flared headlight openings and trimmed fenders for additional tire clearance. Although safety wasn't much of a consideration back then, the single hoop roll bar behind the driver provides minimal protection. To keep the driver inside in the event of a rollover, the doors were welded shut, which is the extent of the safety features on the car. In fact, the five-gallon military-style fuel can strapped in the rear is downright dangerous considering the bumping and banging these cars did running dirt back in the '40s and '50s.

As Moody's first stock car, he drove the car to the track, taped the headlights, raced, then drove it home if it wasn't too badly damaged. Current owner Bob Pendergast hasn't been able to find much information on the car, but he does know that Moody drove the car mostly in the New England area.

Power comes from a potent 239 cid flathead engine, which had been bored .040" over for a total 250 cubic inches of displacement. Air/fuel is mixed by a single Stromberg 97 carburetor. With the exception of an Iskendarian camshaft, most of the engine is stock, so total output is estimated to be about 100 horsepower.

The rest of the powertrain consists of a three-speed manual transmission, and a stock 3.78 geared rear end. The suspension is somewhat archaic, with buggy-style transverse springs and ancient Houdise shocks. The stock bumpers were removed and replaced with some heavy battering-ram-style homemade steel bumpers.

At left is a photo of a young Ralph Moody standing next to his car (he's on the left) as he raced it. Above is a closeup of the restored version by Bob Prendergast.

CURTIS CRIDER'S FORD COUPE

Curtis Crider was one of the finest stock car drivers to ever run on an oval, and this is one of the cars he drove between 1951 and 1957. Afterward, it was driven by a young driver named Cale Yarborough. Talk about an impressive pedigree!

This '40 Ford coupe was built by the Yon Brothers in 1950. The car was built to run strictly on short tracks, which it did with great success.

The coupe is powered by a 1948, 59AB flathead Ford engine with displacement bored to 296. With a full complement of typical aftermarket performance parts—heads, exhaust, camshaft, multi-carbs, etc.—the output is an impressive 250 horsepower.

The frame was stock, but it was "plated and boxed," meaning reinforced for extra strength. The suspension was pretty much the factory stock unit except that the springs had a few extra leafs for increased stiffness. As for modifications to the body, the doors were secured by being welded shut, the lights were removed and the recesses filled in. The wheelwells were also enlarged, and the stock bumpers were replaced with sturdier steel pieces.

According to Crider, "These cars lasted a long time compared to today's stock cars. We kept rebuilding the car whenever it was wrecked, which was more often than I care to admit, so there wasn't much left of the original parts and pieces by the time I quit running the car." As you can see, he's restored it to near-perfect condition.

Crider's flawlessly restored '40 coupe is just as he raced it. Built by the Yon Bros., it was later raced by Cale Yarborough as well. Crider is at right just after the restoration was completed.

THE EVOLUTION OF THE MODERN STOCK CAR

3

After the formation of NASCAR, the sport started to mature in both public perception and the ever-increasing technology of the cars. Supported by a sharp crew of promoters and technical people, NASCAR quickly grew in popularity, and Detroit began to take notice. In fact, the rules of NASCAR can be credited somewhat with the development of performance in the modern passenger car, at least through the next few decades.

Early Grand National rules dictated that all equipment on the cars be stock. This included almost all engine components: heads, manifolds, camshaft, pistons, carbu-

retors, ignition. It also included most chassis parts and running gear. You couldn't even use tubular steel exhaust headers, although you could run an open pipe off the manifold, eliminating the muffler.

Needless to say, an auto company that wanted to look good on the NASCAR track had to provide some pretty powerful stock equipment, and the "technology race" was on. The manufacturers began working in their research labs, and with hot rodders like Ed Iskendarian, to develop parts and engines that pushed cars to speeds that were never thought possible. So it makes sense that any technical look at stock car racing surely

The starting field of a 1951 race on the Daytona Beach course shows a majority of Olds 88s, a model and engine that dominated the first two years of the decade in Grand National racing. Courtesy Daytona Racing Archives.

"Although the debate rages on about speed and power vs. driver talent, it is generally agreed that it is easier for a mediocre driver to win with a superior engine, than it is the other way around."

The Oldsmobile "Rocket 88" engine (shown is the 1950 version), was the most powerful engine built by General Motors at the time. With a compression ratio of 7.55:1, it developed 135 horsepower. In racing trim, the engine proved to be highly successful, winning many races and dominating the 1950 and 1951 NASCAR seasons. Courtesy Oldsmobile.

should start with a peek under the hood at the magnificent engines that have evolved over the years.

THE ENGINES OF THE '50s

Perhaps one of the foremost reasons behind the growth of the sport of stock car racing was the almost daily development of new technology. Although engines were important during the early days (the flathead Ford pretty much dominated), it wasn't until the mid '50s that the engine wars began to heat up. As Detroit developed faster, more powerful engines, they turned to stock car racing for some of their "unofficial" research and testing, as well as for marketing exposure. After awhile, the brand of engine was just as important as the car, at least in the minds of the fans. Engines began to dominate, and a great deal of attention was

focused on developing this new technology. Although the debate rages on about speed and power vs. driver talent, it is generally agreed that it is easier for a mediocre driver to win with a superior engine, than it is the other way around. What follows are some of the more notable engines that have been significant milestones in modern stock car racing history.

Olds Rocket 88

One of the first engines to dominate was the Olds Rocket 88 V8. The engine was introduced in the 1949 Olds 88 and was used in Cadillacs that year as well. The 303 cubic inch engine was putting out 135 horsepower, but the Olds 88 car was relatively lightweight. It could go 100 mph, and 0–60 in just 13 seconds, which was very impressive for the period.

In stock trim, the engine was perfectly

Hudson Hornet's dominated for a variety of reasons, mainly because of chassis and body advantages. However, the 232 cid flathead six was no slouch, and enjoyed major factory support, so there were many factory performance racing parts available. The engine could pump out a maximum of 210 hp @ 4500 rpm. The car shown above is a recreation. Phil Kunz photo.

designed for racing with hydraulic lifters, an over-square bore-stroke ratio, forged steel crank with six counterweights, cast aluminum pistons, full-floating wrist-pins and a compact, durable cast iron block. It also offered a two-barrel, downdraft carburetor mounted to a dual-plane intake manifold.

All of this was good enough for Olds to dominate NASCAR for the 1950 and 1951 seasons. Race officials made the Olds teams use the stock hydraulic valve lifters, which gave fits to the mechanics because of their tendency to pump up at engine speeds over 4000 rpm. The Olds also had to make do with a 2-barrel carb. The fact it was still able to dominate despite these technical handicaps says a lot about the technology of this engine.

The Olds 88 was the choice of a number of heavy hitters in 1950, including Red Byron, Bob Flock, and Buck Baker. But the top Olds 88 teams included Fireball Roberts, who finished second in the points, and fourth-place points finisher Curtis Turner—

both men would go on to become major players in NASCAR Grand National racing. In 1951, the Olds 88 domination continued with Fonty Flock finishing second with eight wins, followed by brother Tim Flock in third with seven victories.

Hudson Hornet Engine

The Hudson was introduced in 1949, and the car would prove to be a milestone. More on the car itself is on page 52. But the engine was also significant. The flathead six was 232 cid cubic inches, and because Hudson was so supportive of stock car racing, their engineers developed a special parts list as long as an arm. The list included an aluminum high compression head, dual carbs, high performance camshaft, high rate valve springs, heavy duty pistons, rods and oil pump, and dual low-restriction exhaust manifolds. Hudson called it the "7X" engine, and with these mods, it was capable of 210 horsepower at 4500 rpm. It may not sound like much today, but coupled with the

Chevy's 265 cid small block released in 1955 was so revolutionary that it immediately rendered just about every other engine obsolete. One of the bigger racing advantages was the higher rpm limit. Photo courtesy GM.

Ford's answer to the Chevy was this Y-block V8. Racers could get a special dual 4-barrel carb setup as well as a few other high performance parts. Ford wouldn't rate the engine, but estimates were 300 hp after racers were done tuning it.

unique Hudson body, it was enough to allow the Herb Thomas Team to dominate NASCAR racing from 1952 to 1954.

The Small-Block Chevy

In 1955, Chevrolet unveiled their 265 cubic inch small-block V8 engine, which changed the world forever. Although there had been V8s for decades, the new design was so revolutionary that it rendered nearly every other engine design obsolete—virtually overnight. But aside from the design, it was the performance that captivated engineers, the public and racers alike.

From the outset, the 265 cid engine did things no other stock engine had done. It developed 180 hp at 4800 rpm with 8:1 compression and a 4-barrel carb. Most important, the ultralight valvetrain could turn 5500 rpm or more—in stock trim!

Racers already knew that the more they could rev their engines, the more power they had. But they also knew the more they revved the engine, the better chance they had for valvetrain failure. It's still that way today. The ability to wind up to a higher rpm before shifting would give the Chevy engine a tremendous advantage in racing. There was now a new benchmark for performance.

In 1957, Chevy increased displacement to 283 cid and added Rochester fuel injection as an option, partly in response to the supercharged version of Ford's 312 cid engine. In stock form, the engine could produce one horsepower per cubic inch—the first factory stock engine with added options to make this claim—but just by adding open exhaust, you could get over 300 hp without too much effort. At a timed run on Daytona Beach (the flying mile course, not the NASCAR track), the Chevy was recorded at 130 mph.

Ford

Ford, of course, could not let this development go unanswered, and responded with their 292 cubic-inch Y-Block in 1955. The engine was equipped with a 4-barrel carb off

Fords like this 1956 Ford Customline stock car, equipped with the V8 Thunderbird Special engine, frequently battled Chevys and Chryslers throughout the mid-50s, but Chevy seemed to have the upper hand. Bob Fairman photo.

the assembly line, but NASCAR racers could get a special dual 4-barrel carb setup for competition. The engine also featured a special solid-lifter cam, high-rate valve springs and dual exhaust. Ford declined to rate the horsepower output of this engine, but racers were thought to coax as much as 300 hp out of it with a few modifications.

In 1957, Ford increased displacement to 312 cid as part of their "Police Interceptor" package. The engine was rated stock at 285 hp @ 5000 rpm, and featured the dual 4-barrel carbs previously only available to racers as stock. Later in the '57 model year, Ford added a belt-driven Paxton supercharger for NASCAR racing to counter the new fuel-injected 283 Chevy. This motor could pump out 330 horsepower in stock form, and ran 131 mph in a timed flying mile run at Daytona. When the Chevy and Ford met on the track, the Ford was faster on tracks with long straightaways, like the superspeedways, while the Chevy was quicker on shorter tracks. The thought was at the time, that

the small-block Chevys could rev quicker than the Fords. This proved to be true for many years until the Ford developed engines that could rev as fast.

Ford and Chevy slugged it out from race to race, and the factories dumped millions of dollars into development. Pretty soon, only those so blessed with the factory dollars were winning, which began to make NASCAR uneasy. This expensive, elitist type of competition went against the spirit of NASCAR competition and stock-style racing, so right in the middle of the 1957 season, they banned superchargers and fuel injection. All cars were required to run a single 4-barrel carburetor, a rule that still stands today. NASCAR's philosophy is for a level playing field between all brands competing as well as within any and all brands. One good way for any team to mess up the show is for them to be the dominating one and have any sort of clear advantage over the rest of the competition.

It was the custom in the 1950s to carry the engine horsepower on the hood as the Russ Truelove Mercury demonstrates in this photo.

Chrysler 300s dominated in '55 and '56 with their awesome Hemi engine, which produced up to 355 horsepower with performance parts. Tim and Thomas Flock, along with Buck Baker, powered these cars to victory many times during those years.

Chrysler

Chrysler introduced their first "Hemi" engine in 1951. Nicknamed for its hemispherical heads and unique valve positioning, the engine would go on to become a standard in drag racing where it and later its design, built by aftermarket businesses, would power Top Fuel and Funny Cars over the 200 and 300 mph barriers. The one-of-a-kind design would later return to NASCAR in mid '60s and into the aero wars of the late '60s and early '70s.

In 1951, this engine developed 180 hp with a modest 7.5:1 compression ratio.

Chrysler didn't really get serious until they were awakened by Chevy's small block in 1955. They then unveiled their first real power pack engine, which was for the C-300 sport coupe. By adding a dual 4-barrel carb, a long duration, solid-lifter cam and dual exhausts, the horsepower was bumped to an astounding 300 @ 5200 rpm—the basis for the C-300 name.

In '56, the Hemi was bumped to 354 cid and 340 hp. An optional engine package boosted output to an astounding 355 hp, more than one horsepower per cubic inch! Eventually, Chrysler would increase displacement to 392 cid and output to 390 hp.

How good was this engine? In a case of "getting it right the first time" the Hemi and 300 model Chryslers would dominate NASCAR racing in 1955 and 1956 (more on this later). Tim and Thomas Flock, as well as Buck Baker, literally blew away all other competitors these two years. Even though the car was far bigger and heavier than the Chevys and Fords running against it, the awesome Hemi more than compensated. The Hemi engine had the "most usable" horsepower of any other passenger car at the time, and it translated directly onto the track, especially on fast superspeedways.

As an excellent example of the adage "racing improving the breed," Chrysler discovered that the oil in the standard oil-bath air cleaners would shift to one side during hard cornering, leaving the engine without oil and unprotected during the long sweeping turns. This certainly did nothing to promote engine life. This discovery led to the development of the first pleated, non-oiled air filter for a U.S. production-based car.

By the end of 1956, Chevy and Ford had decided that Chrysler's reign had to end, and had stepped up their involvement. Chrysler was soon beaten by cubic dollars. Some sources say that Ford and Chevy were each spending $2–$3 million a year on NASCAR racing in '56 and '57, an amazing figure for the time. It began to pay off soon, as both

Ford produced a 368 cid engine that was very competitive.

"The Hemi engine had the most usable horsepower of any other passenger car at the time, and it translated directly onto the track, especially on fast super-speedways."

Ford and Chevy began to dominate.

When NASCAR put a lid on this technology, the Automobile Manufacturer's Association (AMA) bowed to pressure from the government, insurance companies and public to stop the emphasis on speed and power, and effectively banned direct factory competition in racing. This also indirectly slowed the development of horsepower and cubic inches.

The manufacturers complied—at least publicly. NASCAR continued to flourish, but how they got new technology from manufacturers reverted back to how it was done in the early '50s. The high performance parts the factories produced—heads, cams, carb setups, exhaust, etc.—were available only over the counter, and not as an option on cars sold off the showroom floor. In this way, the factories were covertly able to continue battling each other on the track.

Big Blocks

In the late '50s, nearly all of the manufacturers had a big-block engine. Chevy produced their first one, a 348 cid W block, in 1958. In stock trim it only produced a mild 280 hp, but if you went down the option list

(remember the AMA ban), there was a Super Turbo Thrust option that produced 315 hp. Ford countered with their 352 cid FE big block, while Chrysler was set to unveil the 413 cid engine. However, it wouldn't be until the '60s when the awesome power potential of these big blocks would be fully realized.

THE ENGINES OF THE '60s

In 1960, after three relatively quiet years, Ford broke ranks with the AMA (at least publicly), by unveiling the high performance option for their 352 cid engine, which they rated at 360 hp @ 6000 rpm. However, this engine was no match for Chevy's 348 cid engine.

The Chevy 409

Then in 1961, Chevy released the fabled 409, which was essentially a bored and stroked version of the 348, with a beefier bottom end that consisted of stronger rods, harder bearings, forged pistons, and something new called a *windage tray*, the first time something like this had been used on a production engine. A windage tray is a flat

41

"The 409 was very successful on NASCAR tracks. Junior Johnson, Ned Jarrett, and Johnny Rutherford were three of the top 409-powered drivers during this time period."

Chevy turned their 348 cubic inch truck engine into this screaming 409 cid big block which produced an equal number of horsepower. It was the first engine to use a windage tray. John Farquhar photo.

sheet metal tray-shaped device mounted under the crankshaft and above the oil in the pan. It's designed to keep the oil from splashing onto the crankshaft, thereby slowing it down by friction. This allows the crank to maintain momentum and not lose speed, keeping engine revs up.

The 409 also had 11:1 compression, large passage aluminum manifold, the newly introduced 600 cfm Carter AFB aluminum 4-barrel carb and special low-restriction exhaust manifolds. A long duration solid lifter cam was used with standard valves and high-rate springs.

In 1962 and '63, Chevy added some important improvements to the 409. These included new cylinder head castings with larger ports and valves, dual 4-barrel carbs, redesigned piston domes for better combustion, a redesigned camshaft and still-higher rate valve springs with dampers. The 409 was very successful on the NASCAR tracks. Junior Johnson, Ned Jarrett, and Johnny Rutherford were three of the top 409-powered drivers during this time period.

Ford 406/427

In 1962, Ford introduced the famous 406 cid engine. The extra cubes, plus larger exhaust valves and a beautiful new triple 2-barrel carburetion system, boosted output at least 20–30 hp over the 390 cid (the successor to the lackluster 352). The three Holley 2-barrels had a total airflow of 920 cfm. They were mounted on a big passage, aluminum dual-plane manifold.

Toward the end of '63 model year, Ford released the 427 NASCAR engine. The biggest feature was the new dual 4-barrel carburetion system, with two 600 cfm Holleys with progressive primary throttles and vacuum-operated secondaries.

Marvin Panch and Fireball Roberts were successful with the Ford big-block engines.

Chrysler 426 Hemi

In 1964, Richard Petty showed up at Daytona with an all-new, second generation Chrysler Hemi 426 and history was made. The engine was superior in every way, generating at least 50-75 hp more than the closest rival. It was the most dominant engine in

The 1970 Plymouth Road Runner was one car that used the famous 426 Hemi. The engine was available with a triple two-barrel carb setup or with a single four-barrel version (shown here), which was one that ran in NASCAR. Phil Kunz photo.

any type of motor racing that required a stock engine, and of course, it was made with special parts.

NASCAR rules did not specify a minimum production run to qualify a factory built engine as "strictly stock" in the early '60s. As long as it was built by a U.S. car company, it was considered stock.

Chrysler stretched this concept to the limit with the Hemi. Their idea was to use the wildest, best breathing heads on the 426 cid production cylinder block without changing camshaft location. Special parts exclusive to this new Hemi included bigger forged connecting rods with larger bolts, a high output oil pump, forged counterweighted crankshaft, forged pistons, cross-bolted mains and a deep oil sump. Even the block casting was beefed up. The combustion chambers were true hemispheres, with the spark plug near the center of the dome and the valves inclined across the engine. Big valves were operated by rocker arms facing in opposite directions on two parallel shafts. All of this

added up to a superior combination for racing.

Richard Petty won the first race of the '64 season, the Daytona 500, with the new 426

The 426 Hemi (shown here in a more modern version on the dyno of Kammer & Kammer in Dayton, Ohio) built in 1964 was superior in every way, generating at least 50–75 more horsepower than the closest rival, in stock trim. Petty won the '64 Daytona 500 season operer, and never looked back, dominating the rest of the season.

Ford's response to the Hemi was the BOSS 429. NASCAR had mandated the "500" rule, but didn't specify that the 500 minimum engines had to be in the same car. Ford put them in 1360 Mustangs for the street, but because the Mustang wasn't legal to run in NASCAR, the engine was used in Torino Talladegas and Cyclone Spoiler IIs. These cars didn't have this engine in the street version. These corporate games were typical of the day (and still are used today) to gain any edge possible over the competition. Phil Kunz photo.

Hemi, and the Hemi never looked back for the rest of the season, completely dominating the circuit.

Ford 427 SOHC

In response to the Hemi, Ford unleashed an even more powerful stock block engine, the single overhead cam (SOHC) engine, in 1965. Basically, Ford took the 427 cid NASCAR block, with its side oiling system and cross-bolted main caps, and developed entirely new Hemi-type cylinder heads. The SOHC 427 Ford was a clever bolt-up arrangement, so that any 427 NASCAR engine could be easily converted.

NASCAR Applies the Brakes

The debut of the SOHC engine, along with the dominance of the Hemi, prompted NASCAR to nip this proprietary engine

game in the bud. NASCAR still believed that the circuit should be confined to cars and engines that were near to showroom conditions, so late in 1964, they adopted the "500" rule, which meant that any engine for the Grand National circuit would have to be installed in a minimum of 500 cars and sold to the public through new car dealers.

Ford, which was spending a reputed $14,000 per SOHC engine, immediately withdrew the engine and ran it in drag racing. Chrysler was outraged, especially after having been allowed to run all of 1964. However, they soon put a detuned engine in Dodges and Plymouths on the street.

This 500 rule was responsible for much of the development of the radical NASCAR stock cars during the '60s as well. The Plymouth Superbird and Dodge Daytona were examples of cars with limited street

production to qualify for racing, as were the Boss 429s of '69-'70. In all they produced just 1360 Boss 429 Mustangs with the *shotgun motor*. However, since Mustangs were not legal in NASCAR, the engine was used in Ford Torino Talladegas and Mercury Cyclone Spoiler II models. David Pearson won the '69 championship in a Talladega.

Chevy 427 Mystery Motor

During all of this, Chevrolet was forced to stand by and watch Ford and Chrysler dominate, at least publicly. GM had forbidden any of its divisions to go racing, but somehow, Chevy managed to sneak in a few performance zingers of its own.

In 1963, Junior Johnson arrived at Daytona with a 427 cubic inch Mk IV side-oiler engine that was dubbed the "Mystery Motor" because no one but Chevy engineers knew that it was a stroked derivative of the 409 and 348. The motor also was nicknamed the "Porcupine Engine," because of the staggered angles on the valves. Tuned to perfection, it was worth an amazing one horsepower per one cubic inch of displacement.

The opposition immediately protested the engine because the Mk IV was not a production engine available in any car model, and was therefore not legal under the rules.

Smokey's Chevelle—Chevrolet, noticeably absent since the Junior Johnson Impala #3 in 1963, reappeared with the legendary Smokey Yunick in 1967, again with the "mystery engine." By this time, smaller bodies such as the Ford Fairlanes and slightly smaller Plymouths were making their debut. But Chevy had been long gone for four years. When Smokey decided to make a new car, he chose the 1967 Chevelle body style. The car caught NASCAR by surprise as they had no templates for such a racer and had to make them off a new Chevelle in the parking lot on the spot. Smokey's distinctive gold and black car with the number 13 was an immediate hit with Chevy fans, long starved for someone to cheer on. Although it only ran for part of '67, the mystery motor marked not only the return of Smokey and Chevrolet, but NASCAR's original bad boy, Curtis Turner. Turner had been banned from NASCAR by Bill France Sr. when he tried

When Smokey Yunick showed up at Daytona with a "mystery motor" equipped 67 Chevelle it marked not only another isolated return for Chevrolet but the return of NASCAR bad boy, Curtis Turner. Turner had been banned from racing by Bill France Sr. for trying to form a driver's union. The car and its driver generated quite a bit of interest in NASCAR racing for that 1967 Daytona 500 by winning the pole. Mike Slade photo.

This Holman & Moody, 1969 Ford Torino, shown in the garage area of Daytona, advertises 427 CI (cubic inches) on the hood. It's a Ford factory-supported car. A similar-looking car ran in 1967 with Mario Andretti driving and went on to win. That car had the smaller Fairlane body that was used that year. Rick Rickard photo.

to organize the drivers into a sort of union.

Between the return of the banned Turner and the missing Chevys, the 1967 Daytona 500 held just about every stock car fan's interest. The sleek and distinctive-sounding Chevy rolled off the trailer and promptly earned the pole position. Chrysler and Ford howled, not believing for an instant the Chevelle was legal, but Turner drove a convincing race until the new engine developed problems. Not much later in the year, the car was destroyed at Atlanta Speedway in a spectacular practice accident. Smokey tried to enter the Daytona 500 the next year with a similar car but was unable to qualify.

More Rules

Unable to control engine costs and sizes, NASCAR instituted an engine cubic inch/overall weight rule that changed the direction of engine development and even car size used. In 1967, the Ford Fairlanes, already a noticeably smaller car than the more common Ford Galaxy, were allowed to run the 427 wedge engines with a pair of four-barrel carbs. Chrysler cars could run

the Hemi with only one four-barrel. Lighter Chrysler models used a destroked, 404 cid Hemi, which was the configuration that Richard Petty used to great advantage with his distinctive blue #43 Plymouths. Without any GM cars, it was a two-brand race those days; FoMoCo with Fords and Mercurys, and Chrysler with Dodges and Plymouths.

NASCAR could see that if something wasn't done, cubic inches would continue to climb insanely, as would speeds. A big wake-up call would come in 1970, when Bobby Isaac, driving Harry Hyde's winged Dodge Daytona, clocked an astounding 201.10 mph lap around Talladega, a record that would stand for many years. After hearing rumors of 500 cid monster motors in development, NASCAR enacted a 430 cid limit so the current engines, the 426s and 427s, could still legally compete.

Back to the Small Block

At the time, the Ford/Mercury and Plymouth/Dodge teams were dominant. In 1970 and 1971, Charlotte promoter Richard Howard contracted Junior Johnson to build a

Chevy Monte Carlo to revive the age-old battle between Ford and Chevy. Initially, the engine was a big block because they were still run on the street, so a few of the cars were built just to raise fan interest and sell tickets for the races at Charlotte. Oddly enough, the early Chevy Monte Carlo engines were built by a Holman & Moody (the well-known Ford builders) employee named Robert Yates, who was given permission to moonlight in the evening at Johnson's shop. Yates built the engines for the Monte Carlos and was partially responsible for the return of Chevy to NASCAR. With the tremendous skill Yates possessed, it wasn't long before he would go on to bigger and better things. It is somewhat ironic that most of Yates' future would be as a Ford team owner routinely battling the dominating Chevys he helped bring back to the sport.

From that basically promotional project, Junior Johnson decided to go racing seriously, and signed up Bobby Allison for the 1972 season and had quite a year. When the Chevys, too, had to find a smaller engine, they returned to the tried and true small block, then based on the 350 cid street displacement.

Because Detroit was planning on eliminating big blocks in street cars, NASCAR decided to go the same direction but needed to do so gradually. NASCAR wanted to give an advantage to those who would run the smaller engines, so more people would run them, which would eventually phase out the big blocks. To do this, NASCAR required a smaller, more limiting carburetor for all engines over 366 cubic inches for the 1974 season. This allowed some teams to consider smaller engines, but until engine builders could equal the big block in power and durability, they were still hesitant to race them.

Although Bud Moore developed a Ford 358 small block a few years before, it was the Wood Brothers—with a 366 cubic inch

Today's top teams run through quite a few engines, and top teams have a different set of engines for each type of track. This is a lineup of small-blocks all ready for the next race at Hendrick Motorsports.

Ford engine—that raised eyebrows first. In their first outing with the new small block, David Pearson captured pole position at the 1974 Atlanta race.

With the impressive performance of the their smaller but equally powerful engines, the future of the small block was assured for the Fords. The Mopars, however, were not as fortunate. Their Hemi was pretty much their only engine, and when it was de-tuned, it was no match for the Fords. Most Mopar teams went to the smaller engines out of necessity.

For the 1998 season, NASCAR approved the use of the powerful Chevy SB-2 cylinder head engine. This photo shows one of the early models of this engine. Phil Kunz photo.

The engine is expected to improve performance over the standard, long-standing 187-degree engine. Chevrolet photo.

ENGINES OF TODAY

By the mid-'80s, engine horsepower and speeds had climbed so much that it wasn't long before stock cars were running 220 mph on the straights of Daytona and Talladega, all with a small block displacing 358 cubic inches pushing a 3400-pound car.

Despite the vast advances in automotive engine technology in the last two decades, the NASCAR racing engine of today uses technology first implemented in the '60s and early '70s. The air and fuel is still delivered with a standard 750 cfm double pumper Holley carburetor, which has been around for decades.

What is really reflective of the advances in car and engine building is the age-old apples to oranges comparison. When the speeds at Talladega first hit the mysterious and fascinating 200 mph mark in the first year of racing there (1969), the cars were using 426, 427 or 429 cubic inch engines and 10 inch wheels and tires—a proven combination of power and traction—the staples of any race car. By the time the speeds climbed back up to that 200 mph level again in 1982 and after, the cars had been regulated to 358 cubic inch engines and eight inch wheels and tires. With the advent of aftermarket parts, the influx of money into what was now the Winston Cup Series and the continuing involvement by the factories with their engineers and wind tunnel development, the limitations of the smaller engines and tires were overcome. Bodywork was more streamlined and the marriage of high technology in that area and stronger racing engines has created exciting racing at higher speeds than thought possible. Today's engines run a 14:1 compression ratio, and with some horsepower estimates at 800+ horsepower and 500 lb-ft. of torque, at about 9000 rpm max. Of course, an engine builder would rather give his life than divulge true numbers, but these are relatively close.

The Carb Restrictor Plate

As speeds at Talladega and Daytona escalated, it quickly became apparent any driver would have to clear the 200 mph barrier just to make the races. As mentioned previously, while qualifying for the 1987 Winston 500 at Talladega, Bill Elliott recorded a blistering lap of 212.809 mph. The day of the 200 mph starting field had come. And despite the fact that Elliott had held the qualifying record there for an amazing six straight races, it was the state of racing in NASCAR's Winston Cup. With his 212 mph run, racing had now crossed a different, unknown barrier. The race started with Elliott on his well-earned pole, but what he and the crowd didn't expect was what followed next.

Bobby Allison, driving the Stavola Brothers Miller American Beer Buick, got caught up in traffic and a multi-car wreck—a common occurrence on superspeedways with so many cars carrying so much speed. But what happened next was not in anyone's mind. Allison's car got airborne, twisting and turning into the catch fencing along the grandstand part of the track. The car took out over 400 feet of the safety fence and came dangerously close to the flag stand. Because the fence was knocked down, the race was immediately red flagged and halted. Catch fencing is designed to keep wheels or car parts from leaving the track. It was not, however, designed to keep a 3400-lb. car *inside* the track. Luckily, Bobby's wayward car did not go into the capacity-filled grandstand. That would have changed the face of NASCAR racing forever, or perhaps ended it altogether. This accident, along with Elliott's pole speed and another similar accident by Cale Yarborough, convinced officials that action was needed, and soon.

NASCAR took several steps to keep the racers and fans safe, two of them concerning the engines. One was the return of the very unpopular restrictor plate, a device that had not been used since 1971, when speeds first topped 200 mph. However, it was a quick, effective and proven way to slow a car down. The plate is simply a piece of sheet aluminum placed between the carburetor and intake manifold. With smaller holes corresponding to the holes in the bottom of the carb, the plate greatly reduces the flow of the air and fuel passing into the intake and combustion chamber. It is the reverse of what had been going on all these years: less fuel

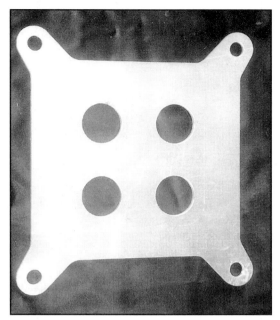

After several high speed accidents that nearly sent cars into the grandstands, NASCAR took the drastic step of curbing speeds on the two fastest superspeedways, Daytona and Talladega. This restrictor plate cut more than 200 horsepower from an engine's output, and has been unpopular with just about everyone—fans, drivers, engine builders—except NASCAR officials.

mixture into the engine means less power—a lot less. In today's modern racing engines, for example, an unrestricted motor easily puts out close to 800 horsepower. When a restrictor plate is added, it not only changes many of the engine's dynamics but drops the horsepower to about 600. The idea worked and the pole speed for the next Winston 500 in 1988 was reduced to 198 mph. The downsides for the racers were a longer "ramp time" for the engine to build up speed during restarts and after pit stops, and the fact that the power wasn't there if a driver needed to use it to get out of trouble. It also tended to bunch up the cars, made passing difficult and created multi-car accidents.

Many driver and owners would have preferred smaller engines rather than use the plates. The airflow over the cars had always been an important factor at Talladega and Daytona, the tracks where plates would now be required. When a driver went to pass on these tracks, he had to have a drafting partner or he would end up being effectively

"But what happened next was not in anyone's mind. Allison's car got airborne, twisting and turning into the catch fencing along the grandstand part of the track."

Johnny Mantz won NASCAR's first superspeedway race, the 1950 Southern 500 at Darlington, in 1950. Mantz bought the car in Florence, SC, changed the plugs and tires, and won the race at an average speed of just 75+ miles per hour after being the slowest qualifier. Mike Slade photo.

slowed down and the cars behind him would easily pass. This created a new style of driving where the driver would literally keep the gas pedal "mashed" down all the way around the track. Imagine driving into a turn that was banked 33 degrees at 200 mph without lifting the gas pedal!

In 1997, in another effort to reduce speeds that were once again creeping over the 200 mph barrier, NASCAR limited the compression ratio to 14:1 after some teams were using ratios as high as 20:1. That's holding for now, but engine builders spend countless hours and dollars to give their driver all the motor they can to win races. It's just the nature of the racing beast.

The other idea NASCAR had for making the cars safer had to do with changes to the bodies of the cars, and that information is discussed on page 122.

THE EVOLUTION OF THE MODERN STOCK CAR

Now that we have an understanding of the development of engine technology, let's examine how the actual car developed over the years. As described in Chapter 2, when NASCAR formed the new Grand National

class, it quickly became more popular than their Modified class. The rules dictated that cars running in the class must be "strictly stock," and so they were. The cars that raced at the track were often driven there. The headlights were taped, a race was run, then the cars were driven home. Talk about low budget racing!

The Fifties

In 1950 and 1951, the Olds Rocket 88 engine, as installed in a Cadillac or Olds, would win most of the NASCAR races. However, the first real "car" to stand out the following year would be the Hudson Hornet.

Hudson Hornet—The first car to dominate totally during this early NASCAR period was the Hudson Hornet. Eager to get his new Grand National class going, Bill France took an enthusiastic driver named Marshall Teague, who had been running a Hornet independently with a Smokey Yunick-built engine, to Hudson in Detroit to sell them on the idea of a factory racing program. Recognizing that this was an opportunity to gain an edge in the new, emerging performance market, Hudson went for it.

Hudson already had the chassis. In 1949, they had introduced their unique "step-down" chassis. The step-down used a perimeter frame with semi-unit shell construction. You stepped over the frame rail when entering the door. This allowed car height to be reduced, lowering the center of gravity. Careful matching of springs and shocks and the lower center of gravity resulted in outstanding handling for those days—perfect for racing.

The problem was putting together the list of "stock" parts to ensure the Hudson stayed out front. The Hudson people put in charge a young engineer, Vince Piggins, to develop their newly formed and aptly named "Severe-Usage Parts Program."

All of the stock car tracks were dirt then, which was very hard on parts. In cooperation with Kelsey-Hayes, Piggins developed

Marshall Teague was running his own Hornet, with an engine built by Smokey Yunick, when Bill France Sr. took him to Detroit to pitch Hudson on an official factory program. Hudson went for it, and the Hornets would dominate from 1952 to 1954. This is Teague after winning a 1950s race on the Daytona Beach course. Courtesy Daytona Racing Archives.

the first reinforced wheel. Up to then, racers had been reinforcing the wire wheels with boiler plate—which tended to break spindles. Other "Severe Usage" parts Piggins and his group developed included larger diameter rear axle shafts, shot-peened spindles and steering arms, and much more. These components were soon adopted by other teams as well.

When coupled with the famed "7X" flathead six engine, the Hudson Hornet would dominate NASCAR from 1952 to 1954.

Tim Flock and Herb Thomas took their Hudsons to a 1-2 points finish in the 1952 season, each garnering an impressive eight wins. Thomas then turned the tables and won the '53 title with an overpowering 12-win performance in his Hornet. Dick Rathman, also in a Hornet, took third with five wins. Amazingly, Thomas would win 12 times again in 1954, but he still had to settle for a runner-up finish in the championship to winner Lee Petty in a Chrysler.

In all, Thomas won 39 times in his Hudsons, making it one of the most successful nameplates in NASCAR history, and certainly the first major one. With its outstanding handling and superior aerodynamics, the Hudson did have a significant advantage. Also, because the frame rails were outside the rear wheels, which was unique, Marshall Teague and the Herb Thomas Team employed an unusual driving technique. The Hudson pilots would actually lay the right rear fender against the guardrails and nail the throttle. Where the other stockers had to go low in the turns, the fastest line for the Hudsons was high and wide! Sparks would fly and the cars would be gouged down the right side, but they won races that way. The resulting tortured bodywork became known as "Darlington Stripes," named after the track where this technique was most often practiced.

Herb Thomas's Hudson Hornet

One look at the Hudson Hornet design of the early 1950s quickly reveals that its sleek lines most likely had an unfair advantage over the squarish shapes of the competition. And this was in the days before the importance of race car aerodynamics was clearly understood.

The machine shown here is the car that won the 1951 championship, piloted by NASCAR Champion driver and car owner Herb Thomas. A young Smokey Yunick built the potent powerplants for this low-slung machine. The Hudson was also possibly the most powerful engine of the time, aided greatly by the Twin-H Carburetion System which had been encouraged by another Hudson driver, Marshall Teague.

The Hudson won the NASCAR Championships for four straight years from 1951 thru 1954. A measure of the domination of the Hudsons came from the fact that they won 13 AAA/NASCAR races in 1951, a startling 48 the following year, and 46 in 1953. Even when the factory Hudson racing program went away in 1954, there were still plenty of the machines around and they were run. Thomas, using year-old equipment, finished second to Lee Petty in his Chrysler for the Grand National Championship the year after the factory shut down the operation.

The domination of the Hornet came mostly from its low center of gravity, which added greatly to the handling of the model. The Hudson had a strong and reliable rear end/axle assembly, and an excellent selection of rear end gear ratios. This alone allowed the car to be tuned to each and every track it raced. The transmission was also reported by the teams to be very reliable.

But the technology was moving swiftly and it wasn't long before the Chrysler 300 and new 1955 Chevy overcame the Hudsons and they were no longer able to compete—both on the track and in the marketplace. However, the Hudson Hornet established a racing legacy that won't be forgotten.

Herb Thomas drove this '51 Hornet to 7 victories and the championship, which was only the beginning of his domination. He would go on to win 8 in '52, 12 in '53 and 12 again in '54. In all, he won 39 times in Hudsons. Bob Fairman photo.

Technical Evolution—As popular as the Grand National class was, it became apparent that the chassis of these cars were not designed to withstand the speeds and forces generated by racing. To get around the "strictly stock" rules, the factories were developing high performance parts for cars that weren't originally designed to handle them. Parts began to break, often with catastrophic results. It was clear to NASCAR that something had to be done before the government stepped in, so they began to slowly allow homemade improvements in chassis design for the sake of safety.

Racers began to use truck parts when they could, because they were stronger and built for heavy duty use. Truck brakes, which were much larger and designed for stopping heavier trucks, were used to slow down the relatively heavy sedans, which were going at triple digit speeds. Axles frequently broke during hard cornering, and the solution was to swap for a set of truck ones. In some cases, parts were swapped with those of larger, luxury models. Ford sedans used parts from their much larger Lincolns and Mercurys. The Plymouths and Dodges often switched to somewhat beefier Chrysler parts.

There's an old saying that says "give 'em an inch, they'll take a yard," and racers began to take advantage of NASCAR's allowance of stronger parts. Soon, cars were being modified in a variety of ways, and resembled their factory counterparts less and less each race.

Tires were becoming a major problem. Special purpose race tires had yet to be built, and the stock tires available clearly weren't up to racing stress. To keep an eye on the condition of the right side tires at speed, drivers used trap-door devices that could be lifted with a wire or lanyard to actually view the condition of the rubber. Once the white color of the tire cords appeared at racing speed, it was time to hit the pits, pronto!

During the '50s, simple roll bars evolved into roll cages. The primary concern was to provide added safety for the driver, but it wasn't long before roll cages were integrated into the frame to stiffen the chassis. A more rigid chassis meant better cornering ability.

Although drivers had long ago used bucket seats from military airplanes, they went back to use another military device: seat belts. Pilots not only used lap belts, but shoulder harnesses as well. It didn't take long before these, too, were mandated by NASCAR.

As power increased under the hood and speeds rose, other stock pieces needed to be reinforced or replaced. The extra g forces often tore out the wheel centers, especially on the right side. Either beefed-up stock wheels or heavy-duty truck wheels were used as standard equipment by the late 1950s. Another area to go quickly was the factory shocks. Racers initially installed bigger shocks, then tried multiple shocks per wheel. On some cars, as many as four were used on each wheel, but usually there were just two. Dual shocks were used on the rears until the 1980s, when they were replaced by more effective gas-filled shocks. Today, shock absorber technology and tuning has become so sophisticated that almost all shops have at least one shock absorber dyno and a team member who specializes only in this area. That's how critical dampening has become to handling.

Chrysler Dominates—After Hudson, the next car to dominate was the Chrysler 300. During 1955 and 1956, these Chryslers

Hudsons could also run well on dirt, like this '54 model. Courtesy the Harvey Collection.

This original '56 Mercury NASCAR stock car was driven by Russ Truelove on the Daytona Beach course. During one of those races, it flipped six times.

In addition to the Hornets and Chryslers, Tim Flock also drove this Mercury.

The immaculately prepared Chryslers by Carl Kiekhaefer were so dominant in '55 and '56 that all other teams thought they must be cheating, and the fans were unhappy because there wasn't much close racing. Above, Tim Flock in a Chrysler 300 (on the inside of the turn) leads teammate Speedy Thompson (in a Dodge, #500) through the north turn of the Daytona Beach course in 1956. Courtesy Daytona Racing Archives.

would be at the top of the podium more than any other manufacturer, especially those prepared by Carl Kiekhaefer and sponsored by his Mercury Outboard Motor Company. Kiekhaefer was one of the first racers to substitute beefier taxicab and truck parts for the stock components to withstand the higher stresses of racing.

He was also one of the first to approach racing as a business rather than a recreational pastime. Kiekhaefer hired top crews and drivers and insisted on total professionalism, from car preparation to clean uniforms for the driver and crew—no dirty T-shirts allowed. He also was one of the first to realize the importance of quick and efficient pit stops and insisted that his crews practice regularly to get times down. He also was one

Carl Kiekhaefer and his monster Chrysler 300s changed the face of NASCAR racing, bringing a sense of respectability and professionalism to the sport. He made his crew wear uniforms, and put the cars in covered transporters rather than on trailers. Mike Slade photo.

Kiekhaefer spared no attention to detail; his cars were always prepared to perfection (not unlike another top car owner, Roger Penske). This is a near-flawless restoration of Flock's 1956 car.

The trunk on this 300B Chrysler was still functional, so to keep it from flying up, a bungee cord was installed. Not exactly what you'd call a high-tech fastener! Remember, these were factory-built cars taken directly from the showroom floor and converted into racing machines with limited modifications.

of the first to haul race cars to the track in immaculate transporters, something that amazed his competitors. In fact, many credit Kiekhaefer with bringing professionalism and some respect to the sport of NASCAR.

The talented Tim Flock won the second title for Chrysler (Lee Petty won the first in 1954) in 1955 driving for Kiekhaefer, then Buck Baker won the title the next year for a total of two years in a row for Kiekhaefer's cars. Baker would go on to win again the next year but that would be in a Chevrolet. The team was also campaigning Dodges at the same time, and that brand added eight

victories during the 1956 season, which was in addition to the 22 of 29 Grand National races won by the dominant Chryslers that same season.

Take a closer look at the 300, and you'll wonder why it was so successful. It was huge and heavy, and most of the credit went to the awesome Hemi engine, which had by far the most usable horsepower of any stock American car at the time. Still, with that huge mammoth grille and wide wind blocking front end, it is hard to see why it won.

Much of the Chrysler success came from the superb management style of owner Karl Kiekhaefer, who thought no detail too trivial. He demanded perfection from his drivers, perfect car preparation from his crews, and even had a weatherman employed to provide humidity and other data for even more precise engine tuning. The team's success was so overwhelming that other teams claimed they were cheating. While the cars were not all that much superior to the rest of the field, they were in the highest state of preparation and that was their advantage. The performance level of cars on the street had averaged out among the factory car builders. Attention to detail on almost every component of a good car with a great motor was the secret in the early days of "strictly stock" cars.

The consistency of the Kiekhaefer team

"Take a closer look at the 300, and you'll wonder why it was so successful. It was huge and heavy, and most of the credit went to the awesome Hemi engine, which had by far the most usable horsepower of any stock American car at the time."

The NASCAR convertible division gave fans an unobstructed view of the drivers. Here, Marvin Panch is trying to engage reverse so he can turn around, as Larry Frank, heading the right way, exits the north turn at Daytona Beach in 1957. Note that Larry Frank's car has no rollbars, an illustration of the lack of safety rules at the time. Courtesy Daytona Racing Archives.

Curtis Turner also ran convertibles. This is a fully restored 1956 Ford. Despite Turner's awesome driving talent, the Chevys dominated the short-lived series.

also created considerable booing from the fans for the overwhelming domination. Just ask Jeff Gordon about that: He also experienced it in the 1990s.

The Short-Lived Convertible Division— With the tremendous resurgence of the convertible in America starting in the mid-1950s, NASCAR briefly added a convertible class to the series in 1956. The Chevys dominated, winning the title in all four years of the class. Bob Welbon won three of those titles. The Chryslers and Dodges stuck to Grand National events.

Although some of the convertibles featured a single rollbar behind the front seat, not all of them did, and the danger was obvious. Therefore, NASCAR pulled the plug on the series after the 1959 season.

The '57 Chevy—The 1957 Chevy design has been described as one of the most popu-

This 1959 Chevy was driven to victory at the '59 Southern 500 by Jim Reed and gave Goodyear its first major stock car competition victory. Bob Fairman photo.

"As the decade drew to a close, the 'strictly stock' cars began to deviate more from stock with each race."

lar street cars ever produced. It was equally as popular as a NASCAR racer. Buck Baker drove one of the machines to the title in 1957, finishing in the top ten an amazing 38 out of 40 times, with 10 total wins. A year later, using the same body design even though it was an old model, such legends as Fireball Roberts, Frankie Schneider and Speedy Thompson drove '57 Chevys to win 25 of 51 races. The new Chevy small-block engine was one of the big reasons for this success. But a lesser known fact is that the new engine was set back farther in the '57 chassis than previous models, which helped with weight distribution and resulted in better handling.

Chassis Tuning Tech—As the decade drew to a close, the "strictly stock" cars began to deviate more from stock with each race. Although it wasn't visible from the grandstands or the outside of the car, many changes had taken place in the chassis and suspension areas. Chassis were reinforced with steel plate and bars, and stronger spin-

dles and hubs were developed just for racing. The new parts made the cars not only safer but, coupled with better chassis adjusting, faster as well. In the early 1960s, adjustable screw jacks were used to fine-tune each spring and corner of the car. The screw jacks, also known as weight jacks and load bolts, were installed into the frame over the centerline of the spring. They were a threaded rod turning through a nut welded onto the frame and pushing a steel plate and cup holding the top of the spring. Raising or lowering the frame over the spring effectively adjusted the spring's rate. If a driver needed more "bite" on the right rear or less "pushing" (the act of the car going straight and not turning) he might adjust the spring. While originally designed for coil springs, they were also fashioned for the leaf springs used in the rear of some cars.

These adjusting devices really helped to fine-tune the suspension to each track, and increase cornering speeds. Faster cornering meant more launch coming onto the

"When the teams rolled into Bill France's new Florida track, no one was quite sure what to make of a track this size and shape."

Pontiac ruled from 1960 through 1962, winning 59 races and 71 pole positions. One reason was the torque advantage the Pontiac motors had, but another is the talent: Pontiacs were driven by top drivers such as Junior Johnson, David Pearson, Joe Weatherly, Marvin Panch, Banjo Matthews and Fireball Roberts. Roberts, who always carried number 22, was well known to NASCAR fans during the 1960s. Here is Fireball's '62 Pontiac. Rick Rickard photo.

straightaway, which translated into more overall top speed and lower lap times. The chassis was now evolving into a stiffer unit that required more durable suspension parts. Leaf springs were also modified with a fabricated hanger that featured multiple holes to raise or lower the ride height in the rear. This device allowed for the spring rate to be adjusted at the rear as well. It had the same effect the screw jack did on a front coil spring. There were soon homemade and aftermarket sway bars of different sizes available to match different tracks, and they too were adjustable. For example, a track like Daytona required a larger diameter unit to combat the incredible loads race cars and drivers had never seen, much less imagined.

The Sixties

Pontiac Rules—During the 1960 through 1962 seasons, Pontiac race cars were very dominant. Though they were still built by

their owners as opposed to the race car factories that would come shortly, their slightly bigger engines also had more torque to move them around the track even more effectively. The first sign of this was at the inaugural Daytona 500 in 1959. When the teams rolled into Bill France's new Florida track, no one was quite sure what to make of a track this size and shape. Until now, the biggest track was Darlington, built in 1950, which was only a 1.3 mile track and had turns banked only 23 and 25 degrees depending on which turn you were in. By comparison, Daytona was 2.5 miles in length and banked at a whopping 33 degrees! The Pontiac driven by Cotton Owens nabbed the very first Daytona pole with an at-the-time-unheard-of speed of 143.198 mph.

With the considerable driving talents of such stars as Junior Johnson, David Pearson, Joe Weatherly, Marvin Panch, Banjo

Junior Johnson (#27) leads Fireball Roberts (#22), both in Pontiacs on the high banks of Daytona at the 500 in 1962. Trailing is Richard Petty in his '62 Plymouth, a position he and other competitors were in during Pontiac's domination that year. Courtesy Daytona Racing Archives.

Matthews and Fireball Roberts, Pontiac was the brand to beat in 1960–1962. During that time they won 59 races and 71 poles with Weatherly winning the title in 1962.

Fireball's Ford—In 1963, the characteristic light purple Number 22 Ford of Fireball Roberts was about as well known as Dale Earnhardt's black Number 3 Monte Carlo is today. That year, he finished fifth in the points with four wins and 11 top five finishes in only 20 starts of the 53 races possible.

The reason for the strange color was because Ford wanted to make a big statement that Fireball was defecting from the successful Pontiac group. Because there were no cars that color in NASCAR Grand National Racing, the superstar got the strange shade and, needless to say, a lot of kidding from his competitors.

One technical innovation resulted from this Ford: The engine ran pretty hot, and threw off a lot of heat into the cockpit. Fireball solved the problem by laying a blanket of asbestos on the front floorboard, which is a technique still used today. Asbestos is still used in many of today's modern forms, as are other high tech materials such as those used in the space program. Heat is a bigger problem; as on the street, the engines of today just run hotter.

Tragically, Fireball would be killed at Charlotte during the World 600 the following season in a 1964 Ford.

Junior's '63 Impala—As mentioned on page 45, the 1963 Impala driven by Junior Johnson was famous for its "mystery motor." Johnson drove the wheels off the car, and it displayed awesome speeds, times and horsepower. With Ray Fox turning the wrenches, the Impala made quite an impact, although it was one of the few Chevys being

This is the 1963 Ford driven by the late Fireball Roberts to his second Southern 500 victory in 1963. Roberts set a record speed of over 129 miles per hour. The engine ran so hot that Roberts put asbestos on the firewall and floorboard to keep the cockpit cool—a technique still used today. Bob Fairman photo.

Junior Johnson drove this 1963 Chevy to seven wins, ten fast times and nine track records with no factory support! Johnson won $65,710 with this car during the 1963 season, an amazing sum of money for that year. Bob Fairman photo.

Joe Weatherly's '64 Mercury advertised on the hood that horsepower output was 410, but in reality, the Bud Moore Engineering-built 427 was pumping out between 460 and 470 horsepower. Bob Fairman photo.

run that year. Unfortunately, while it was a star that year, it faded quickly and pretty much signaled Chevy's absence from NASCAR for the next four years.

The Chevy Impala was too big and heavy to stay competitive. With the factory not actively involved in racing at the time, the Ford and Mopar teams were ahead in the development of faster body styles utilizing more aerodynamic features to help the car get around the track. Ford, as one example,

came out with what they called its 1963 1/2 Ford Galaxie with sloping rear window and roof pillars that were much more suited to racing on the bigger tracks. Chevy's roofline at the time was more abrupt and therefore less effective in the wind. Much like today, it was the bigger tracks that got more attention for the simple reason of speed.

The Fox/Johnson Chevy was only one car, as opposed to the factory effort that would deliver six or more cars to the track ready to race and win. So while the limited, but game effort by Johnson, Fox and maybe even Chevy was outnumbered, it was also a matter of playing catch up with the other teams. Very few major sports allow a player to come back in after an absence and be a top runner. In racing it was and always will be a matter of technology.

During these seasons, teams often displayed the horsepower of the car on the hood, or at least, a close approximation. Obviously, no one would give away their true numbers, so many drivers would quote the factory rating. Joe Weatherly's '64 Mercury stated that there were 410 ponies under the hood, but in reality, the 427 engine was probably putting out between 460 and 470 horsepower.

Building Cars from Scratch—Up until the early 1960s, the conversion of street cars into race cars was done pretty much by the race teams themselves. NASCAR driver Curtis Crawfish Crider recalls a time in 1961 when he purchased a brand-new Mercury from a dealership, drove it home, stripped it down and built it into a race car in only 13 days. He then took the car to Darlington for the Southern 500 and had the fastest Mercury at 119.854 miles per hour. But that kind of activity was starting to cease with the formation of companies that built racing parts and complete, purpose-built, turn-key race cars from scratch.

As speeds rose, so did the severity of the wrecks. Drivers were still, as a whole, faring well with all the safety devices decreed by

THE GOLDEN BOY

One of the most illustrious NASCAR drivers was "Golden Boy" Fred Lorenzen. He earned that nickname when he became the first stock car driver to top $100,000 in prize money in a single season, which was 1963. That year, he had 6 victories from 29 starts, and finished third in the points standings. His total take for that year was $122,587.28.

Lorenzen was most often behind the wheel of his famous #28 Holman & Moody-prepared factory Ford, a restored example of a 1966 model which is shown here. The car shows the state-of-the art for the mid 1960s time period.

After Lorenzen drove the car in '66, it was purchased and driven by Wendell Scott, who drove it for one season and junked the car in 1967. The car was stored for 17 years before it was restored by master race car restorer Kim Haynes. He did considerable research on the car and everything is as close as possible to the way it was.

The car carried a stock Ford frame and factory sheet metal, but no rear spoiler, tricked-up body, or ultra wide tires. Even so, the long-track versions of this car were capable of 170 mph on the superspeedways.

The car's correct 427 cubic inch engine was long gone when Haynes got the car, but he was able to find a suitable block and accomplish the build-up. He also located one of the special large input shaft transmissions. Fortunately, the floating rear end was still with the car. Because the original body was badly rusted, it was necessary to acquire a factory body.

Many say, including Lorenzen himself, that he retired much too early, well before his prime.

NASCAR, but the cars were taking a terrible beating, causing teams to take longer to rebuild them. It was the same way with building new race cars. With speeds hitting the 170 mph mark in the mid-1960s, NASCAR allowed for the creation of totally built race cars. In the past, the cars started out as street cars converted to race cars. Teams would often buy a partially stripped car and rebuild it into a race car. In the days of factory involvement during this transition time, the factories would offer "bodies in white," a partially built car ready to convert into racers with less work. Even during the factory pullout from racing, these "bodies in

white" were still showing up, often delivered secretly during the night with no paperwork or return address.

From the racer's point of view, it was taking longer to rework an existing car than to build one from scratch, so that's what they did, building race cars from the ground up and finishing them off with factory body parts. They even prepped the cars for each race.

Holman & Moody—Although a private company, Holman & Moody was the unofficial extension of Ford racing in the early 1960s and built all their race cars and parts. Holman & Moody consisted of Ralph

Johnny Rutherford, three-time Indycar champ, raced stock cars throughout the '60s. This is his '66 Chevy prepared by Ray Fox Engineering.

Moody and John Holman, and using Moody's personal experience as a driver, they devised a new rear spring design for better rear axle torque control that incorporated a special spring seat fabricated onto the axle housing. H&M also changed the entire steering geometry to acclimate the car's handling to different tracks. Teams were figuring out the geometry of all those moving chassis parts under the engine and coming up with some good racing ideas—as were the factories. To illustrate just how innovative the H&M team was, consider how they solved the overheating problem plaguing the differentials of the cars. The diffs were turning far more rpm than they were designed for, and they would literally ignite, especially during pit stops. Holman & Moody's solution was to install a power steering pump driven by a yoke and pulley off the differential housing to circulate the differential lubricant to a Cessna aircraft oil cooler located in the trunk. The heat was dissipated by ducting cool air and by adding an electric blower originally used in the car's HVAC system. The oil was then routed back to the differential. This is one of the first uses of a "remote oil cooler system" so common today, especially on engines.

Ford Dominates '66-'67 Seasons—The 1966–1967 Ford Fairlane, first of the downsized cars, was one of the strong contenders as title winners Ned Jarrett ('66) and Junior Johnson ('67) each won 13 times, giving Ford a total of 48 wins over the two-year period. Even more amazing was the fact that 32 of those wins came in a row, including Indycar driver Mario Andretti's Daytona 500 win in 1967.

Petty's Satellite—The biggest challenger to the Fords in 1967 was Richard Petty in his Plymouth Satellite. Petty was one of the first to use an adjustable torsion bar suspension. Most other racers still used screw-jacks on a chassis with coil springs in the front and leaf springs in the rear. But Petty's setup effectively was a "controlled" control arm system. The reason for Petty using the torsion bar suspension was the fact that the Mopars used that system on the street and NASCAR still wanted the teams to utilize the same system that came under the body style. Instead of a coil or leaf spring, the torsion bar system limited the movement of the control arms that held the spindles much as the springs regulated the movement of their control arms. The bar was installed into the corresponding pocket of the frame and preloaded with torque, thereby earning its name. As the bar pushed the control arm, the action of arm fighting back as the car was under load pushed back. The bars were used in the front of the Mopars while leaf springs were used in the rear.

The torsion bar suspension would fall by the wayside when the Mopars would eventually leave NASCAR. Then, the choice of any team running was either the Chevy front and rear coil springs or the Ford front/coil and rear/leaf spring systems.

The combo of Richard Petty and the Satellite was almost unbeatable as they captured a record 27 victories in that '67 season alone (in those days, NASCAR ran more than 50 races a year, sometimes as many as 70). This is also a record that will most like-

ly never be broken, because NASCAR no longer runs as many races in a season. This success was even more astounding given the two-ton weight of the Satellite, and the fact that it was as aerodynamic as a block of wood. This domination was testimony both to the awesome talent of Petty and the brute horsepower of the second generation 426 Hemi.

Another late 1960s concept that was adopted was the use of older proven components and design on later models. For example, Ford NASCAR models used the reinforced, front control arm design from the 1965 Galaxie well into the 1970s. GM cars as well as some Fords adopted the longer rear trailing arms from a GM pickup truck to go with their Chevelle front end suspension. That particular design had triangulated upper and lower control arms as opposed to Ford's single pivot lower arms and strut design. Oddly enough, what NASCAR would end up with and use to this day would be a combination of the Ford passenger car suspension on the front with the rear suspension derived from the early 1970s

Chevy/GMC truck. The front was and is a single pivot lower control arm and coil springs, while the rear consists of long, rear control arms on coil springs with a Ford rear end housing and gear set. Today, those components are still being used but no longer come from the factories in Detroit. Instead, they are hard-core race parts finely honed over the years for both performance and longer life and fabricated by outside manufacturers for such racing.

Aerodynamic Super Cars—Much of the development of NASCAR race equipment at the factory level was nothing more than brute horsepower. Even if a car is not as aerodynamic as its competitors, more motor can compensate. Chrysler's success with the 426 Hemi and Ford's remarkable comeback in '66-'67 with the 427 dual-quad tunnel port engine were evidence of this.

Airflow wasn't given much thought up until this time, mainly because speeds weren't high enough for it to become much of a problem. Frankly, the cars raced during the mid-1960s were as aerodynamic as a brick. The front ends were flat and vertical,

Richard Petty's 1967 Plymouth Satellite captured an amazing 27 victories during the 1967 season. At the time, the NASCAR schedule had considerably more races on its yearly schedule—48 to be exact. It's highly unlikely Petty's record will ever be broken as the current Winston Cup schedule only features 30 to 34 races per season. Mike Slade photo.

The Ford Torino was popular with late 1960s NASCAR and short track drivers alike because of its aerodynamics. Just look at the sloping rear deck. This short track '68 model used a 427 cid engine. Ford dominated both the '68 and '69 NASCAR seasons. Courtesy Harvey Collection.

"Suddenly, race car builders began looking at the shape of the body— not only the power potential of the engine— when choosing a car to campaign on the circuit."

pushing air much like a snowplow. These blunt front ends created a turbulence at higher speeds that began to affect handling greatly as it whirled under the car.

One of the first builders to address this was Smokey Yunick, whose mind never stopped looking for an edge of any kind, legal or not. He was one of the first to devise a full belly pan under the car to smooth airflow and reduce drag as it passed underneath. The result was so successful that it was promptly banned by NASCAR. This of course, didn't deter Smokey, who then decided to smooth out the stock floorpan as much as possible. He also widened the stock front bumper and changed the angle to create the same downforce effect as an air dam.

These innovations launched a new area of development and research as racers and factory manufacturers began to look at managing airflow as a way to increase speed and improve handling. "Coefficient of drag," or "Cd," once a term only applied to airplanes, was heard often around the pits.

But there was another trend afoot in the mid-'60s that was changing this picture. This was the increasing popularity of high

banked superspeedways on the NASCAR Southern circuit, where cars could hits speeds up to 200 mph. Tracks like Daytona, Talladega, Atlanta and Charlotte put new emphasis on high speed aerodynamic performance. Suddenly, race car builders began looking at the shape of the body—not only the power potential of the engine—when choosing a car to campaign on the circuit.

Chrysler's Charger 500—Most will agree that it was Chrysler that was the first to give race teams some special low-drag aerodynamics to work with. The Dodge Charger had been redesigned for 1968, with sleek styling and a tunnel-back layout at the rear window, much like the fastbacks of only a few years earlier. Wheel opening lips were flush. The quarter panel and roof C-pillars swept back, but the window notched down steeply between the rear roof pillars. Despite its racy looks, this roof pillar layout was bad from an aerodynamic standpoint.

There was a lot of turbulence in the hollow behind the window. Chrysler's fix was to throw a gently sloped window across the gap between the C-pillars, and extend it back farther on the rear deck, flush mount-

The street version of the Ford Talladega was almost identical to the race version. In fact, the street version shown here was designed by Ford with racing in mind. It carried very few luxury options and was available in 1969. Phil Kunz photo.

ing it. The change could be made on the original Charger body line with relatively simple tooling. Additionally, the grille was moved forward, flush with the front end. This further helped the coefficient of drag factor. The overall result was a big reduction in aerodynamic drag when combined with the rounded body sides and flush wheel-opening lips.

Chrysler's Charger 500s were released to NASCAR teams early in the '68 season. The "500" designation represented the number of cars Dodge built to make the model eligible for Grand National racing as stated by the homologation rules. The cars were said to be 2-3 mph faster than the original Chargers on the superspeedways.

The Dodge Daytona—This was only the beginning. Encouraged by the track record of the 500 model in 1968, Chrysler engineers went much, much further in 1969. They set out to clean up the Charger body. Using scale models in the 7 x 10 ft wind tunnel at Wichita University, they designed a pointed nose for the 500 body that reduced the drag coefficient by a full 23%. Admittedly, it wasn't very practical for the street. The new nose extended 18 inches far-

ther forward and eliminated the front bumper. Try to get away with that today! Also, the headlights were concealed to reduce the Cd further. The nose was actually a separate triangular hard rubber piece with a small radiator opening located directly in the middle.

But this unique nose, while reducing drag, also unloaded the rear tires, which made the car prone to oversteer and extremely unstable at high speed. The fix was a unique rear wing to give downforce. The wing was supported at the ends by vertical struts two feet above the deck, like some sort of airplane wing. The wing was mounted on aluminum uprights, with a standard tilt of about 11 degrees, but some teams adjusted it as high as 14 degrees. Each degree of deflection was worth about 50 pounds of downforce, so up to 650 pounds could be realized, which was needed on some superspeedways. As mentioned, the sloping nose created its own downforce, so much that without the rear wing, the rear tires were light. The Daytona had a Cd of .35, which was unheard of for the time period.

But this wing did the job. The new '69 Dodge Daytona was at least 6-8 mph faster

This show car is a nearly exact reproduction of the Richard Petty number 43 Hemi Superbird. These cars dominated as long as NASCAR allowed them to. Bob Fairman photo.

than the '68 Charger 500 with the same horsepower.

Ford Continues Domination—But this success didn't translate all that well to the track in '68 and '69 when the Fords dominated once again. Although Richard Petty's early success is usually associated with Mopar, he ran a Torino Talladega in 1969, which was a shock to his Plymouth fans. He simply couldn't pass up the superb aerodynamics of the Talladega. Ford's approach to the conversion was similar to Chrysler's: Stick an extended sheet metal nose on the front of a standard body to reduce front-end drag, and provide a minimum grille opening to cool the engine on the street. Ford's nose wasn't as tapered as the Chrysler's, so it wasn't as efficient aerodynamically. But it only extended 12 inches forward and didn't need the huge rear wing. The bumper was designed flush-tight to the fender so that there was no break in the airflow at speed. It wasn't that particularly sleek-looking, but it ultimately got the job done. These Fords began the season with the 427 Shotgun engines, but would later move to the potent Boss 429 engines. NASCAR decreed that

enough of the engines had been produced, despite the fact that the engine was only available in Mustangs. The holmogation rule stated that a minimum of 500 cars and engines had to be produced to be eligible, but it didn't specify the engines had to be in the same vehicle! Talk about loopholes!

Petty had eight wins (out of a total of 11 for all Talladegas being raced) in 1969 along with 21 top-five finishes, which was only good enough to finish second to David Pearson, who was also piloting a Talladega prepared by Holman & Moody.

The Seventies

In 1970, Plymouth unveiled their version of the Daytona, called the Superbird, and Chrysler got it right this time. Although the Superbird looked like a duplicate of the Daytona, there were some subtle, yet significant differences. First, the Superbird's adjustable wing was taller, had more rake and was mounted further forward. The wing was taller not because it was better for performance, but so that the trunk lid would clear. The height therefore needed to be at least 25 inches.

The huge rear wing added a great deal of down-force, increasing high speed handling in the turns, but also causing the tires to wear faster. However, the Superbirds were still the cars to beat. Phil Kunz photo.

Bobby Allison at full speed at Talladega, in a 1971 Ford Torino prepared by Holman & Moody. Although the sloping roofline was certainly streamlined, it still had trouble competing against the Superbirds. Mike Slade photo.

Up front, another difference was that the Superbird's front end had a shorter chin spoiler. The little Road Runner cartoon character decal was the final telltale for those who still had trouble distinguishing it from the Daytona. Almost four times as many Superbirds were sold in 1970 than the '69 Daytona, so making the 500 minimum NASCAR quota was a little easier.

One problem with the design of the winged race cars was the tendency to wear the tires much faster than normal because of the increased downforce. Also, there was the "bubble scoop" on each fender above the front tires, which was designed to evacuate air from under the fenders. But the design failed, and in fact created problems with turbulence under the car. However, NASCAR wouldn't allow teams to remove them, but they were allowed to seal them up.

However, there's no question that the Superbirds and the Daytonas were the cars to beat in 1970. Petty came back from Ford to run these new cars, but the season belonged to Bobby Isaac. As mentioned on page 46, Isaac drove the wheels off Harry Hyde's Daytona, clocking an astounding lap of 201.10 mph around Talladega, a record that would stand for many years. He also went on to win the NASCAR Grand National Championship. In 1971, Richard Petty would do the same in his Superbird.

In 1971, Cotton Owens, a famous NASCAR driver turned owner, unveiled a new Plymouth Roadrunner with many innovative chassis designs that would set a new trend. The front suspension consisted of twin Regal Ride shocks with torsion bars, while the rears had twin shocks as well as leaf springs. Also, in a bold new move, Owens moved the dry sump oil tank from just the behind the left front wheel to behind the driver. This not only helped proportion the weight and reduced the amount of heat going to the driver's feet, but greatly reduced the chances of an oil fire and oil getting through the firewall to the driver in the event of wreck. An added bonus was less oil for the track crew to clean up after a wreck. Owens also attached engine headers to the body with springs to make it easier to change engines, and to help dampen engine vibrations.

Also competitive during '70 and '71 were

Cale Yarborough
SPECIAL
428

A pair of street version Mercury Spoiler II models that served as the basis for an awesome, and extremely aerodynamic, NASCAR racer. The design was very similar to the Ford Talladega. East Coast consumers could order the special Cale Yarborough edition (upper right), while West Coast consumers could only get the Dan Gurney edition. The street versions used the 428 engine. David Tucker photo.

Ford's Talladega and Mercury Cyclone cars, although they didn't dominate like '68 and '69. Through the 1971 season, they visited victory lane 15 times, and were most effective on the superspeedways. However, more often than not they finished second to the Plymouth Superbirds.

Ford's Cyclone Spoiler II—The Cyclone Spoiler II street version was available with either red or blue body-length stripes. Then, there was the racing treatment of the models that really got the public's attention. The Spoiler IIs sold on the East Coast carried the Cale Yarborough autograph sticker on the front fenders, while the Western versions were signed by Dan Gurney. The street versions also came stock with the 351 Windsor engines rated at 290 horsepower, but like the Talladega, the engine would not be used in the Spoiler II race version. The model incorporated the same extended fenderwell front

end as the Talladega, and was one of the first stock cars to be tested in a wind tunnel. There were also the same Talladega-style rolled rocker panels that set the Cyclone down an inch closer to the pavement, thereby dropping the car even lower for better handling.

In race trim, the Spoiler II was equipped with the 429 Hemi Ford engine, and the car/engine combination proved that it could definitely run up front. Cale Yarborough was the best Cyclone driver with three wins and 11 top-five finishes in only 19 starts during the 1970 season.

In 1970, Ford decided to cut back its racing activities, and withdrew official factory support. The 1970 Torino street car design, although sporty looking, was about as aerodynamic as a cardboard box! Therefore, a number of teams went back to their older model Spoiler IIs and Talladegas with continuing success. Each model had four wins during 1970, running against the new Superbirds, which got six wins. Then, they too went away.

The 1970 Monte Carlo—The 1970 Monte Carlo model arrived just after the wing wars, but because of its somewhat chunky appearance, it didn't get much attention from the racing community. In fact, when it was finally raced, it was as a promotional gimmick and not as a truly competitive effort. At the time, GM was not directly involved in racing as a factory effort and fans as well as track owners were getting bored with watching a two-car race between Ford and Chrysler. Richard Howard, the promoter of the Charlotte Motor Speedway, thought he could entice the legions of Chevy fans to come to the race if they could root for one of their own, even it didn't stand much chance of winning. But in just a few years, the Monte Carlo would evolve into a very successful race car, and would go on to be the most successful nameplate in Winston Cup history. One reason the Monte Carlo proved to be successful was that the engine was set back four inches more than other models, changing the center of gravity and the weight distribution for much better handling, especially on short

tracks, where more rearward weight is desirable.

Although the Monte Carlos started out as an attraction, by late 1971, they had become serious contenders. By the time the 1972 season started, Bobby Allison and Junior Johnson teamed up with the distinctive red and gold #12 Monte Carlos sponsored by another new name to racing, Coca-Cola. Together they won 10 of the now-reduced 31-race schedule, finished second 12 times and earned 11 poles. This consistency put them in second place for the points total. While they were the point men for the return of Chevy, they also didn't get along very well and split up when the season ended. Bobby went on his own and Junior hired Cale Yarborough to drive the new Chevelle Laguna S3 bodied cars.

Wood Brothers—After the Spoiler II,

This '72 Torino driven by George Follmer was about as aerodynamic as a brick! Ford withdrew official factory support in 1970, so racers went back to year-old Talladegas and Cyclones because they were more streamlined. Get a load of those pants! Mike Slade photo.

Donnie Allison, in the Wood Brothers Mercury, is rubbing door handles with his brother Bobby in the Holman & Moody Ford. The track is Talladega, the year 1972. Mike Slade photo.

Even though the sheet metal on the right side of his car was completely ripped off, Benny Parsons went on to finish the Rockingham race and win the 1973 Winston Cup championship. Mike Slade photo.

When Chevy redesigned the Chevelle in 1973, it was immediately adopted by a number of stock car teams, including this Coca-Cola-sponsored machine driven by Bobby Allison. Mike Slade photo.

Ford rolled out a new car based on the Mercury for the 1971 season. It was a sleek design and with its long fastback and sloping hood, it quickly became a favorite. The design remained basically unchanged through the 1974 season and showcased the talents of Bobby Allison and David Pearson, the latter in the famous Wood Brothers number 21 machines. The distinctive Wood

Brothers cars wore pearl white paint on the sides and a deep red metal-flake roof. Like the bright blue of Richard Petty, the distinctive paint job was so well known, the car really didn't need a number.

During a four-year period, from 1971-1974, the Wood Brothers Mercurys won 38 times with 39 pole positions. Two of those wins came from the incomparable A.J. Foyt driving for the Wood Brothers. Power was applied by the potent 427 Ford "Wedge Head" engines.

Although the Wood Brothers were very competitive whenever they showed up at a track, they actually never ran a full schedule, instead picking and choosing their races carefully. It would not be until 1985 with Kyle Petty driving, that the Stuart, Virginia, team known for their impressive pit stops would take on the full schedule.

Roger Penske—In 1974, Roger Penske introduced some braking technology that would vastly improve the performance of

Two of NASCAR's all-time greats at speed: Richard Petty is chased by Bobby Allison during the 1974 American 500 at Rockingham. Mike Slade photo.

In 1974, Roger Penske introduced 4-wheel disc brakes and AMC to NASCAR. The Matador, driven by Bobby Allison, captured one win, 10 top five finishes and three poles in its two seasons of racing. Allison poses next to the car prior to the 1975 Daytona 500 Rick Rickard photo.

The Wood Bros. pit crew springs into action at Darlington, 1976. The Wood Bros. perfected the art of the pit stop, and were so good that they were hired as consultants to train pit crews in Indycar racing. Mike Slade photo.

the cars. Bobby Allison drove Roger Penske's Matador, introducing not only four wheel disc brakes but American Motors to NASCAR. Prior to this no one had tried the aircraft-style brakes in NASCAR with any success. Penske had used American Motors Javelins and AMCs in road racing with Mark Donahue driving with great success. Moving to the NASCAR Winston Grand National Series, Penske brought these innovations with him in hopes of an advantage. It worked, however slightly, with one win, 10 top five finishes and three poles. Not too bad for the first new marque to compete in NASCAR in quite a few years. The car created interest in the sport that was already growing out of its traditional Southeastern fan base.

From that time in the mid 1970s up to 1980, there were no major changes to the NASCAR stock car. The normal rate of evolution moved along at its own speed with hardly any noticeable changes. Mopar was beginning to pull out of racing, and Richard Petty stayed in, electing to run under the General Motors banner starting in 1979. It was now, basically, a two label race—Ford and GM. Ford still had their Ford Thunderbirds and Mercury Cyclones while GM had Chevys, Pontiacs, Buicks and Oldsmobiles.

The Eighties

The 1980s completely belonged to GM, with Pontiac getting one (1989), Buick three ('81-'83) and Chevy five ('80, '84-'87) cham-

Bill Elliott, in car number 9, leads the pack at Charlotte in 1980. Elliott's Winston Million victory in '85 and his '87 championship would turn out to be the brightest moments for Ford during the '80s. The decade was dominated by GM, which won all other titles.

pionships. Many younger NASCAR fans probably relate General Motors, including Chevy, Pontiac, and Oldsmobile, to its successes in the mid-to-late 1990s. But those a little grayer of beards will tell you of 14 straight years of success starting in 1976 and lasting through the 1989 season. In fact, with the exception of a Bill Elliott Ford title in 1988, it could have stretched through the 1980s decade. During that era, there were eight titles won by Chevy and Chevy-powered GM drivers; Cale Yarborough, Richard Petty, Dale Earnhardt, Terry Labonte, and Darrell Waltrip. The Yarborough and Petty titles came during the 1970s, while all others took place during the 1980s decade. Chrysler, sadly, withdrew from NASCAR completely in 1975. It was the end of a magnificent era, and as of this writing, they still have not returned, despite many rumors over the years that they would. Will the company ever come back to Winston Cup? Only time will tell, but its many fans sure wish it would

happen, and soon.

Buick—The first few years of the decade belonged to Buick, except for Earnhardt's lone 1980 championship in a Chevy Monte Carlo. A sloping front nose design brought the Buick Regal on strong for the 1981 season with a number of top drivers using the model, including Darrell Waltrip, who took the crown in '81 and '82. Buick did win the '83 championship with Bobby Allison in the Miller High Life #22 car with now-NASCAR Chief Inspector Gary Nelson as his crew chief. The Buicks were powered by Chevy corporate engines, which displeased Chevrolet because they weren't getting any credit for it.

A small group of drivers stuck to the Buick Regal body styles during the 1984–1988 seasons, most notably Bobby Allison. Allison was very much involved as a consultant to Buick in those days, providing many design suggestions that greatly influenced the 1988 Regal. But Buick's

Buicks would have their greatest success in NASCAR during the early 1980s. Here, Terry Labonte (#44) in a Monte Carlo has a slight edge on Ron Bouchard's Buick in 1984 action.

The then-new Thunderbird design, which was first introduced in 1985, would have a long and effective tenure and would last through the 1997 season before being replaced by the Taurus. This 1987 photo shows the sleek new T-Bird design compared to the Pontiac design of the time. That's Alan Kulwicki in #35 leading Michael Waltrip. Mike Slade photo.

Bill Elliott & The Small-Block Ford Thunderbird

One of the speed demons of the '80s, and a man responsible for indirectly bringing about rules changes to limit speeds, was Bill Elliott. The Elliott family, located in Dawsonville, Georgia, and well out of the usual Charlotte, North Carolina, loop of race shops, were not originally factory-supported. Their small-block combination did well, winning 11 poles and 11 races in 1985. The results were significant because Bill Elliott won the initial Winston Million—a brand-new program from the series sponsor that offered a million dollar bonus to the winner of three of the sport's four biggest races. The Coors #9 Ford Thunderbird, owned by Harry Melling, won the Daytona 500, Talladega Winston 500 and the Darlington Southern 500, creating a few new nicknames for the driver: Awesome Bill from Dawsonville and Million Dollar Bill. One very important footnote on these wins concerns the one at Talladega. After dropping to four laps down from the leaders, Elliott

used his Ford and some well-placed caution flags to not only catch the leaders, but pass them and go on to win.

Talladega seems suited for Elliott as well. A few years later, in 1987, he would set the all-time fastest lap for a NASCAR Winston Cup car at 212.809 mph, which raised a few eyebrows with officials and set in motion serious talks about limiting speeds. The record will likely stand the test of time as these days, restrictor plates are used there and at Daytona, and NASCAR officials will change the rules once again if speeds start creeping up once more.

Georgian George Muse now owns the car and it's been restored back to its original state. Muse explained that the car was campaigned for several years in ARCA before it was retired, and he bought it shortly thereafter..

Muse wanted the car to be exactly the way it was when it took the checkered at Darlington, so he went to the place where it had been originally painted, Melling Racing. They were able to paint it to the same colors and specs, and the Thunderbird does indeed turn back the clock to 1985.

days, as well as those of Oldsmobile, were numbered. Some say it was the brass at Chevrolet that made the call for the ouster as they were not only fighting Ford for valuable manufacturer's points, but their own in-house corporate cousins. Pontiac, with its performance image and long-standing relationship with NASCAR, was able to withstand the pressure. NASCAR already knew that a two-car race would not sell as many tickets as a four- or five-car race, but GM was getting tired of racing and cut the Buicks and Oldsmobiles from the program.

A New Monte Carlo—Chevy debuted an all-new Monte Carlo in 1983, and although it took some refining, it would turn out to be the dominant car of the next two decades.

Gone was the vertical air-stopping front end, replaced by a more sloping front grille that flowed the air quickly over the steeply raked windshield. Darrell Waltrip, Terry Labonte and Dale Earnhardt would all campaign a Monte Carlo with great success, resulting in four championships.

In 1987, the Monte Carlo received a sloping rear window to improve the aerodynamics, which immediately blew away the competition. It gave Earnhardt just enough of an edge to dominate the season.

Thunderbird—If it weren't for "Awesome Bill from Dawsonville," the '80s would have been pretty dismal for Ford. Although he won the Winston Million in 1985 with a Thunderbird, Elliott wouldn't see bigger

A new-generation Monte Carlo returned in 1995 with a new-generation driver, Jeff Gordon, at the helm. The two proved to be a potent combination, winning the title their first time out. It would be the first of a string of championships and numerous victories and records. Chevy execs stated they worked more closely with racers on the initial design of this model than on any other in stock car history. Randy Jones photo.

success until 1987, when the new 'Bird was introduced. Although he didn't win the championship, Elliott clocked the fastest lap in NASCAR history, an astounding 212.809 miles per hour around Talladega. This foretold the next season, when Elliott would win Ford's lone NASCAR championship of the 1980s.

The Nineties

Chevy countered the new Thunderbird by replacing the Monte Carlo with the Lumina,

The Lumina was the first model allowed to race that was front-wheel-drive in stock, factory form. The racing version was the standard rear-wheel-drive. It was the perfect foil for the T-Bird. Dale Earnhardt won four championships in one.

a model far more aerodynamic than the first Monte Carlo, but not without some controversy. It was the first production front-wheel-drive car allowed to run in the series, although it had to be modified to be rear-wheel-drive for the track. The Lumina would dominate the series with Dale Earnhardt at the wheel, winning the title in '90, '91, '94 and '95.

A Rejuvenated Monte Carlo—An all-new Monte Carlo returned in 1995, a new generation car with a new generation driver, Jeff Gordon, at the helm (among others). Gordon and the Monte Carlo won the title their first time out, and have been the team to beat in Winston Cup racing since.

A large part of this instant success of the Monte Carlo can be attributed to the close working relationship between GM and the NASCAR teams that would run the new car. Racing engineers and GM stylists worked very closely to build a car that would be a winner on the track from the very beginning. Although built to be a mass market five passenger production car, there was no mistaking the heritage and marketing intent of the new Monte Carlo. GM executives indicated that they worked harder on this design than on any other NASCAR model. In fact when the next generation Pontiac Grand Prix was

KEEPING THINGS EQUAL

One of the reasons NASCAR has always been so popular is because of the close, flag-to-flag competition. Having a race where the leader runs off and leaves the rest of the field is not much fun to watch, nor is it much fun to see the same team win race after race. NASCAR, as well as other top stock car organizations, does everything it can to maintain close racing and to ensure that there will be as many cars as possible on the lead lap at the finish line.

NASCAR then constantly tweaks the rules to keep the cars as equal as possible. Body templates, like those shown at right, are used before and after the race to make the cars keep within very close specifications for height, width and spoiler angle. Currently, NASCAR rules specify that all race cars have 110-inch wheelbase, a 60-inch width, a 51-inch height, and a four-inch ground clearance. There have been times when NASCAR actually impounded examples of each model after selected races and carefully measured their aerodynamic and downforce characteristics in a wind tunnel. The findings of these tests resulted in certain changes to the cars to keep them equal on

the track. The changes usually involved the height of rear deck spoilers, to either increase or decrease the level of downforce of the cars. The front air dams are also examined and adjusted.

Another interesting change in the rules took place in 1997, one that illustrates just how far NASCAR is willing to go to keep the cars equal. In previous years, the weight rule was that all Winston Cup cars had to weigh 3,400 lbs. minimum, not including the weight of the driver. Therefore, smaller, lighter drivers, like Mark Martin and Jeff Gordon, had an advantage over another driver who may weigh much more. Rather than make everyone go on a diet, each driver was weighed and placed into different weight categories—those over 160 lbs and those under. Drivers weighing less than 160 lbs must add 50 lbs of lead weight to the left side of the car. Of course, the lighter guys didn't like it, while the heavyweights thought it was just fine, thank you.

released the next year, one Pontiac team owner said privately the Monte Carlo was designed to win races while the Grand Prix was designed to sell cars.

The design was four years in the making, and it was not without some problems. When the final model was finished, it almost wasn't allowed to race. First, the rear deck turned out to be too narrow for the NASCAR rule book. NASCAR mandated that the trunk width be widened. This, of course, brought forth howls of protest from the Ford camp, who said the extra area would result in more downforce from a non-stock configuration. NASCAR allowed the

change, and the rest of the Monte Carlo story is in the record books.

As of the close of 1998, the Monte Carlo is the most successful nameplate in Winston Cup history, with an astounding 264 wins. The new Monte Carlo has won four straight Winston Cup Championships ('95-'98), with Terry Labonte getting one in '97 and Jeff Gordon the other three. All four championships have been for car owner Rick Hendrick, who is the only owner in history to get four in a row.

The Other GM Guys—But the Chevy wasn't the only guy in town. The latest version of the Pontiac Grand Prix arrived in

The Taurus was unveiled with great fanfare in 1998. It would be driven by the likes of Rusty Wallace, Dale Jarrett, Mark Martin, Jeff Burton and others in its inaugural season. The car was not without controversy, and marked the return of a four-door to stock car racing, something which hadn't been seen since the 1950s. Despite a frantic R&D schedule and a great deal of body massaging and changes to conform to the rules, the Taurus was very competitive in its first season. Mark Martin was in the hunt for the championship during 1998, but had to settle for second to winner Jeff Gordon and his Chevy Monte Carlo.

1996 and was similar to the Monte Carlo, but it didn't win right out of the box. With minimal massaging and rules adjustments, it too became a winner even though the Pontiac teams numbered only about five or six during any given year.

The most significant Pontiac teams during the 1990s were those driven by Kyle Petty, for Richard Petty after he retired in 1992, and by Rusty Wallace, Ward Burton and Bobby Labonte. Wallace, however, switched to Ford in 1994.

The Ford Taurus—During the mid to late 1990s, you had to feel sorry for the Ford guys. The factory was definitely caught sleeping when the new Monte Carlo came out. The Ford Thunderbird that raced through 1997 was aerodynamically the same as the one they introduced in 1987. Even though NASCAR helped with some favorable rules changes, and even though some minor face lifts improved aerodynamics, the T-Bird was definitely getting long in the tooth. At the time, Ford had been planning

an all-new T-Bird, but it wouldn't be available until 1999 or 2000, so the situation was looking pretty bleak. In 1997, Ford announced it was discontinuing the Thunderbird, citing poor sales as the reason. The Thunderbird, however, did serve well. When it was officially retired, it had a career total of 191 wins.

However, Ford had planned to race the Taurus, but just not so soon. Because of their T-Bird cancellation decision, they had to race the model a full year before they had originally planned—1998. To make matters more interesting, they went racing with the four-door model that was already their sales leader. There was no other two-door, or for that matter any model at all, that was available. It marked the first time since the 1950s that a four-door model had run in NASCAR.

The technical challenges were enormous. Normally, stock sheet metal parts such as the hood, roof and deck lid are used along with the A, B and C pillars posts that connect the roof to the rest of the car. Not so for the new

Kenny Irwin in a Taurus (#28) leads Sterling Marlin in a Monte Carlo (#40), who is just edging by the Pontiac Grand Prix of Ward Burton, at Rockingham in 1998. These three nameplates will most likely be slugging it out well into the next millennium. Bob Fairman photo.

"So far, they have been very successful, because NASCAR is arguably the most competitive racing series in the world."

Taurus. The hood was about five inches too short, the roof panels were too long and the rear deck lid was made of aluminum, which was not allowed by NASCAR. Ford ended up making separate steel sheet metal parts— just for racing—to conform to the new rules. The new Taurus also needed to have its wheelbase increased 1 1/2" to bring it up to the NASCAR minimum of 110 inches. The length of the hood was increased, the roof was reduced and rear deck lid material was changed from aluminum to steel. In order to enable the Ford teams to build all their cars for the 1998 season, Ford actually produced all the steel body pieces for the race car configuration.

The introduction, testing and finalization process of a new model race car normally takes about 2 1/2 years, but the Taurus introduction was accomplished much more quickly.

When the new car hit the track for the 1998 season, it was very competitive, especially on intermediate tracks like Charlotte, Atlanta, and Michigan, as well as the new speedways in Texas and California which were also intermediate tracks. The Fords dominated the top ten in points with Mark Martin finishing second and Dale Jarrett third.

As NASCAR Winston Cup racing approaches the end of the century, it appears that the Monte Carlo, Grand Prix, and Taurus will still be battling each other. No matter what, though, recall that NASCAR's key to success has long been close competition and race cars kept as equal as possible to retain that winning formula. Throughout the 1990s, the organization continuously made changes to the cars so that one model wouldn't run away from the other. So far, they have been very successful, because NASCAR is arguably the most competitive racing series in the world.

The Wind Tunnel as a Racing Tool

Starting in the early 1980s, large, full size wind tunnel testing became an important engineering tool in top race car design. Teams, often with factory funding and engineers, would routinely take their cars to one of two full size wind tunnels and flog their cars for better drag, downforce and aero numbers. A dent in a contour here and a little body filler there made for a slicker car especially around the bigger tracks like Daytona and Talladega. They soon learned they could also massage their cars for intermediate and even short tracks and augment their particular needs virtually at will—all within the confines of NASCAR body templates, of course.

Soon, the factories thought about using the wind tunnel for their upcoming cars, and eventually, even the street

The wind tunnel is a big part of NASCAR technology today. This is a 1996 IROC car being tested.

versions "did the wind." In fact, the wind tunnel was one of the main tools in designing the new Chevy Monte Carlo aero-nose in the early 1980s which put the model ahead for such a long time. The nose had a distinct split personality as it flowed great on the street version of the Monte Carlo SS, but worked even better at the lowered stance of a race car. Coincidence or not? But Ford kept working with the big wind and came up with its super sleek 1985 Thunderbird design. With the downforce that was missing from the General Motors models of this time period, GM went back to the wind tunnel. As a result, they found additional downforce by redesigning the rear window treatment, playing it out over the rear deck lid of their Monte Carlos and Pontiac Grand Pries. And so it continued into the 1990s with the Thunderbird, Monte Carlo and Grand Prix carrying out their coefficient of drag battles both on the track and in the wind tunnels.

In the mid-1990s, NASCAR itself started using the wind tunnel to compare the aero-dynamic characteristics of the Monte Carlo, Thunderbird, and Grand Prix.

Immediately following a few selected races, the leading cars of all three brands were confiscated and run through extensive wind tunnel sessions. The right-off-the-track information was shared with the car owners but not the general public. After that, NASCAR came up with rule adjustments it felt would make the cars as close as possible on the track. Some of these changes even limited the tracks where certain spec cars could compete. Over the course of the season, NASCAR repeated the tests at different sized tracks. All in all, it was another move to continue massaging the rules for equal racing. Most adjustments to the car were limited to the front valance (air dam) and the rear spoiler. By adjusting these two critical items, a better shot at equality was attempted and often achieved.

Bending and Breaking the Rules

As long as there are rules, there will always be racers trying to bend, or even break them. Stock car racing has produced many innovative builders and designers who, when asked, would not exactly call it cheating. Call it "tricks of the trade," or whatever, but most racers are not above looking for loopholes in the rules, and once found, going right through them. What follows is a list of attempts made throughout NASCAR history to gain "an unfair advantage" as they say. Most of these rule-bending techniques were identified and penalties were levied, and if a rule didn't exist to make it illegal, NASCAR made one up as soon as possible. Through the years, though, NASCAR has made it more and more difficult to vary outside the lines of the rules. They've also made more costly to get caught with a sliding scale of fines that grow as the number of tricks are found out. You have to admit that they are definitely interesting!

1. Changing body shape. One team slightly lowered the roof line and raised the rear deck for better aerodynamics. The slight body changes created better aerodynamics, but the deviations were quickly noted and disallowed. Highly accurate, laser-cut templates quickly point out the altered body panels.

2. Engine glazing. During the 1950s, no engine porting was allowed, but some builders lacquered the intake ports until they were as smooth as glass. The technique wasn't against the rules, but deemed "not in the spirit" by officials.

3. Cutting manifolds. An engine modification of cutting the intake/exhaust manifolds in half, smoothing out the passages, and then brazing them back together so inspectors wouldn't suspect the handiwork. Open headers eliminated the exhaust manifolds. Intakes are pretty much wide open except for the restrictor plate units that have to meet certain gauge tests for opening size and depth.

4. Casting numbers. A super-illegal undertaking was the welding of the legal casting number on an illegal block casting. Trained eyes know which blocks have what characteristics.

5. Replacement chassis parts. In earlier days, a number of teams substituted stronger non-factory A-frames and axles due to the increased pressure on these components as the performance of the cars increased. It was more a question of reliability rather than cheating for speed, but illegal nonetheless.

6. Narrowed bumpers. Bumpers were narrowed to increase the efficiency of the airflow around the front of the car. The same was later tried with headlight openings and covers, narrowing them until it was evident the normally square or rectangular shape was not much more than a vertical slit. The narrowing resulted in less car cutting into the oncoming air, effectively reducing drag and adding speed. The rule of thumb at the time was for every inch a car was narrowed, it would gain one mph at Daytona. Measurements were checked to keep the parts true.

7. Nitrous oxide. The use of performance-increasing nitrous oxide was often tried as it literally gave the engine an instant blast of power, at the push of a button. Many times the gas allowed a driver to get by a competitor on the straightaway and lead into the turn. Some competitors were hiding the gas in rollbars.

8. Grille flaps. The insertion of flaps to cover the grille opening blocks the air going into the engine compartment. This helps in two ways; it makes the air work over the body, hopefully creating more downforce. By eliminating the air in the engine compartment, there is less lift on the front end and that helps handling, too. The trade-off is no air going to the radiator so it can't be used for long periods of time without damaging the engine. The flaps would almost have to be visible to work, and blind areas of the car are checked with mirrors. Another creative but illegal trick.

(continued next page)

(Bending and Breaking the Rules continued)

9. Lead weights. The use of lead weights inserted in various car locations for better handling. There was also the capability to jettison the weights before the end of the race. Sometimes this was done with weight that was in the form of shot or tiny little balls of steel or lead. One old racing story has the driver confirming to his crew chief over the radio that he dropped the weight by saying "bombs away." Weights are supposed to be mounted inside the main frame rails only.

10. Illegal moldings. Innovative sheet metal molding to provide better aerodynamic flow or to increase downforce on the car, providing better handling in the turns. The templates used for inspecting the car do not cover every area of the car, so those that are not policed are open to what is often called "creative rules interpretation."

11. Hydraulics. Hydraulic lowering of the car by the driver while at speed reduces drag and improves the center of gravity for better handling. Various points on the car such as the corners of the rear quarter panels are measured and cars are checked thoroughly for such devices. One driver had such a device and hid it in his car's fire bottle for extinguishing fires. Because of where the device was located and how it negated the use of the fire bottle, thus making the car more dangerous to drive, the amount of the fine was substantial.

12. Soft tires. Softening of tires with brake fluid or other illegal liquids makes them stick to the track better. Inspectors use a "sniffing" device much like the ones used to detect natural gas leaks.

13. Changing tire codes. Vulcanizing or even super gluing the legal tire ID code onto a softer compound car. Durometers are often used to check the hardness of the rubber.

14. Increased fuel capacity. Larger fuel cells which might provide for one less pit stop over the course of a 500 mile race. Fuel cells are checked for outside measurements and how many gallons of fuel they can hold. The maximum is 22 gallons.

15. Post-race weight gain. Adding weight to the car after the race in order to pass post-race inspection. A variation of this was the lead weight that was disguised as a roll of duct tape sitting in the car while it went across the scales only to be removed before qualifying or the race. Cars go from inspection to the track within a confined area of the garage and under the close scrutiny of numerous inspectors. Coming off the track, it's the same thing and no crew members are allowed to do anything to the car.

16. Lightweight bumpers. Aluminum bumpers were used to reduce weight on the front and back ends of the cars because using the weight where it does the most good is different from having to mount it in one consistent place. Along these same lines, fiberglass hoods and rear deck lids were also tried. Magnets are now a part of the tech inspection.

17. Decrease rollbar thickness. One very dangerous trick was to build a car with the wall thickness of the roll bars less than what was required. While it may reduce the weight above the centerline on the car and improve overall handling, it put the driver at great risk if the car was involved in a crash and could not provide protection. Ultra-sound detectors are used as well as drilling a small hole in one of the tubes of the cage to check the wall thickness. Some of the museums that are part of the stock car world often have their own displays of illegal and confiscated parts. It's always interesting to visit these displays and see the actual parts.

THE MANY TYPES OF STOCK CARS

4

Most people associate the term "stock car" with the Winston Cup NASCAR race cars that are seen on TV throughout the year. While these types of cars epitomize the sport and industry, the world of stock car racing actually encompasses a wide variety of race cars. Stock car racing is not unlike a pyramid. At the top, you have Winston Cup, and at the bottom, you have the grassroots level of the sport, a multitude of cars, classes and series ranging from Modifieds to ASA cars and Late Models. And within that pyramid, stock car racing has different levels where a driver, mechanic or a car owner can "work"

their way up to the level they choose to stay at. It's a well-known fact that most drivers, mechanics and car owners of NASCAR Winston Cup racing didn't just walk into that lofty level of the sport; they worked their way into it. The drivers and mechanics did it by learning and showcasing their talents up the "racing chain," with wins and consistent results. The car owners used these lower level series to establish themselves as proven and profitable business entities.

Many forms of stock cars race in different regions throughout the United States. Some are exclusive to just a few race tracks and geographic areas. Because there are so many

Stock car racing is a vast world of motorsports that includes more than just Winston Cup cars. Shown below is one of the top entry-level forms of stock cars, Dirt Late Model. The action is always exciting, as Kevin Weaver demonstrates at Brownstown Speedway in Indiana. Tony Hammett photo.

This Street Stock uses a vintage Monte Carlo body and a small-block engine. The performance of many of these cars is surprising considering the amount of money invested, which is usually the bare minimum.

Street Stocks also find their way onto dirt tracks around the country. Needless to say, there is a lot of fender-banging in this level of competition.

some classes will be able to run slicks and open exhaust, for example, while the same car in another area must run street tires with a stock-style exhaust in place. One track may call their Street Stock class "Detroit Iron" or "Spectator Stock," while a neighboring track may label them "Action Cars" or "Bombers. " So depending on the cooperation between track promoters, it can be either easy or difficult to run the same car at different tracks within the same region. Generally, the number of fans that show up is directly proportional to the number of cars—the more cars, the more fans—something not lost on savvy promoters. On the other hand, some tracks compete for cars and fans on the same night, so they keep the rules strictly separate to discourage their "regulars" from jumping to the other track.

On the other side of the coin, the more expensive cars may have rules that closely follow those of national organizations. One example is the extremely popular IMCA Modifieds described shortly. Local tracks basically use the same rules with few changes. With these cars, drivers can compete in a variety of regions and nationally, if they choose, with basically the same car.

The common denominator of all stock cars are the restrictions on chassis and engine modifications, which dictates speed, and on the purses at the end of each evening. Some classes race for nothing more than bragging rights and a trophy, while others offer a pretty substantial purse.

STREET STOCK CARS

Depending on the particular track and part of the country you're in, there will be one or more support classes that run among the main events. These classes are often an entry-level, grassroots form of racing for beginners or amateurs on a limited budget.

One such class is most commonly known as "Street Stock," although it is called many different names in various regions.

interpretations of what a stock car is, it isn't feasible to cover all of them in individual technical detail. And the rules governing one broad class of stock car, such as a Street Stock or Figure 8 racer, may be different in the Midwest than, say, the South.

The evolution of some of these cars has caused them to lose their identity with a particular brand or street model, contrary to the guiding philosophy of NASCAR. While the number of different classes across the country seems enormous, it's more often the different names that add confusion than the number of classes. Many of the rules are very similar, but not identical, which is why

Troy Talley powers his battered Street Stock around Thunderbowl Speedway in Valdosta, Georgia, during 1996 competition. Tony Hammett photo.

However, the idea is similar: low-budget race cars with minimal modifications. Many of the cars are little more than an existing passenger car with few modifications, the amount of which vary from track to track. Most feature a full, welded-in roll cage, five-point seat belts, welded doors, no glass or windows, and some high performance suspension and chassis components. Most of these classes stipulate that street tires must be used, which therefore limits speeds, costs, and traction.

Usually, the interiors of these cars have been gutted down to the bare essentials. Because there is so much fender banging in these classes, there is little point in spending a lot of money on exotic paint jobs. Duct tape and hand-painted lettering are more likely the norm. The class closely resembles the "strictly stock" class that raced in NASCAR's first few seasons. The main difference today is the advanced safety equipment and better construction of the cars, even if they are "beaters."

Road Hogs

One of the lowest forms of the Street Stock class is the "Road Hog" or "Detroit Iron" class popular in Kentucky and other Midwestern states. In this class, you'll often find old luxury barges, big Lincolns, Fords and Chevys that were popular in the '70s. We're talking big cars weighing between four and five thousand pounds. Not exactly what you'd call a "lean and mean" racing machine!

Most of these cars were rescued from the junkyard for one last shot at glory. The cars retain their stock engines and suspension and many of the Hog teams invest well under $1000 in the cars. It's definitely an entry-level class, but the fan enthusiasm and tight racing make it popular.

With many true amateurs driving these types of cars, it's not surprising to see a lot of fender banging, spin-outs and blown engines. These machines are raced on both dirt and pavement.

ENDURO STOCK CARS

The Enduro class is a broad term with one common denominator: it is perhaps the most grassroots form of racing. You don't need a whole lot of driving experience or a big budget to compete.

Enduro racing could best be described as a mad dash around an oval for a few laps, with

Mini Stocks are another economical way to go racing. The mini stocks have long been a starter class for many pavement stock car racing drivers. The Ford Pinto has been one of the more common cars raced in this class, along with Vegas, Mustangs and Camaros. Some tracks even allow small pickups in this class, as long as the engines are four-cylinder.

as much fender banging as possible. After watching a few of these races, it seems as though the "enduro" name stems from how long a car can last before being crashed off the course or broken down. Sometimes, as many as two hundred cars show up to run, which makes for crowded conditions on a 1/2 mile oval, even if there are separate heats. You can imagine what happens as the cars crowd into a turn. Just about anything goes, much to the delight of the fans. Of course, depending on the particular track rules, the cars must be equipped with basic safety equipment, including a minimal roll cage, safety belts, a fire extinguisher and dri-

ver's safety gear. The brand can be anything, old or new, American or foreign. Another way to describe Enduro racing is that it's basically a "Demolition Derby" run in a circle!

MINI STOCKS

Mini Stock is another one of those catch-all terms that encompasses a class of racing where the cars are essentially the same, but differ in certain respects depending on the region of the country and sanctioning body they run. Mini Stock drivers are either inexperienced beginners just starting out, pros who couldn't cut it in the higher levels (either financially or talent-wise) and have stepped down, or just experienced amateurs who like the cost-per-racing-smile ratio. You get a lot of bang for your buck.

This class includes body styles that have long since been discontinued, such as the Vega, Pinto, Arrow, etc. However, you'll also find more modern body styles from Mustangs to Camaros. Some sanctioning bodies and tracks allow fiberglass bodies to run that don't resemble any make or model.

Mini Stocks are usually powered with four-cylinder engines of the same brand as

Dennis Franklin at speed at Cherokee Speedway in South Carolina, in a Plymouth Arrow Mini Stock racer. Tony Hammett photo.

The next move up from Mini Stocks used to be the more sophisticated Pro-4 class as typified by this machine. The rules dictated that engines be limited to four cylinders, but other than that, just about anything was legal, allowing for some very interesting interpretations.

the body. Some simple modifications are usually allowed for a slight boost in power. Depending on the rules, these can include a larger carburetor, engine blueprinting, a slight overbore, and performance headers. The rest of the powertrain, such as the transmission and rear end, is usually stock.

Minor body modifications are also usually allowed (in cases other than the fiberglass bodies mentioned), and many cars run front and rear spoilers. Detroit certainly never had this in mind when these models were first designed, but with little modification and money, these cars can be transformed into impressive racing machines. With the number of subcompact cars easily outnumbering the older and heavier full size cars sitting in junkyards, this class can be extremely economical. Besides, many of those bigger cars are highly sought for demolition and figure eight classes. They also put on a great show with excellent competition.

In many Mini Stock classes, you'll also find cars with small truck bodies, such as the Chevy S-10, Ford Ranger, Dodge Dakota and various imports such as Nissan and Toyota.

ARCA Pro-4

The next level up in stock cars used to be the ARCA Pro-4 class. The cars in this class were generally considered to be very innovative, which produced some leading edge technology that has worked its way into other levels of racing. Unfortunately, the class was terminated by ARCA in favor of mini trucks, but its contribution to racing technology certainly deserves mention as there are still a few small regional tracks that have retained the class.

Just about anything went with this class as far as body configurations were concerned.

One of the slickest Pro-4 machines ever built was this so-called "Batmobile," an example of how innovative this class could be. Bob Fairman photo.

This full-bodied Pro-4 racer shows its slick exterior while underneath it hides a potent Cosworth Ford race engine. Phil Kunz photo.

Figure 8 racing is not a stock car sport for the faint of heart. The cars, though, are fairly sophisticated and do have quite a bit of heavy metal for protection, like the beefy front bumper on this car. Phil Kunz photo.

Some had a standard stock-car-appearing front end with normal front fenders. Then too, one could race an open-wheel-style front end. There have been Pro-4 cars with one side open wheel, while on the other side, the wheels were enclosed. Like we said, just about anything went.

The engine rules permitted a variety of four-cylinder engines, but the most common were the 2.0 or 2.3-liter Ford engines once used in Pintos and other models in the '70s. However, considerable modifications were allowed, and engine output was as high as 300 horsepower.

The Pro-4 class also had some very unique

engines; one of them being a Ford Cosworth engine equipped with side-draft carburetors and capable of turning 9000 rpm. Another interesting power plant was a 2.2 liter Dodge Daytona engine capable of 225 horsepower.

The cars were, in fact, so highly developed that they often held the overall track record at many of the Midwestern short tracks they toured. It is unusual to think of a car with a four cylinder engine going faster than a bigger and more powerful V8, but it did happen and quite often. Part of the reason was the highly developed chassis that helped the smaller engine. These very lightweight chassis were as high tech as any super Late Model and ran soft-compound racing tires for better grip in the turns. So between a favorable power-to-weight ratio and the use of some hardcore racing parts, the lighter cars were often the faster cars.

FIGURE 8 CARS

The cars that run in the Figure 8 class can be compared to that family member who is politely referred to as "eccentric." While it seems to be all about show business, Figure 8 racing is taken quite seriously at many tracks.

Figure 8 tracks are usually laid out on a standard oval track with straightaways going diagonally through the infield, with an intersection in the center. When two race cars arrive at the intersection simultaneously, something or someone has to give—and most of the time it's sheet metal and suspension pieces. And while it is usually taken less seriously by most of the fans, just about any Figure 8 racer will be a dedicated and devout participant.

Jerry Brown of Louisville, Kentucky, is one of the best Figure 8 drivers in the nation, and most of his preparation centers on the frame itself—for safety reasons. He uses one and three-quarter inch steel tubing for the main frame parts and cage. However, other sections are lightened or use lightweight components. Four heavy bars in the driver's side door provide as much protection as possible.

With all that sturdy construction, these cars often take the hits and keep on racing. The bumpers on many of these machines are built like battering rams, with the front one also serving as protection for the radiator and engine. Most tracks allow drivers to run any model car they choose, while following a street stock rule book with only extra protection on the driver's door. Other tracks often do race a full-fledged race car with racing tires and plenty of hard core racing parts. Some tracks wet their surface down with water to slow speeds and hopefully reduce the severity of impact. Others let 'em rip on the same tacky racing surface as the oval trackers. Years ago, Figure 8 was such a popular novelty that ABC telecast the championships from historic Islip Speedway in New York on Wide World of Sports.

DWARF/LEGEND CARS

In the 1990s, stock car racing seems to have followed the trend set by corporate America—downsizing. Promoters, in an effort to attract fans and participants alike, have created some very interesting classes. Two of the most successful are the Dwarf and Legend cars. The Legend car design was conceived by Charlotte Motor Speedway's owner Bruton Smith and his promoter, Humpy Wheeler. These cars, which are approximately 5/8ths scale models of pre-war coupes and sedans that ran from the late

This Figure 8 racer looks new and scratch-free. But given the nature of Figure 8 racing, chances are it won't last this way for long. The Figure 8 class is one of those classes that has a widely diverse rule book that varies from region to region. Bob Fairman photo.

Humpy Wheeler and Bruton Smith, of Charlotte Motor Speedway, designed the Legends class for national racing. Cars are powered by Yamaha 1200cc motorcycle engines, but only weigh a max of 1150 lbs.

The Dwarf car is similar in concept to the Legend, but has some notable differences. Outwardly, there are no fenders, unlike the Legend. They also have a slightly more powerful 1250cc Kawasaki or Suzuki engine, but also weigh more, up to 1400 lbs. This car, lettered like Terry Labonte's Winston Cup car, is shown at Volusia County Speedway in Florida. Phil Kunz photo.

'20s through 1940, have become immensely popular. Many short tracks run either class as a support race to main events. Although they look toy-like, these cars are quite capable, and can run some very impressive speeds.

Although Dwarfs and Legends are similar in concept, there are many differences in how they are constructed. One of the main differences between the two cars is that the Legend cars have a complete body, including fenders. Dwarf cars do not have fenders. Although the engines are small, the cars are very light, so the power-to-weight ratio is significantly high. The cars were also designed to be affordable. The engines and suspensions are relatively simple, and the price of a race-ready Dwarf or Legend is between $12,000 and $15,000 at the time of this writing.

Normally, Legend cars run mostly on paved tracks but the Dwarfs (with that open wheel look) are regularly seen running both pavement and dirt.

Both the Dwarf and Legend cars are exactly the same size with a 73-inch wheelbase. The widths of both cars are identical at 60 inches. The body styles used on the cars are restricted to certain eras. The Dwarf cars must run body styles based on cars built from 1928 to 1940. The Legend cars are based on cars built between 1934 and 1940. Each car type must have a complete roll cage and door bars welded to the frame, not bolted in. Fuel cells are also mandatory. Another of the major differences between cars is that the Legends' bodies are constructed of fiberglass while the Dwarfs' are made of aluminum.

The allowable weight range is somewhat different, with the heavier Dwarf cars having a 1200–1400 pound range, while with the Legend cars, it's a 950 to 1150 pound range.

The main frame rails of both cars are fab-

Legends cars are fairly sophisticated, with welded tube frames, disc brakes, coil-over shocks—all this despite a relatively low cost of around $15,000. Shown here are several Legends in various stages of completion at a production facility.

"Although they look toy-like, these cars are quite capable, and can run some very impressive speeds."

ricated from one by two inch mild steel tubing of .120 inch wall thickness, providing both a stiff chassis for superior handling and maximum safety. So while they may be very similar in outward body style, appearance, and chassis construction, they are not playing on exactly equal terms when it comes to equipment.

Both cars use Japanese production motorcycle engines, with the Legends specifying Yamaha of no more than 1200 cc's and Dwarf cars allowing both Suzuki and Kawasaki at 1250 cc's. When it comes to fuel, Legend cars run strictly pump gasoline while Dwarf cars can run gas or alcohol. Unlike motorcycles that use chains, both types of cars are shaft driven to the rear wheels like a street car. Getting the power to the rear wheels is the stock, five speed manual transmission, shifted by the driver's hands more like a car than a motorcycle.

Between the light car and strong engine, speeds are likely to surprise some fans and even some drivers. Like any other race car, they are geared to and limited by the track's

size, but can quickly get to 80 mph on short tracks and even 100 mph on the straights of a full-sized course. Legends cars use BF Goodrich performance street tires but allow for tread shaving to reduce tread "wiggle" and increase traction. These cars, although considered a "spec" series (one where certain specifications are to be met and never varied), are allowed some liberties within the rules for chassis adjustments.

BANDOLERO MINIATURE STOCK CARS

After the success of their Legends cars, Smith and Wheeler developed a new class called the *Bandolero*. The Bandolero is similar to a go-kart, weighing only 450 pounds with a starting price of about $7,000 for a complete car.

Like a go-kart, there is no active suspension (no shocks or springs), which is one reason for the low cost. However, there is a full body made of fiberglass and resembling a stock car. The engine everyone must use is a two-cylinder Briggs and Stratton that pro-

The Super Mini Cup cars are a half-scale version of Winston Cup cars. They are powered by a Honda motorcycle engine and are gaining in popularity.

duces nearly 40 horsepower. However, the chassis is of tube-frame construction, and the 10-inch tires are specially made by Hoosier. The rear wheels are chain-driven, like a go-kart.

SUPER MINI CUP CARS

With the popularity of Winston Cup cars, it was not surprising that a smaller-scale version of those cars would soon be developed appear. The class is called *Super Mini Cup*. They are actually half-scale versions of the Winston Cup cars and are considered to be a starter class to develop new driving talent—just as Indy Lights cars are to CART racing. These cars are not "go-karts," but actual race cars.

Super Mini Cup cars feature a complete MIG-welded roll cage and chassis. There's also an extremely tunable suspension with front upper and lower control arms, adjustable coil-over shocks, a rear panhard bar, and rack and pinion steering.

Power comes from a 13 horsepower Honda GX 390 motorcycle engine which is capable of driving this classy little mini-machine to speeds of more than 100 miles per hour on pump gas! The 60-inch wheelbase cars also carry a rear-mounted fuel cell,

aluminum seat, slick racing tires (although the cars can run on dirt with dirt tires), a five-point safety harness, and a hand-made fiberglass Chevy or Ford body.

The nice aspect of this type of racing is the minimal cost required to get into one of these cars, which is about $8,000 at the time of this writing. The rules are tight, with no modifications allowed to the engine, and a minimum weight requirement of 410 pounds.

The series is run by the Miniature Motorsports Racing Association (MMRA), which was established in 1996, and sanctions races on 45 tracks nationwide.

MODIFIEDS

The Modified class, as you may recall from Chapter 2, was the first class sanctioned by NASCAR. This type of race car has continued to be popular through the years with many different types of models and sanctioning bodies coming about. The Modified has become somewhat of a standard term for hundreds of classes across the nation, with cars running on both dirt and pavement tracks.

So once again, the term "Modified," or "Mods," as they are sometimes called, can

The Modified division is NASCAR's first and oldest class. It exists in many forms, but the official NASCAR version is the Featherlite Tour. These big-block powered Modifieds run mainly in the Northeast. Shown here is seven-time champion Billy Pauch at Flemington Speedway in New Jersey. Courtesy Flemington Speedway.

be rather ambiguous. Once racing became a sport of dedicated cars separating dirt from pavement, along came the surface-specific dirt and pavement Mods. And if that wasn't enough, division within each of those categories produced even more types of Mods. From the NASCAR Featherlite Tour Modified class to the IMCA Modified, and with many local types included, the term Modified covers quite a bit of ground.

There have also been a number of Modified races with large purses and there will undoubtedly be more in the future as the sport grows. Here are the facts and figures on these stock car classes with roots that go back to the very beginning of stock car racing.

NASCAR Featherlite Tour and Pavement Modifieds

These cars are basically from NASCAR's oldest class. They are currently referred to as NASCAR Featherlite Tour Modifieds, although they have been called many different names in the past (Modified is the common link). Similar to their ancestors, these cars are open-wheeled, with no fenders, and a just about "anything goes" approach to racing. These Modifieds put on a very compet-

itive show during the regular season, mostly in New England. They also race annually in Florida and Virginia at special events.

Unlike their predecessors, however, these cars are far from stock, and in fact are almost "unlimited." They are purpose-built race cars, with lightweight tube frames powered by massive big-block engines, bored out to as much as 500 cubic inches with more than 800 horsepower outputs. Between the chassis and the custom-made suspension components, the cars look like they are scraping the ground. With less suspension travel taking place on a smooth paved track, NASCAR and other pavement Modifieds can improve their handling with a lower car and center of gravity. And the fact that they are custom made means that they can get around the factory parts to put the chassis exactly where they want it—as close to the surface as they can.

The bodies may have the tag of a Chevy or Ford, but this identifies the engine more than the bodywork. The bodies are all custom sheet metal, and are not based on any particular make or model car. By and large, these Modifieds do not look much different than their predecessors from the '40s and early '50s; however, they are much, much faster.

A great field of Northeast Modifieds gather at Martinsville Speedway for competition. Mike Slade photo.

As with most every type of race car in America, "the Mods," as they are commonly known, have produced some memorable races and drivers over the years. The Modifieds have become so popular that they race in special events at local tracks for sub-

stantial prize money. These are races that are not necessarily sanctioned by NASCAR. It's also not unusual to see national sponsors on the cars, trailers and uniforms of these Northeastern Modified race teams.

Modifieds are purpose-built race cars, with lightweight tube frames powered by massive big–block engines bored out to as much as 500 cubic inches. Horsepower output is over 800.

Richie Tobias blasts out of a turn at Hagerstown Speedway during the DIRT Octoberfest 250 in 1994. Tony Hammett photo.

This photo of Northeast Modifieds was taken in 1984, and shows how much the cars have changed since, mostly in the body style. However, they are just as powerful as ever, and the show is also exciting and fun to watch.

Dirt Modifieds

Like their pavement clones, Dirt Modifieds are derivative of the very first Modifieds, but have never gotten off the dirt track. They too can be sanctioned by any number of organizations, and the cars can take many different forms. They also run primarily on the East Coast and in the Northeast U. S. Often, these cars will run in a support race for sprint cars. These dirt trackers use custom-made race chassis with big-block engines. It is not uncommon for these cars to power-slide their way through the turns much like a sprint car, with the car flung sideways and throwing a rooster tail of fresh dirt.

Economy Modifieds grew out of necessity. As the popularity of their big-block brothers grew, so did the cost, pricing them out of reach for many former competitors. Also, there needed to be a class for older Modifieds. Economy Modifieds have smaller engines, and smaller tires, and are less expensive to race. However, the racing is still great to watch.

The front suspension on an E-Mod is basically stock with a "front clip" from a passenger car. The rest of the frame is custom-built, tubular design.

Like the Featherlite Pavement Modifieds, there are several subclasses with smaller engines and more limited rules that offer less expensive racing with the same thrills and spills. Open-wheel cars are much more likely than full-bodied cars to get airborne, especially if the exposed wheels touch. With close racing and their hair-raising slides through turns, it's no wonder Dirt Modifieds are so popular with the New England crowds.

Economy Modifieds

Once the regular NASCAR and regional Modified attained a level of popularity that warranted it, the creation of Economy Mods came about. Fans and racers alike supported the Modified classes and as they grew, it became more expensive to compete. With the shear number of cars waiting for better budgets to race, the idea came up for a new class of Mods. Some are even older cars that have been rendered obsolete by the fast-moving technology. Like the Featherlite cars, they are open-wheeled, custom-made race chassis cars with racing tires. They are, in some cases, identical in appearance to their big brothers but upon closer inspection, have smaller engines and smaller, often harder tires that last longer. Those are the two areas that affect costs the most—

engines and tires. Where the bigger mods have big blocks of 500 cubic inches and the biggest tires available, the smaller Econo-mods have small blocks for power and a smaller spec tire. And as the class split on pavement tracks, so did the dirt mods, too. A similar spin-off happened across the country with sprint cars as well.

IMCA Modifieds

By far the most prolific of the Modified type of stock car in the country today is known as the IMCA Modified style of car. The cars run both pavement and dirt with minimal differences. A few of the major sanctioning bodies for these cars are IMCA (International Motor Contest Association), UMP (United Midwest Promoters) and I-Car. These organizations regularly hold regional special events offering big money for the local racer willing to make the tow. Also, many local paved and dirt tracks run the rules of IMCA Modifieds without any sanctioning body overseeing the competition. A measure of the interest in these cars is the driver's list for UMP, where 1000 Modified drivers are on record. The names of the classes these cars race in often vary as the basic IMCA rules may have been copied or changed to suit the track and the region's competition. After local tracks first buy into the IMCA franchise and get their classes and car counts established, they will sometimes drop the franchise and slightly change the rules and come up with a new name for the class.

Like their Econo and big-block brothers, these cars also have an open-wheel front end with a portion of a body. From there, the similarity ends. The biggest difference is that these cars run on both dirt and paved tracks with basically the same rules. When it comes to the cars themselves, IMCA mods, or rules that closely emulate these cars, utilize a stock, OEM front frame section called a clip that generally has to extend behind the firewall before it can be converted to a weld-

Most E-Mods run Chevy small-blocks, mainly because of the availability of parts. However, a small number are racing Ford small-blocks, like this one above.

ed, rectangular tubing section to support the rear suspension and roll cage. They can also use a body that's sometimes closer to a recognizable street car body by starting with a OEM roof.

The power for an IMCA or IMCA-style car comes from small-block engines that are mostly Chevys with a few Fords and Mopars. There's no fuel injection or other exotic engine parts and rules usually limit the carburetors to one 4-barrel or sometimes even a two-barrel carb. The single carb is often mounted on a cast-iron intake manifold or an aluminum aftermarket intake, again depending on the rules. Headers are almost always used and some even allow for open pipes depending on the track's required sound levels. Fuels will also vary with rules as to pump, racing gas or alcohol. Changes to the engines are usually rather limited and cubic inch limits vary from one set of rules to another. Generally, however, small block engines are limited to under 400 inches. The power of these engines is usually in the 300–400 horsepower range and is then sent through OEM manual four-speed transmissions to beefier, OEM rear ends. These rules are designed to limit not only the power but the costs of building and maintaining a race engine/car and coupled with the spec tire rules at the tracks, greatly reduce costs.

Some tracks even have a claiming rule on

Late Models is a broad category, just like Modifieds. Dirt Late Models run obviously, only on dirt tracks, and are specially built to do so. Although the Dirt Late Models are far from stock-appearing on most of the body, many are now adopting stock front ends to coincide with the brand of engine. This Ford-powered Dirt Late Model, for example, has a Thunderbird nosepiece.

The most prestigious event for the Dirt Late Models is the World 100 classic race at Eldora Speedway in Ohio. The event has been held annually since 1971 and attracts over two hundred cars. Staton photo.

the engine where a racer can "buy" his competitor's engine for the established claiming price. Failure to sell often causes the refusing racer some sort of suspension from the track. The idea is to have a cap on just how much money is spent on the engine, not investing more money than the established claiming price.

The reason for the popularity of these cars is simply cost. With the front OEM clip, D.O.T. tires and stock-style engines, parts come from cars of the street and junkyard as opposed to expensive, hardcore racing aftermarket parts. Many IMCA and IMCA-style teams will quickly point out if it were not for this class, they could not afford to race.

Despite their OEM parts, they often weigh in close to the Late Models (2300 lbs.).

That's because they are slightly smaller in chassis width, length and their rather limited body dimensions. Like Late Models, they are not equipped with anything much more than they need and usually put on a good show. While the class is designed for average racers to build their own cars from OEM frames and clips, there are a few companies that specialize in building IMCA legal chassis and parts starting with those same OEM parts.

Unlike many other types of racing, converting IMCA cars from dirt to pavement and even pavement to dirt is relatively simple. The open front end as well as a liberally designed back frame section both allow for plenty of suspension travel. That means it's just the difference of springs and shocks and the spec tires to match the rules from one surface to another.

But like every other class of stock car racing, there are some exceptions with the IMCA Modifieds too. Some tracks allow the cars to have any engine that will bolt directly to the factory motor plate, while at other tracks, racing transmissions and even quick change rear ends are allowed. It's the evolution and discretion of the track operators that dictate the limits of these popular and competitive cars.

LATE MODEL STOCK CARS

The term "late model" also encompasses a wide variety of stock cars with styles and subclasses that change from region to region. However, the class can be categorized generally into those that run on pavement, and those that run on dirt. Also, the evolution of a class of car is affected by rules changes. One example is a promoter who is faced with dwindling car counts in his Late Model division. To reverse the evolution of the class and roll back costs, he may ban certain more expensive equipment on the cars, thus actually changing the classification, but retain the same class name. So while one

One of the best in the Dirt Late Model class is Donnie Moran, shown here at speed. Note how low the car is to the dirt track, even though it is deeply rutted. Extra space in the wheelwells allows for increased suspension travel. Rick Rickard photo.

may normally assume a Late Model will have an alloy quick change rear end, for example, some tracks may not allow it and still call their cars Late Models.

Dirt Late Models

Dirt Late Model racing exploded during the 1990s, partly because of the increased national exposure from cable and satellite TV, but mostly because of the close competition and low cost. The Dirt Late Model sport recently went national, when two of the major sanctioning bodies—STARS, and Hav-A-Tampa—got together to devise enough universal rules to allow the stars of these series to move between the two groups without having to radically alter their cars.

Body & Chassis—Dirt Late Models all share the same basic body shape and style, almost like a spec racer, but they don't resemble a stock production car, unless the car is from a sanctioning body that mandates a "stock'" appearing nose. For example, if there is a Ford engine in the car, either a Probe, Mustang, Taurus or T-Bird nose piece is required. If it's a Chevy, then a Camaro or Monte Carlo nose may be mandated. The nose doesn't have to be from a stock produc-

tion car; it just has to be fabricated to resemble one.

Dirt cars often run on tracks that are deeply rutted, with holes and pits in the racing line. To run in these conditions, dirt track cars need more suspension travel and ground clearance to keep from bottoming out. The increased suspension travel on a

A view of a typical rear suspension system for a Dirt Late Model stock car. Note the coil-over shocks and the horizontally mounted shock, which dampens rear end movement on bumpy dirt tracks.

99

Builder CJ Rayborn showed up at Atomic Speedway in 1992 with this radical, ultra-lightweight Dirt Late Model for the Hall of Fame 100 race. Note "boxy" shape, with straight body panels. This type of construction is very inexpensive to replace in the event of an accident or fender bender, which happens frequently. If you aren't banging fenders, you aren't racing hard enough. Tony Hammett photo.

dirt car requires more room between the tire and the body, so the wheelwell opening is much larger.

As for the tires, dirt track tires have a tread, usually in the form of a waffle or her-ringbone pattern.

On dirt tracks, there is a steady stream of mud, dirt clods and rocks flung from the tires, so a windshield would likely crack or shatter. Instead, dirt cars usually use a fine meshed wire screen in place of a windshield to protect the driver.

The shape of these cars can best be described as "sleek and straight." The sides are straight and vertical with the top of the cars straight and horizontal, almost like a low-profile rectangular box, with a sloping nose. There has been talk in the past of making these cars more "stock appearing," but the teams have argued that because of the extensive fender banging and crashes in most races, it would be very expensive to keep the stock sheet metal looking good. The current bodies use easy-to-replace panels that are relatively inexpensive.

For safety, the cars are designed so the front end will crumple to absorb most of the impact, and divert most of the damaging force away from the driver. Many times, a crashed car appears to be more badly damaged than it really is.

These cars still look similar to the "Wedge Car" designs of the mid-1980s, which were much larger machines with aerodynamic body panels and wings, along with trick, high performance, custom-made suspen-

Dirt Late Models go fast enough to be concerned about rear downforce. To achieve this, these cars use a rear deck-mounted adjustable spoiler like the one shown above.

Some Dirt sanctioning bodies do not limit cubic inches, while other only allow small-blocks. Some classes require the engines to be mostly stock, while others require a fully prepped, aluminum race engine to be competitive. There are as many engine configurations as there are classes. Shown at left are two typical engine layouts used in Dirt Late Model.

sions. However, the costs soon got out of hand for the original concept of that class, so the cars were "downsized" to keep them relatively affordable.

Depending on the part of the country and the sanctioning body, there are some interesting body styles allowed, notably the convertible racers that basically have no roof, just a simple roll cage around the driver. Some other configurations only require that the driver's compartment be enclosed, while the rest of the car is encased in flat sheet metal panels, from the nose to the rear deck.

A number of different types of suspension are in place with the modern Dirt Late Models including coil-over shocks, torsion bars, and even some leaf springs, or combinations of them.

Engine & Drivetrain—There are as many varieties of engine configurations as there are classes. The less-expensive classes require cheaper iron blocks and allow few modifications, while the Pro classes may allow fully-prepped aluminum blocks with the best race components money can buy.

The track size and layout often dictates what engine will be run. Many of the major Dirt Late Model organizations have no cubic

Wheel-to-wheel Dirt Late Model action between Wendell Wallace (6M) and Jack Boggs (B4) shows just how exciting this type of racing can be. These guys are slugging it out at Volunteer Speedway in Bulls Gap, Tennessee, March, 1997. Tony Hammett photo.

inch limit on the engines. The top money races will often feature aftermarket, aluminum small blocks used in configurations from 400 to 500 cubic inches, not unlike the ones used in sprint cars. These engines are capable of 700–800 horsepower. However, there are some groups that provide a one-hundred pound weight brake when a smaller engine (like a 360 cid engine) is used.

These cars use a two-speed manual transmission. The most common is the Brinn transmission, which uses a 1.88 first gear ratio with a direct drive set-up that goes directly to the rear end. Again, it's very similar to the arrangement used by a modern sprint car but still retains the ability to start on its own and move off from a dead stop.

The lower of the two gears brings the engine revs up quicker, and is better suited to maximize torque for better acceleration coming off the turns. When the engine approaches its rev limit, the transmission shifts to a direct drive for better top speed.

These transmissions are coupled to a quick-change rear end like the ones used in Sprint cars. The reason is to allow for very quick changes of rear end gearing between heats to tune the car for a given track, or to adjust to the changing track conditions that occur between events and heats. Crew members can literally change the gearing in a matter of minutes, without having to remove axles and such. Experienced teams have learned to anticipate just how much a track will change during the course of an evening, and have selected the gears accordingly.

At some pavement tracks, there are minimal rules for the late models and just about any type of aerodynamic device is allowed, such as this roof-mounted sprint car wing. Needless to say, this car will really stick to the track at speed.

This class has evolved through the years, from a time when the cars were constructed by hand, to a number of prominent Dirt Late Model manufacturers, notably GRT, Rocket, and Rayburn among others.

PAVEMENT LATE MODELS

There are obvious differences between dirt and pavement stock cars for all divisions and Late Models are no exceptions. The major difference between the two models is the body. Pavement Late Models resemble a stock car more than the dirt versions. The nose is a one-piece fiberglass, plastic or a combination thereof that is riveted onto the front fenders and covers the heavy front bumper tubing. While not an OEM piece, it actually resembles a stock front end rather than replaces it. These pieces have been in use for years, starting with the second-generation Camaros in the early 1970s. They are easier to mount to the car, easier to clean up in the event of a wreck and are actually cheaper and lighter than a factory assembly; always a serious racing factor. With a regulated nose piece, the cars do look more stock and fans can easily tell a Chevy from a Ford

making the "car in the driveway at home" association stronger.

Another distinctive difference is the windshield. Pavement cars almost always use a windshield made of durable Lexan® plastic; dirt cars use screens.

Pavement Late Model body styles range from those similar to Dirt Late Model, like the one shown above, to those that closely resemble their factory counterparts. In fact, several Pavement Late Model sanctioning bodies use factory body templates to ensure uniformity with the street version. The rules of many of the larger sanctioning bodies, though, are similar enough to allow teams to move between tracks and series with little modification, just as with the Dirt Late Models.

Technically, the pavement cars are very close to the Dirt Late Models with the only changes being for the difference of the paved track. Pavement Late Models have very limited suspension travel, with minimal ground clearance to lower the center of gravity for better handling. Another more obvious difference is the wheelwell opening, which is narrow for pavement cars. And, the tires are slicks, with wear indicators instead

Pavement Late Model stock cars may be required to maintain some identity with a factory model. This one shown here is actually trying to copy Dale Earnhardt's famous #3 Monte Carlo.

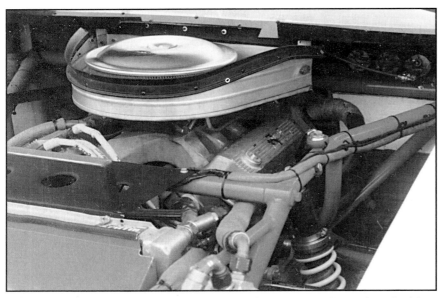

Most Pavement Late Models run small-block Chevys, normally aspirated with a single 390 or 500 cfm carburetor.

Dick Trickle used the ASA circuit to make it to the big time. He has been rated as one of the best short track drivers in ASA history. This is Dick in a 1979 race in his famous number 99 Firebird. Courtesy ASA.

of a tread pattern. The majority of these cars use V8 engines with the suspension using high-tech, yet similar components.

Some of the prime short track Pavement Late Model series include the Hooters Cup Series (exclusively in the Southeast), the NASCAR Featherlite Southwest Tour (Southwest United States), NASCAR Slim Jim All Pro Series (mostly in the Southeast), Southern All Star Asphalt Series (mostly in the Southeast), All Pro Auto Parts MainEvent Series, and the Castrol CAS-CAR Series that runs in Canada.

Although the engine rules for the Pavement Late Models vary from organization to organization and state to state, most all cars, regardless of series or sanctioning body, run Chevy-powered 355 cid (max) small block race engines with a 390 or 500 cfm carburetor. Horsepower range is 400–425.

The standard wheelbase is 105 inches for these cars which use four-speed transmissions.

American Speed Association (ASA)

As stated above, this country is blessed with a number of excellent Pavement Late Model organizations which have served as feeder systems to the big time for a number of years. Probably the top such organization is the Indiana-based American Speed Association (ASA). Many of today's Winston Cup drivers such as Mark Martin, Rusty Wallace, Dick Trickle, Ted Musgrave, Alan Kulwicki and others are ASA graduates. Much of the ASA success has come from the close relationship between the ASA race car and its production counterpart.

For many years, ASA was known as a "Pony Car" circuit with Camaros, Firebirds, and Mustangs doing battle until 1990. Since then, the models competing include the Chevy Monte Carlo, Pontiac Grand Prix, Ford Thunderbird, and now, the Ford Taurus.

Engines—In 1981, ASA was the first to

In 1992, ASA mandated that the chassis must come from approved chassis builders as a spec racer, with no privately built cars allowed. The body was subject to the same restrictions. Bob Fairman photo.

adopt the 9:1 compression rule to curb rising costs. Keeping the compression to this lower level limits the extent of engine modifications and increases durability.

ASA has also allowed the use of V6 engines, making them legal from 1992 through the 1999 season. The reduced compression rule seems to have been the way to go as even NASCAR has used it in many of their divisions all the way to Winston Cup cars. When using V8s, ASA cars have run small-block Chevys, Fords and the occasional Mopar. V6 action was divided between Buick, Chevy and Ford much like the V6s of NASCAR Busch Grand National racing.

The year 2000 season will see a change in direction as far as ASA engine rules are concerned. Plans call for requiring a nearly stock LS-1 Chevy engine. General Motors believes that such an engine would be capable of providing 450 horsepower, which is approximately the same as the current ASA V6 engine.

The engine is unique in that it will introduce fuel injection and electronic engine management for the first time in stock car

racing. Both ASA and General Motors feel that the engine will reduce costs since the engine will not contain a significant number of aftermarket racing components. And unless Ford comes out with a similar engine (an unlikely scenario) all ASA cars—regardless of body brand—could be required to carry this engine. This uniform concept, of course, has detractors and its ultimate success remains to be seen.

Chassis—Starting in the 1992 season, ASA introduced a new rules package involving the chassis and the body. The chassis now had more rigid rules and had to come

V6 Chevy engines, like the one here, have been the engine of choice since 1992. ASA rules permitted extensive modifications for these engines, so power output was about 450 horsepower. However, for 2000 and beyond, ASA has mandated the use of the Chevy LS-1 V8 engine, in mostly stock trim. The move is an effort to reduce cost and equalize competition. Bob Fairman photo.

ASA tech inspection is just as rigorous as NASCAR. Cars must conform to exact specifications, even though they are all built by a handful of chassis builders.

Driver safety is paramount; ASA mandated in '92 that the rollcage be moved forward the seven inches. Extra protection was also called for in the footwell. Bob Fairman photo.

from assigned chassis builders as a spec car; no home-builts allowed. The body, consisting of fiberglass panels, also had to come from designated suppliers and was basically for ASA only. The body actually looks like the Detroit version it's supposed to be. A Monte Carlo looks just like a Monte Carlo and a Taurus looks like a Taurus.

This is done in two distinctive ways. One is through the restriction of body modifications, allowing no chopped tops, bubbled wheelwells, extreme sloping front ends or flipping up rear body sections—all otherwise standard body modifications used in racing. The other way is the mounting of the

body in relation to the chassis. Instead of lowering the body down over the chassis as race cars normally do, the bodies in ASA racing were now mounted quite a bit closer to the height seen on the streets. Based on a 105-inch wheelbase and a slightly more narrow chassis than before, the cars sit taller on the track and have the wheels tucked under the car more than they used to. This goes against the standard racing look of a car that's been lowered, uses wider than stock wheels and tires and often has had other noticeable body changes. To do this, the chassis had to be redesigned to move the roll cage forward on the chassis to fit the new body and still offer the driver the best protection. ASA also added extra protection in the foot areas of the cockpit for the drivers, continuing their high safety standards. The cars still maintain their 2800-lb weight minimum and all the chassis components are that same.

The components of the body are made of fiberglass and Kevlar making for a stronger unit together and as individual pieces. The body parts have flanges molded into them for assembly with pop rivets that are fast, flush-mounted and easy to hide. The hood and roof have been reinforced with Kevlar

ARCA was founded in 1952 by John Marcum and is still going strong today. Shown above are a group of ARCA cars at speed on the banks of Salem Speedway in Indiana in the late '60s. The racing was always close, just like NASCAR. Courtesy ARCA.

Racing at such high speeds on short tracks will lead to the inevitable. Two ARCA competitors make contact at Salem Speedway, in 1988. Kevin Horcher photo.

making them stronger. This all but eliminates the body "ripples" seen at speed in those areas. Windows are still made from another remarkably strong but light material; Lexan. This see-through type of plastic is best described as similar to the bulletproof glass seen in banks. It will take more impact without shattering like glass and is even lighter than glass.

The gamble for ASA's new look in the early 1990s has paid off as ASA races are regularly televised to plenty of fans across the country. At the track, the crowds still show up and ASA racers are still making

their way into NASCAR.

Automobile Racing Club of America (ARCA)

The Automobile Racing Club of America (ARCA) Bondo Mar-Hyde Super Car is the closest thing to a NASCAR Winston Cup car. Despite that, or maybe even because of it, ARCA Super Cars still have their own, distinct personality.

John Marcum, who had long dreamed of having his own racing series, formed ARCA in 1952, and today it is one of the top stock car organizations in North America.

ARCA is the only major stock car series that still runs on both dirt and pavement, just like old times. Here, the ARCA boys get down in the dirt at the Springfield Fairgrounds track in Illinois, in 1994. Kevin Horcher photo.

ARCA has always been a training ground for top Winston Cup drivers. Many ARCA cars in the past were one- or two-year-old Winston Cup cars. Also, because ARCA runs on many of the same tracks, it provides future Winston Cup drivers with invaluable experience. ARCA photo.

ARCA cars still run at state fairgrounds dirt tracks, a tradition as old as stock car racing itself. Here, ARCA cars are "running the rail," at the Illinois State Fairgrounds, in Springfield, Illinois, in 1995. Kevin Horcher photo.

Marcum, a close personal friend of the France family, served an apprenticeship of sorts in the early years of NASCAR before going home to Ohio and forming ARCA. From the start, his series closely resembled NASCAR but raced mostly in the northern part of the United States and Canada.

Today, Marcum's dream is still going strong in the hands of his family. ARCA is one of the more diverse series, racing all over the tracks of the Midwest, NASCAR's speedways and even on state fairgrounds, where the roots of stock car racing are.

Unlike NASCAR, however, ARCA competitors generally have "day jobs." A race winner enjoying the victory lane celebration often ends up discussing that win around the water cooler with co-workers on Monday morning. The same may hold true for his crew members, car owner and family.

Racing ARCA has been beneficial for more than a few Winston Cup stars over the years. Drivers such as Bobby and Davey Allison, Ken Schrader, Dick Trickle, Jeremy Mayfield, Mark Martin, Darrell and Michael Waltrip, Kyle Petty, Ernie Irvan, Tim Richmond and others have raced ARCA to sharpen their skills. One of ARCA's most famous graduates is Benny Parsons, a former cab driver from Detroit. He was the

ARCA has always followed the example set by NASCAR—perhaps too much. Like NASCAR, top ARCA competitors began building separate chassis for short tracks, intermediates and superspeedways. This, of course, made it much more expensive to compete, leaving the "little guys," behind. This went against the very spirit of ARCA, and the organizers took action. Beginning in 1999, ARCA phased out the use of a short track chassis, and all teams had to run the same type for each race. This had many tuning advantages, but above all, it took away some of the "money advantage," enjoyed by teams with deeper pockets, and evened out competition. Tim Steele, shown above, dominated ARCA in the 1990s.

ARCA Rookie of the Year in 1965 and went on to become the only driver to achieve a championship in both ARCA and Winston Cup racing.

While those drivers reflect the modern age of ARCA, names such as Fonty Flock, Bill Rexford, Darrell Dieringer, Don White, Ernie Derr, Nelson Stacy, Charlie Glotzbach, Curtis Turner, Tiny Lund, Fred Lorenzen, and Ron Hutcheson competed in the series a few years before NASCAR's modern era, which began in 1972. The proximity of the Midwest helped draw Indy 500 racers into ARCA stock cars with names such as Roger Ward, Tony Bettenhausen, Johnnie Parsons, Troy Ruttman, Bill Cheesebourg and Danny Sullivan.

The Super Cars of ARCA have always followed rules very similar to Winston Cup for running ARCA races on superspeedway tracks like Daytona, Talladega, Charlotte, Atlanta, Michigan, Texas and Pocono. When ARCA ran short tracks, they began to build special short track chassis, but with the same full-size steel bodies used on bigger tracks. ARCA changed the rules in 1999, phasing out the short track chassis altogether. This allowed some of the less-financed teams to use one or two cars for running the entire season—no matter what type of track. The added bonus was that ARCA Super Car drivers would learn how to tune a single chassis much faster than having to constantly change from track to track. Above all, costs were reduced, which allowed for better competition.

Today, ARCA has grown to four touring divisions and it holds races across the country. It is one of the true stepping-stones to Winston Cup racing, and because the differences between the cars are so slight, many Winston Cup teams use ARCA for research and development on their own cars. On the other end of the scale, ARCA teams often buy and even lease their equipment from Winston Cup teams. It's a mutually advantageous situation, with new ideas tried under controlled environments at many of the

Once again, ARCA has followed NASCAR's lead with a truck series of its own. Their ARCA trucks debuted in 1999, and run smaller, subcompact trucks as opposed to NASCAR's full-size models. This is one of the first ARCA trucks, making an exhibition run at Flat Rock Speedway. J.D. Scott photo.

Whether or not import trucks will be allowed to compete hadn't been decided at the time of this writing, so in the meantime, Chevy S-10, Ford Ranger and Dodge Dakotas fill up most starting fields. J.D. Scott photo.

same tracks.

Quite often, ARCA cars run as support races for NASCAR Winston Cup events, usually running on Saturday. With the sell-out crowds at NASCAR races, being in an ARCA car on the day before offers the highest visibility ARCA drivers and sponsors will see all season. It's also great racing.

ARCA Trucks—As stated earlier, there has been a large grassroots interest in trucks. ARCA looked at the concept, and like NASCAR, decided having an in-house truck series made sense. After running several exhibition races in 1998, ARCA added a full series for trucks in 1999.

Like the NASCAR versions, ARCA trucks are purpose-built for racing from the

ground up, with 108-inch wheelbase, a full-tube racing chassis, three-link rear suspension, coil-over race shocks, and a quick-change rear end. The trucks have stock-appearing fiberglass bodies fashioned in Chevy S-10, Ford Ranger, and Dodge Dakota body styles. The trucks must run the same engine as the body make. The engines produce about 300 horsepower. As of this writing, there was speculation as to whether or not ARCA would allow import trucks to run. One main difference from the NASCAR versions: ARCA trucks are based on smaller, subcompact models while NASCAR trucks are based on full-size models.

NASCAR CRAFTSMAN TRUCKS

NASCAR first raced trucks with a few exhibition races in 1994. The response was so positive that they sanctioned an entire season in 1995. For performance-minded people, trucks are the last frontier. They are still a rear-wheel-drive vehicle; they are built in modular style with a frame and separate, easily replaceable body parts; and best of all, they are built tough to take abuse. Part of the attraction with trucks was what they didn't have—no front wheel drive, no unibody, and

NASCAR Craftsman Trucks debuted in 1995, and have been increasingly popular. Many top teams, like Richard Childress, own a truck team for a variety of reasons. One chief reason is for additional research and development, especially with the engine, because these trucks must run a 9:1 compression ratio in the engine—a rule that many think will eventually wind up in Winston Cup to slow them down.

most backyard mechanics were still able to do much of the maintenance themselves. So when NASCAR did its market research on the possibility of racing trucks, they found a natural winner.

Dubbed "Supertrucks" and sponsored by another name common to being tough, Craftsman Tools, they had a huge success in their first season. All the events were televised; a number of NASCAR-sanctioned short tracks hosted the trucks to sell-out crowds. A few short years later, bigger

At Leading Edge Race Cars, a Charlotte company that "hangs" bodies on race cars and trucks, this NASCAR Chevy truck is shown mid-process. The original factory roof and hood are in place as are the plastic nose and tail sections. All that remains are the hand-made sides and bed cover. Note the beefy and extensive roll cage that is exactly the same found in Winston Cup, Busch and ARCA cars.

Aside from the close racing, NASCAR Supertrucks have become a breeding ground for new talent. This includes all team members—crew chiefs, managers, and mechanics—as well as drivers.

tracks like Texas Motor Speedway with bigger purses started racing the trucks, giving them even more credibility. And so it's been ever since.

A NASCAR Craftsman Truck differs from a Winston Cup car mainly in the body and part of the chassis. With the taller cab, nine inches were added to the upper roll cage. Because the full-size Chevy, Ford and Dodge trucks are longer than cars, the wheelbase was increased. Like Busch Grand National cars, the different wheelbase makes the truck a very different-handling race car on the track than a Winston Cup car, because wheelbase directly affects chassis loading and unloading, and weight distribution. Chassis setups are unique only to the trucks, so every team had to start with a fresh playbook when the series began.

Because trucks race on short tracks, road courses and intermediate tracks, they have become a learning ground for future Winston Cup and Busch Grand National dri-

vers, crew chiefs, team managers, mechanics and other crew members. The Craftsman Truck series has become known as a place to gain valuable skills and knowledge on the road to greater challenges.

Technically, the trucks offer established Winston and Busch teams some research and development in the area of engines. That's because the trucks are already using the 9:1 compression rule. Many believe that NASCAR will eventually adopt this rule across the board to all their divisions and those smart team owners that invest in trucks now will benefit greatly later with advanced knowledge and experience to speed up the learning curve. Having a truck team also is a viable operation on its own if you ask people like Richard Childress, Dale Earnhardt, Richard Petty and Jack Roush. These highly visible Winston Cup names own teams on the truck circuit and utilize the teams for many of their hidden and not so hidden benefits.

Busch Grand National was once called Late Model Sportsman, until Anheuser Busch signed on. It is recognized as a "minor league" to Winston Cup, but the racing is taken seriously. Many top Winston Cup teams have BGN teams of their own, and the drivers race BGN whenever their schedule permits. Mike Slade photo.

"Of all of NASCAR's series, it is the closest you can get to Winston Cup, and the link between today's BGN star and tomorrow's future Winston Cup champion is very strong."

Once NASCAR let the cat out of the bag, it didn't take long for the craze to go truckin' around the country. Today, after a very fast and far reaching growth spurt, there are countless truck classes at many tracks around the United States. From full-size, NASCAR-like trucks to Chevy S-10 and Ford Rangers mini-trucks, these classes vary in rules and specifications from region to region. They've become part of a major grassroots, entry-level form of stock car racing that has become immensely popular during the last part of the '90s.

BUSCH GRAND NATIONAL CARS

The Busch Grand National Series (BGN) has always been thought of as the "minor leagues," if you will, of NASCAR Winston Cup. Of all of NASCAR's series, it is the closest you can get to Winston Cup, and the link between today's BGN star and tomor-

A 1996 field of BGN cars gets ready to take to the track. BGN is a national series. After a short period with V6s, BGN cars now run V8s, but are limited to 9:1 compression ratios. The wheelbase is also reduced to 105 inches, which makes the BGN car slower all the way around—in power and handling. Tony Hammett photo.

One of the most famous graduates of Busch Grand National is Jeff Gordon. Are there others like him running the circuit? Chances are good there are. Gordon is just one of many famous, successful drivers in Winston Cup who have honed their skills in this highly competitive series. Eric Thompson photo.

row's future Winston Cup champion is very strong.

Busch cars have actually been around since 1982, but they were called the Late Model Sportsman Division, which was a regional series confined pretty much to the Southeast. However, when Anheuser Busch offered a long-term committment, the series was renamed in 1985, and NASCAR took the existing series and made it a national, touring one. Eventually, Busch Grand National racing became the second-highest-paying stock car series in the nation.

Like ARCA and the NASCAR Craftsman Truck class, this series is a breeding ground for new talent, of all kinds. All of the skills learned by every BGN team member can be transferred to Winston Cup—they are that similar. Even owners that may not have the resources to fund a multi-million dollar Winston Cup team have found a home in Busch racing.

The equipment used in Busch cars has changed over the years. At first, the cars

were smaller-bodied, based on models such as the Chevy Nova. Ford teams used Thunderbird bodies, but oddly enough, have never won a BGN championship as of this writing. In later years, the body styles would be adapted to more closely resemble the same models run in Winston Cup, which currently includes the Monte Carlo, Grand Prix, Thunderbird and Taurus.

One of the two biggest differences between Busch cars and Winston Cup cars is in the engine. The BGN cars used V6 engines for a number of years, but currently run a small-block V8, but one that is much more detuned than a Winston Cup car. However, BGN cars use the same 9:1 compression ratio used by the trucks.

The other major difference that can be seen from the the grandstands is the shorter wheelbase of Busch cars. Winston Cup and ARCA Super Cars use a 110-inch wheelbase, while Busch cars are only 105 inches in wheelbase. This five inches make a big difference in handling and chassis tuning, but the principles for setting up a BGN car are the same as Winston Cup.

The Busch Grand National Series does have something its Winston Cup brother doesn't have, and that is a record book with more women drivers in it. There have been five different women racing in BGN in more than 150 of the races from 1982 to today. They've led laps, finished on the lead lap, won the pole but never won a race—so far.

The Busch Series is so far-reaching, it has its own spin-off series—the BGNN—with the second N standing for "North." The BGNN races in the Northeast. Since it has the same rules and equipment, it is not uncommon for drivers from both regions to travel to the other tracks to race.

The NASCAR Busch Series races at many of the Winston Cup tracks, which sets up a "beat the big names" kind of race. Winston Cup drivers and teams make a commitment to run all the races of their series so there is no logistical way they could make all the races on both schedules. On the those races

where Busch cars run on Saturday as a sort of opening act, many of the Cup drivers do indeed race. Many Winston Cup teams or drivers personally have their own teams with full-time personnel and multiple cars. When the Winston Cup stars run with the BGN regulars, there is a great deal of incentive on the part of the regulars to beat them, so the racing is often fierce and hotly contested.

Many of today's Winston Cup stars put in many years in BGN before getting their big break. A few past BGN champions that have gone on to Winston Cup include: Robbie Moroso, Bobby Labonte, Joe Nemechek and Johnny Benson.

Other standouts who got their start or honed their skills in Busch racing and went on to Winston Cup success include: Brett, Geoff and Todd Bodine, Ricky Craven, Chad Little, Kenny Wallace, Mark Martin, Ricky Rudd, Derrick Cope, Dale Earnhardt, Harry Gant, Ken Schrader, Mike Skinner, Darrell and Michael Waltrip, Dale Jarrett, Ernie Irvan, Terry Labonte, Rick Mast, Jeff

The cars might be a bit slower; the risks are the same. Busch cars see their share of accidents too. This is David Bonnett, son of Neil, after smacking the wall at Charlotte Motor Speedway, in 1994. Tony Hammett photo.

Mark Martin (#6) and teammate Jeff Burton pace the 43-car starting field for the Transouth 400 at Darlington, 1998. Although today's Winston Cup car is designed to be identifiable with its street counterpart, it is a race car from the ground up. Bob Fairman photo.

Burton, Sterling Marlin, Bobby Allison, Dick Trickle, Bobby Hamilton, Morgan Shepherd, Alan Kulwicki, Tim Richmond, Neil Bonnett, Davey Allison, and the current dominant force in NASCAR, Jeff Gordon.

There are many that say that when you watch a Busch Grand National race, you are watching the future of NASCAR Winston Cup. Those people just might be right.

NASCAR WINSTON CUP

At the time of this writing, Winston Cup cars are a hybrid of state-of-the-art and old technology. Rules are adjusted to keep the series competitive and to prevent any one brand of car from dominating. Although the exterior sheet metal is identifiable with the production counterpart, the chassis, engine and drivetrain are all specially built from the ground up and follow the same general set of rules set by NASCAR. Most every top team racing today builds their own cars in-house, and they build a lot of them. Teams no longer run one or two cars for all tracks for the season. Now, there are cars specially built for superspeedways, intermediate length tracks, road courses, and short tracks. A top team may have as many as 12 cars per driver.

Body

Through evolution of technology, the necessity of improving safety and keeping costs down, today's Winston Cup cars are now worlds away from their street versions. The body of a Winston Cup car, while serving as a rolling billboard, maintains the appearance of its street counterpart in a number of ways and for a number of reasons. In no particular order:

• They are designed to keep the cars looking like "stock" cars right from the dealer showroom with the key word being "looking."

• Unlike the ones parked in our driveways across the U.S. today, the bodies are asked to be able to withstand 200 mph racing speeds and still remain intact.

• The teams want the bodies to go on or off quickly and efficiently as well as cost as little as possible to build, repair and maintain.

• The crew chiefs, OEM designers and drivers want the very best aerodynamic and

"That's quite a bit to expect from some metal and plastic."

The body of a Winston Cup car must fulfill many requirements. It must go on and off quickly so the crew can work on the chassis and engine underneath, be designed to clean up quickly in the likely event of an on-track incident; and be as aerodynamically efficient as possible. How the body is mounted on the chassis is a complex process, known as "hanging the body." For the Taurus, Ford had to fabricate special hood, roof and decklid panels to conform to NASCAR rules. Bob Fairman photo.

downforce package available, which they will continuously massage for even specific track usage in pursuit of winning. Every little nuance and any slight advantage is critical and even necessary to win in racing today.

• In the likely event of a crash where the bodies cannot withstand the impact, that's the job of the chassis and specialized safety equipment. The cars must be built to clean up quickly after an accident on track, and also be designed to be patched together quickly if the damage is minor enough, to continue racing.

• Finally, NASCAR wants the steel bodies to be as equal as possible so no one team or brand has an advantage over the others.

That's quite a bit to expect from some metal and plastic. NASCAR Winston Cup car builders start the body process with the only three pieces that do indeed come from the OEM manufacturer—and even that is subject to change. For GM cars the roof, hood and decklid actually come from the factory. The OEM front, middle and rear roof pillars (respectively called A, B, and C pillars) are usually used but some builders do make their own—it depends on the make, model and just how hard it is to create them. The rest of the body is hand-fabricated from raw sheet metal and plastic pieces by talented craftsmen.

Ford teams also use pieces from the factory but due to the different size and shape of the four-door Taurus, they are custom-made only for racing and would not fit a street Taurus. The street Taurus sheet metal can't be converted to racing because the hood is too short, the roof is too long and although the rear decklid is the right size, it's made of aluminum. Those parts did not confirm to the NASCAR Winston Cup chassis so Ford made steel body panels to the correct size and metal to be used on Winston Cup, Busch and ARCA stock cars.

Hanging the Body—When a team mem-

Tech inspection is very tough in Winston Cup. During tech inpsection in 1997 at Daytona, it was necessary to sand off a little excess material on Terry Labonte's car in order to fit within the body templates.

being fitted to the chassis, NASCAR templates are used to check clearances, fit and the lines of the body. With those factory pieces properly set in place, the next step is to make up the sides of the car.

Body Panels—The front fenders, doors and rear quarter panels are handmade by skilled sheet metal artists with the multiple tasks of proper and legal fit, aerodynamic considerations, some strength, keeping the weight of the panels to the minimum and even specific track application. And they make them from raw sheet steel. They use large, "English wheel" sheet metal fabricating machines for rolling the soft curves around the large Goodyear racing tires. Sheet metal brakes are used for bending ridges and folds into the metal to make them look like a door or fender from a Monte Carlo, Grand Prix or Taurus. These pieces are then precision-matched to the already positioned roof, hood and rear decklid to make up the majority of the body. Again, legal templates make sure there should be no problems getting through inspection at the track.

Nose & Tail—The next step is put a nose and tail on the car. On street cars, the front and tail sections of a car are made of numerous pieces and assemblies that include head, parking and tail lights, grilles, bumpers, fender and quarter panel corners and maybe even lower hood and trunk threshold pieces. For the sake of simplicity in the areas of track clean up, car building and maintenance and NASCAR inspections, the nose and tail pieces are one-piece units made from a type of plastic and resin. The parts are approved by NASCAR so they can be policed better in the on-going battle to keep the cars uniform. They are pop riveted to the front and rear sections of the side body panels and also attached to under-the-body braces that extend from the tubular frame. Under both nose and tail sections are round tubing bumpers that can take quite a bit of punishment, especially on a short track where that

ber or a specialty shop within the industry starts to "hang the body," they start with a rolling chassis—one that has all wheels tires and suspension pieces—sitting on a large, highly accurate flat piece of metal called a *surface plate*. With the chassis poised at what is called "ride height"—the same exact stance the chassis will have on the track during racing—a number of highly accurate plot lines are measured and marked throughout the chassis and where the body will be mounted. The first piece to hang is the roof panel, complete with pillars, mounted to the cage and firewalls. Then comes the hood or decklid, mounting off the roof pillars and frame pockets for the front windshield and rear window. As each of these pieces is

Of course, sometimes the damage is a bit more severe, so it can't be so easily repaired. The impacts sustained by a modern Winston Cup car are enormous, yet drivers continue to walk away from crashes that defy logic. The reasons can be attributed to the safety features built into the chassis. Note that in this car, both the front and rear have been completely crushed, while the driver's compartment remains intact. The areas containing the fuel (rear) and engine (front) are designed to be isolated from the driver's compartment because of the possibility of fire. Kenny Schrader ended up doing numerous end over end flips and rollovers at Talladega at close to 200 mph without any serious injuries.

kind of action is commonplace.

Final Touches—With the outer body in place, the sheet metal wizards then turn to finishing the body with *crush panels*. During a crash, crush panels do exactly what their name implies. They are smaller pieces of sheet metal that connect the outer body with the chassis and driver's compartment, sealing off the driver from any dirt and debris as well as fumes coming from the outside. Covers for the pockets that hold the lead weights in the main frame as well as covers for the battery and engine oil tank storage compartments need to be not only put in place, but sealed for zero leakage. The areas of the engine and fuel tank compartments must be completely isolated from the driver's compartment because those are the areas in which fires usually originate. There are no holes in the firewall separating the engine from the driver, as even a tiny hole could act as a cutting torch and intensify the flame when an engine fire takes place at racing speeds. This is a practice that is recommended in all race cars.

Sometimes teams have to change bodies. It may be a new model body to be used, or it may be they have switched brands. They can often take the entire body off the car in one piece and install the new one on the old chassis. Imagine what a racing collectable that would make—a complete body in one piece!

But when a completely new body comes along, such as the case of the Ford Taurus, the act of just changing the sheetmetal over an older, and most importantly, different-sized chassis and roll cage isn't enough. Roll cages these days are fitted to the bodies and will match the pillars of the car to provide both a better fit and to take advantage of the new body's lines. It's kind of like putting on an old jacket after gaining weight—it's just not going to fit right. The different contours of the new body's roof, front windshield and side pillars often dictate where roll bars can go within safety guidelines. The safety aspect of today's cars with their smaller window openings also presents a clearance problem for drivers exiting in a hurry after a wreck. Moving the bars to provide the maximum clearance is a NASCAR rule that has allowed many a driver to live longer.

Once the body creation or replacement is

NASCAR tech inspection is very rigorous. Cars must be within exact specifications before and immediately after the race. Because aerodynamics are so important in NASCAR racing, especially on superspeedways, extra attention is given to the body. Templates cut to within fractions of an inch are set over the car to ensure it is within specs. Above, Jimmy Spencer's Ford Thunderbird is measured.

complete, the car is handed off to the body shop, where they will make it look perfect for inspection, the fans and the corporate logos it will receive.

Tech Inspection—At the track, the bodies go through vigorous NASCAR and ARCA inspections prior to practice, qualifying and the race itself. After the race, NASCAR and ARCA will inspect a random number of top finishers (it varies to keep the racers guessing) to ensure any illegal cars being caught. Body inspections include an ever-growing number of templates to fit the body with varying clearances. The most noticeable of the templates is the biggest one that runs the length of the car, starting from the leading edge of the hood down the middle of the car to the spoiler on the rear decklid. There are templates for doors, across the front and rear

of the roof and almost any area of the body. Despite, or maybe because of the templates, the teams spend quite a bit of their research and development budget trying out different ideas on various body parts. Most of this work is done in the wind tunnel, where results show up quicker with technical instrument monitoring. At the track, during testing, similar body modifications are also tested for driver response as well.

Spoilers & Air Dams—The spoilers on the rear decklids are regulated to car make and track size. The specifications are usually formulated by NASCAR and ARCA in conjunction with the front air dam called a *valance*. These two devices, which were developed strictly for racing, can affect speeds with just a slight change in angle or height. They are often used when a subtle

"Despite, or maybe because of the templates, the teams spend quite a bit of their research and development budget trying out different ideas on various body parts."

Front and rear air dams and spoilers are closely regulated in terms of ground clearance, height, angle and size, among other things.

difference is needed between the brands to keep them closer to equal. If one car has an excessive amount of rear downforce, it can be reduced with a smaller rear spoiler. Those cars lacking a small amount of front downforce can receive a longer front valance.

The front valance size controls how much or how little air goes under the car as opposed to pushing the front of the car down increasing front end traction. This is done by raising or lowering the bottom edge of the valance, affecting the size of the valance in relation to the ground. Moving the valance's bottom edge towards the track surface reduces the air going under the car that can contribute to front end lift, thereby increasing downforce on the front end.

The same holds true for the rear spoiler. Its size can increase or reduce rear downforce and traction. When it stands taller from the

NASCAR has worked continually over the years to enact safety devices and regulations, such as restrictor plates and roof flaps, to limit speeds and keep cars on the ground. Although a car has not gone into the grandstand at this writing, crashes still occur frequently.

rear decklid, it stops more air and pushes down on the rear of the car increasing traction.

The spoiler has also helped to regulate racing speeds by just getting in the way. At the two biggest tracks of Daytona and Talladega, where speeds are purposely held back by a number of methods, the rear spoilers are brought up to a taller angle to create more drag, like a set of flaps on an airplane. Teams got around that for a while by using rear shock absorbers that would "settle down" the rear of the car at speed, thus dropping the spoiler out of the path of the 200 mph air and decreasing the car's overall resistance.

Safety Devices—The body of a Winston Cup car (as well as BGN and ARCA cars that run on the superspeedways) has a number of relatively new modifications in external safety equipment that came about from a 200 mph incident at Talladega. As described in detail on page 48, Bobby Allison's Miller Buick became airborne at over 200 mph during the 1987 Winston 500. That in itself was not totally uncommon—Cale Yarborough

had done the same thing at Daytona after recording one of the first laps at the same speed. However, in both incidents, as the car turned sideways into the 200 mph airstream, it lifted up and became completely airborne. With Cale, he was the only car on the track and was coming out of turn four at Daytona where there are no grandstands. When Cale's airborne Hardee's Monte Carlo came back to earth, he spun wildly around the track, bouncing off the crash walls before coming to a stop. He was okay.

Bobby was not so lucky. Again, as described on page 48, his car nearly went into the packed grandstand, which would have been a major catastrophe that could have ended stock car racing altogether. The cars needed to be kept on the ground.

First came the return of the restrictor plates in 1988, not seen since 1971 when speeds first hit 200 mph. This is also detailed on page 48.

But NASCAR knew that they would have to play with aerodynamics to keep the cars on the ground as well as reduce speeds. A year later, in 1989, small raised strips of sheet metal following the length of the roof were added to help keep the cars on the ground. The high profile of the strips face the sides of the cars so they are mostly out of the air when the car is going forward and the strips are only an edge. When the car is sideways, the strip faces into the air and works like a rear spoiler, catching the air. As NASCAR saw the strips working, they extended them further down across the back window and rear decklid for more drag when the car is sideways. In 1992, NASCAR was still in pursuit of keeping the cars on the ground at racing speeds that were now in the 190 mph range at the two tracks. That's when they brought about the side skirts located along the bottom of the car's rocker panels. Now, with the small rails on top of the body acting as a sail and pushing the car back towards the track when the car is sideways, the skirts would keep the air from going under the car. When the car is sideways, air moving under the car causes

lift. The skirts greatly reduced the dangerous amount of lift.

The same rule about lift held true for the interior of the car. Air going into the side window openings but not being able to leave the interior as quickly due to the size of the window openings created lift on the underside of the roof. So the cure for reducing air going into the car's passenger compartment or greenhouse, was to put a passenger window in place. The new, passenger side windows also utilized two sets of quick release hardware operable from the inside by the driver and the outside by safety crews. But even with the passenger windows installed, the cars still showed some degree of lift when getting sideways at those high speeds.

In 1994, roof flaps were mandated on all superspeedway cars and only two years later, on all tracks. The assembly, licensed by NASCAR and built to their specs, consists of two flaps mounted on the roof. One lines up with the width of the roof while the

Rusty Wallace receives quick service from the Penske crew. The car features the latest safety devices up through 1998, which include roof strips, a roof flap and side skirts along the rocker panels. All are designed to keep his car on the ground in the event of an accident. Courtesy California Speedway.

One of the primary keys to success is testing, testing and more testing. Top teams test whenever they can. They are continually looking for shock, spring and suspension setups that will provide the best handling for each individual track. Tires and engine tuning techniques are also tested. Here, a group of unpainted, then-new cars waits to test at Daytona in a Chevy factory test, in 1994.

other follows a 45 degree line perpendicular. When air is forced into the greenhouse by the sudden sideways movement of a spin, a minimum of five pounds of air pressure pops the flaps open. There are steel cables on the flaps to keep them from being ripped off in the extreme air flow, and once open, they relieve the air pressure inside the car, virtually eliminating most of the lift. The car continues its sideways movement and, hopefully, stays on the ground. When the flaps stay open, the driver will need to return to the pits to have crew members put them back in the down position if he is still able to race.

Chassis & Suspension

Winston Cup cars are heavy, with a minimum weight requirement of 3400 lbs. The wheelbase must be 110 inches, the height 51 inches, and the track no more than 61 inches. Minimum ground clearance is three and one-half inches. All specs are routinely checked before qualifying, before the start of the race, and even after the event.

The chassis is constructed of 0.125" rectangular steel for the main rails and 0.095" round tubing for chassis bracing and the extensive roll cage.

Roll bars include four, door-protecting bars on both sides of the car for side impact crashes and a complete cage around the driver to protect from all angles of impact. The cage goes well beyond the simple loop seen in the early days and is reinforced and stiffened extensively. In 1996, NASCAR and ARCA mandated a bar to run in the middle of the upper, roof rails of the cage further tightening the cage and protecting the driver if the roof sheet metal is ripped off in a violent crash. To further protect the driver, there are bars that reinforce the cage from sideways and front and rear forces. On the front of the cage, these bars extend down off the top of the cage into the engine compartment to connect to the loop around the engine. The bars around the engine are not to protect the engine but to reinforce the chassis and suspension mounting points. The bars off the back of the cage extend down into the back seat area and again connect to the frame. Like the front, the bars then go around the fuel cell gas tank and this time, they are for protection as well as chassis and suspension mounts and stiffening. When all the bars are in place according to NASCAR and ARCA rules, the finished assembly provides the maximum protection for the driver and a very stiff chassis for the suspension to work off of.

The front suspension is an independent A-arm setup front with a full floating style axle and hub assembly with reinforced axle housing out back. It's a pair of simple designs that basically came from Detroit in the late 1960s. The front end designs came from the early model Chevy Chevelles or full size Fords depending on where the steering is in relation to the front crossmember. What used to be known as a front steer car had the tie rods, Pitman/Idler arms and center link in front of the chassis crossmember. Those cars with the steering gear behind the crossmember or towards the rear of the car were known as "rear steer." NASCAR still mandates a circular ball steering box whereas most cars on the street have rack and pinion steering.

Shocks & Springs—Shocks and springs are the very soul of any oval track car's suspension. They vary greatly from car to car as well as track to track. Because the car is always turning left, the right front spring generally needs to be the stiffest as it is getting most of the car's load input. That would also dictate that the left front would be the softest corner to spring. The rear springs are much closer to each other in spring rates than the front. There are a handful of theories on springs and shocks and the hardest part for anyone setting up a car is figuring out which information to use. Then there's

This is what's known as a "rolling chassis." It is a complete frame and roll cage assembly with all front and rear suspension pieces installed so the car can actually be rolled around the shop. This version, seen at the Geoffrey Bodine/Joe Bessy Power Team shop, is a used racer that's been bead blasted to clear it of all paint and sealers in preparation for receiving a new Chevy Monte Carlo body.

The key to handling on an oval track is in the shock valving and spring rate. These two areas are different from front-to-back and side-to-side. The shock and spring setup is also different for each track. Also, the driver may have a preference to set the car up to drive "loose" (oversteer) where the back end swings out during cornering, or they may prefer a slight "push" (understeer), where the nose of the car pushes straight slightly rather than turning. Bob Fairman photo.

the driver's preference; some like the car to be slightly "loose" where the back end wants to swing around. The opposite of loose is "push" where the car doesn't want to turn but instead tends to go straight. Any oval track car has to find the delicate balance between the two so a driver can enter a turn as hard as he can and lose the smallest amount of speed possible. Once into the turn, the driver needs to be able to drive out of the turn under as much power as possible without the car getting loose or pushing. The more momentum a driver can preserve and the less speed scrubbed off, the faster the lap.

All springs are coil type in NASCAR Winston Cup, Busch Grand National and ARCA Bondo Super Cars. The shocks are gas filled and, like the springs, are seemingly endless in selection. The purpose of a spring and a shock are more different than people would think. Springs are designed to offset the forces that are loaded onto the

chassis as it moves around the track on both the straights and turns. Even though a car may be on the straight, it is still always turning. That's because the fastest way or "line" around as track is a delicate combination of reducing the angles of the turns with the best line for maintaining momentum. As the car corners harder and softer on various parts of the track, the spring has to absorb those forces and keep the chassis loads evenly spaced so as not to overload any one particular corner of the car. Not only is the spring carefully selected for its *rate,* or how many pounds it takes to compress the spring one inch, but it is adjusted via the weight jacks or load screws. These are threaded rods going through the frame that adjust the rates of the springs. Instead of the spring "pushing" against the frame as in a street car, it pushes against the plate or cap on top of the spring which is touching the weight jack. By raising or lowering the frame just above the spring, the rate of the spring is changed. As seen at the track or on TV, a crew member turns a ratchet wrench somewhere in the back window area to make these changes during a pit stop. Often called adding a "round of bite," it's a good indicator of how good or bad a car may be handling. Seeing a crew member giving the weight jack numerous turns clearly shows a major chassis adjustment.

The purpose of the shock absorber on a race car is to dampen and control the movements of the spring through loading and unloading forces as it goes around the track. That sounds simple, but the key is to come up with the correct shock valving as it compresses and extends. If the shock cannot dampen the spring's movements as quickly as the spring moves, and loads are not distributed smoothly, the spring loads and unloads roughly and unevenly. That causes momentary loose and push conditions and loss of traction. When traction is lost, the driver has to back off the gas pedal and lose momentum and even track position. That

means shocks have to have the right ratio of push and pull resistance on the spring. To further evaluate shocks, most teams have a shock specialist that uses a shock dynamometer to accurately rate each shock.

The springs and shocks are not the only things adjustable on the suspension of these cars. In the front, there is an anti-sway bar extending from the lower left control arm across the width of the car to the right side, lower control arm. That bar is also adjustable for the amount of resistance it creates as the suspension moves through its up and down motions. In the back, there is a panhard or track bar that pretty much does the same thing. Even though the rear wheels are not independent like the front, the track bar does load off one side and reinforce the other to help create the resistance needed. When one quickly adds up the amount of adjustments for each corner of a race car and multiplies them by four, it is quickly apparent that a good crew chief that knows how to

make a car fast is a valuable commodity indeed.

Rear Ends—The rear ends of today's Winston Cup, Busch Grand National and even ARCA Super Cars exclusively use a suspension design that originated with Chevy trucks in 1968. The long, angled control arms almost reach the driver's seat and hold the coil springs and rear end housing. The longer control arms of the truck style offer a softer angle of motion and as such can deliver traction better. It works like the see-saw in a playground. The longer the plane or control arm, the lessor degree of arc it goes through. Once the supply of truck parts was exhausted, a few aftermarket companies that sell parts to racers started supplying made-for-racing control arms that were stronger than the original arms. The same holds true for the rear end housing itself. Based on the design of a 10-inch Ford rear end, it quickly became cost-efficient to use the made-for-racing pieces rather than

If handling goes off during a race (or if it was never right from the start), pit crews can make adjustments during a pit stop by turning the weight jack located at the rear of the car. This is often referred to as "adding a round of bite."

Jeff Gordon's "Rainbow Warriors," get ready to change tires. Tire science is a matter of choosing the right compound for the conditions, and a matter of choosing the right stagger and air pressure.

for different tracks. Carbon fiber brake pads are often used and it seems like horsepower, there are never enough brakes for a driver. They allow a driver to go into a turn harder and reduce just enough speed to keep the momentum going. On the road courses and short tracks, it's not uncommon for a driver to have to slow down to 50 mph for a turn.

Tires

Tire science has become so exact that there are different tires used for different tracks. Choosing the right compound and stagger to suit a given race and track is often the difference between winning and losing. As the track changes in the course of the race, so do the tire requirements. Driver and crew must communicate how the car is handling at all times so proper adjustments can be made during pit stops. When a tire is changed, the crew measures temperature and wear so they can calculate wear and handling characteristics.

Inner Liners—One of the most significant developments in tire technology has been the tubeless inner liner, introduced by Goodyear in 1990. The inner liner concept, which they first introduced in the '60s, was to give the driver some measure of control if the outer tire blew. The early versions were called the Goodyear Lifeguard Safety Shield, but were more like a tire within a tire. The new tubeless inner liners can actually be reused.

When it comes to putting a price on a race-ready, competitive Winston Cup car, one can usually count on spending at least $125,000 per car without the engine. With teams having upwards of a dozen cars in their stable, it's easy to see why budgets for the top teams include sponsorship deals in the $10 million range.

modify an OEM unit. Today, the parts that make up the front and rear suspension of a stock car come from a stock car supplier rather than the local GM or Ford dealer.

Brakes—Brakes are not all that important on long and intermediate ovals other than to brake going in and out of the pits. On short tracks and road courses, brakes are obviously much more important, and on those cars you'll likely see additional brake cooling devices not seen on the speedway cars. They are, of course, hardcore racing disc brakes and sometimes teams use different brakes

STOCK CAR TRACKS

5

Any successful formula has key ingredients, and in stock car racing, a major ingredient is the track. There are many tracks in stock car racing that have become as famous as any other area of the sport—from the drivers and cars to the owners or races. They are more famous than the towns they inhabit, some of which might not even exist if it weren't for the revenue each track brings in.

There are tracks that have taken on an aura that is almost mystical, with personalities shaped by legendary races, drivers, cars and even the untimely deaths of competitors from the past. For many fans, the annual pilgrimage to witness a race at their favorite track has become a tradition shared by generations of families, who consider a race like the Southern 500 to be as much a part of their lives as any other holiday.

Say the names of big tracks like "Talladega," "Daytona" and "Charlotte," or short tracks like "Eldora" and "Winchester," and a majority of stock car fans will quickly give you the facts, figures and highlights of these famous ovals, or talk about some of their favorite races. Some of the tracks are now gone, while others have changed so much over the years that they do not resemble what they where when first founded.

The kingpin of NASCAR stock car tracks is Daytona, where the season kicks off with the Daytona 500. In this 1959 photo, you can see how steep the banking in the corners is in relation to the flat apron. The corners are banked at 31 degrees. Courtesy Daytona Racing Archives.

Atlanta usually gets a lot of attention because one of its two races is held toward the end of the season, with the championship often on the line. But it also hosts plenty of exciting ARCA action. Shown here is turn four of the 1.54 mile oval, banked at 24 degrees. SMI has been transforming Atlanta into one of their trademark luxury racing facilities. Tony Hammett photo.

However, the contributions these tracks and many others have made to the sport are undeniable. They have provided an arena to help the sport develop and prosper. While this is not by any means a complete list of all of the track facilities that host stock car events (that would require a whole book itself), it is an alphabetical list of some of the more notable ones that stand out for a variety of reasons. We've provided as much information as was available. Where the records are listed, these are valid through the end of 1998, and only reflect the Winston Cup lap and race average speed records. If the track does not hold a Winston Cup race, we didn't list the many records of all the classes that run there. It just would take too much space.

ATLANTA MOTOR SPEEDWAY

P.O. Box 500
Hampton, Georgia 30228

Track Facts
Length: 1.54 Miles
Banking: 24 degrees

Winston Cup Records as of 1998
Lap Record: Geoff Bodine, 197.478 mph/28.074 seconds, Nov. 16, 1997

Race Average Speed: Bobby Labonte, 169.904 mph, November 16, 1997

Take the highly successful Charlotte Motor Speedway operation and move it south and you've just about described Atlanta Motor Speedway. The track was originally built in 1960, and it was purchased by Bruton Smith's Speedway Motorsports, Inc. in 1990. In the last few years, the track has undergone a complete transformation to make it a better world-class facility. The original 1.522 mile oval was redone and enlarged slightly into a 1.54-mile quad oval in time for the last race of 1996 . The original back straight was changed to pit road and a new section was added to complete the oval, along with a new start/finish line. All this came with new garage areas, scoring and control towers. The new quad oval is superfast, with Geoff Bodine's quick 197 mph qualifying record as proof.

Any SMI track is famous for its amenities, and Atlanta is no exception. Three new grandstands have been added—the East Turn, the Richard Petty Grandstand and the North Turn—which have more than doubled the original seating capacity. Also, the Champion's Grandstand has added another 37,000 seats. There are currently 84 luxury suites with another 44 planned, and there are also 46 luxurious condominiums. The condos in particular are first class, offering owners and their guests a clubhouse, swimming pool, tennis courts and exercise room, bicycle and hiking trails, and an amazing six fishing lakes.

The Atlanta Motor Speedway is very significant on the Winston Cup trail, hosting two 500-mile races, with the second one coming near the end of the season. (The Miami-Dade Motorsports complex will now host the last race from '99 on.) Many times, the championship and final point standings have been decided by this very race, which makes for some very exciting competition, a trend that is sure to continue for many years to come.

BERLIN SPEEDWAY
Berlin Fairgrounds
Marne, Michigan

Track Facts
Length: 1/2 mile paved oval
Banking: 5 degrees (turns), flat straight-aways

One of the most significant dates in Michigan racing history is April 28, 1951. This was opening day for Berlin Raceway and nearly five decades later, Berlin Raceway is the longest running track operated by the same promoter. Gene Farber won the first race in a '32 Flathead Ford.

The Berlin Speedway has launched the racing careers of successful drivers such as NASCAR drivers Johnny Benson Jr., Butch Miller, and Jack Sprague, along with three-time ARCA Champion Tim Steele. Chet Mysliwiec founded the track in 1951 and still promotes it today, making him possibly the longest-lasting promoter in the nation. He explained, "We thought that the track might last for a few years after World War II, like many of the other tracks in our area, then fade." That sure didn't prove to be the case! Initially, the track was one-fifth mile dirt, a common size and surface for the era. But it was enlarged to accommodate the increasing speeds of stock cars, up to 1/2 mile. In 1966, the Speedway made the transition to pavement.

Their biggest annual event is the ASA race. It usually draws over 10,000 fans. However, there's plenty of weekly racing during the season, with Late Models, Super Stocks and Sportsman cars bringing in as many as 5,000 fans a each night. Berlin has also hosted ARCA events.

Many of the great drivers in stock car racing have run at Berlin, including Bobby Allison, Darrell Waltrip, Dale Earnhardt and Pancho Carter. Berlin is a very historic race-

way with a rich tradition that has helped shape the world of stock car racing.

BRISTOL MOTOR SPEEDWAY
P.O. Box 3966
Bristol, Tennesee 37625

Track Facts
Length: .533 Mile
Banking: 36 degrees

Winston Cup Records as of 1998
Lap Record: Mark Martin, 125.093 mph, set August 25, 1995
Race Average Speed: Charlie Glotzbach, 101.074 mph, set July 11, 1971

Bristol Motor Speedway, another one of Bruton Smith's SMI tracks, has been dubbed "The World's Fastest Half-Mile." Bristol

These two photos illustrate the steep, stadium-style seats of Bristol Motor Speedway. At top is pit road on the morning of the 1998 Winston Cup race, and at bottom is the track later on. Note also the steep banking and the luxury suites in the bottom photo. The very steep 36-degree banking is partly responsible for the track's claim that it is "The World's Fastest Half-Mile."

"Any serious discussion on the great stock car tracks in history would have to include Brownstown Speedway in Indiana."

Brownstown Speedway in Indiana is a former fairgrounds horse track that has been converted into a national-level stock car track. It holds a number of major events that attract the best Dirt Late Model drivers in the country. James Essex photo.

was originally built in 1961 as a perfect half-mile with 22 degree banking, and at the time, could only seat 30,000 fans. At the inaugural race, Jack Smith was credited with the win, although he actually had a relief driver named Johnny Allen take over before the race ended. In the years since, no driver has had more success at Bristol than Darrell Waltrip, who has won there 12 times, including a NASCAR record of seven-in-a-row.

Bristol underwent its first makeover in 1969, when the length was increased to .533 miles, and the banking to a very steep 36 degrees. In 1992, the track was repaved with concrete, and in 1996, Bruton Smith and his SMI company took over and installed stadium-style seating that increased capacity to an amazing 130,000, unheard of for a short track. When empty, the grandstands look like skyscrapers. When full of screaming fans it's something to behold.

BROWNSTOWN SPEEDWAY
Jackson County Fairgrounds
State Route 250

Brownstown, Indiana

Track Facts
Length: 1/4 mile dirt oval
Banking: 10 degrees

Any serious discussion on the great stock car tracks in history would have to include Brownstown Speedway in Indiana. The track was built on a section of the Jackson County Fairgrounds. With its minimal banking and 1/4 mile size, driver skill is more important than horsepower when it comes to winning. The unconventional size of the track often presents a challenge to newcomers while giving local drivers a distinct advantage. One of the best ever of those locals is top runner John Gill, a Dirt Late Model driver, who calls Brownstown his home track.

In recent years, the track has hosted three of the top Dirt Late Model races in the Central region of the United States, including the Jackson 100, the Hoosier Dirt Classic and the Kenny Simpson Memorial. It wouldn't be a stretch to say that

Brownstown is a premier race track for the Dirt Late Model class of racing.

The Jackson 100 race was named after the fact that the Speedway is located at the Jackson County Fairgrounds. The Kenny Simpson Memorial is named after one of the all-time great drivers who was a former two-time track champion at Brownstown. The Hoosier Dirt Classic debuted in 1984, and the first event was won by Jeff Purvis.

CALIFORNIA SPEEDWAY

9300 Cherry Ave.
Fontana, California 92335

Track Facts

Banking: 11 degrees
Length: 2 miles
Front straight: 3,100 feet
Back straight: 2,500 feet

Winston Cup Records as of 1998

Lap Record: Greg Sacks, 39.183 seconds/183.753 mph, June 21, 1997
Race Average Speed: Jeff Gordon 155.012 mph, June 22, 1997

The California Speedway is one of the newer tracks to host stock car events, and it is significant because it represents how far the sport has come in 50 years. It is one of the most sophisticated, most well-planned tracks to be built in many years. In its inaugural race in 1997, more than 75,000 fans jammed the facility to watch the Winston Cup cars do battle. The California Speedway also hosts a separate combined Busch Grand National and Craftsman Truck event.

The California Speedway is also signifi-

Two views of the California Speedway illustrate just how magnificent it really is. PMI and ISC teamed up to build this state-of-the-art $110 million facility, bringing stock car racing back to Southern California. Bottom photo shows the corporate suites lining pit row. The view is from the opposing grandstand. Courtesy California Speedway.

Above: Morgan Shepard bottoms out on the banking at Charlotte, under the lights, during the World 600 in 1994. Below, the field at Charlotte takes to the track. Charlotte has become "the Mecca of Motorsports," under the tutelage of owner Bruton Smith and his promoter, Humpy Wheeler. Together, the two have developed many promotional events that have helped to add entertainment value to stock car racing.

track's turns are banked 14 degrees, the front straight is banked 11 degrees, and the back straight flattens out significantly at 3 degrees. During its initial 1997 season, it hosted NASCAR Winston Cup, Busch Grand National, Winston West, and Craftsman Truck races.

Without doubt, the $110 million facility will be one of the premier stock car racing facilities in the nation. With more than 16 million people living within 150 miles of the facility, there should be plenty of fans to fill the grandstands, as well as the 100 corporate suites. The project was spearheaded by Penske Motorsports, Inc. (PMI) in conjunction with ISC.

CHARLOTTE MOTOR SPEEDWAY
P.O. Box 600
Concord, North Carolina. 28026-0600

Track Facts
Length: 1.5 Miles
Banking: 24 degrees

Winston Cup Records as of 1998
Lap Record: Ward Burton, 185.759 mph/29.07 seconds, set October 6, 1994
Race Average Speed: Ernie Irvan, 154.537 mph, October 10, 1993

cant because it is the first permanent race track built in Southern California in over a decade. Now, stock cars can race in the largest market in the world, the Los Angeles area, which is something they haven't been able to do since Riverside Raceway, a road course, closed in 1988.

The two-mile, D-shaped oval is exceptionally fan friendly, with a lot of thought given to access, cleanliness, parking and traffic flow. There are over 32,000 free parking places, and a nearby train station for commuting from L.A. and Orange County. The track will eventually seat 118,000 fans, and there's not a bad seat in the house. Views of most of the action are possible from just about any of the grandstand seats. The

Charlotte Motor Speedway is known as the "Mecca of Motorsports," and for good reason. Situated on 2,000 acres, it is the first and best known track in Bruton Smith's Speedway Motorsports, Inc., and the largest outdoor sports stadium in the Southeast. It was built in 1960, and has since set the trends for motorsports facilities that others follow. Smith and his flamboyant promoter, Humpy Wheeler, were the brains behind many "firsts." When they proposed building 52 condos on the outside of the turns people scoffed at the idea—who would want to live there? Now, it seems like all new tracks are doing it, and when SMI builds new condos at other tracks, they are often sold out before the first nail has been hammered.

Charlotte also set the trend for "pre-race" entertainment. Humpy Wheeler has come up with everything from hair-raising stunts such as car and bus jumps over cars, motorcycle jumps and mock invasions by military groups to an actual three-ring circus. Humpy Wheeler and Bruton Smith are also the driving force behind the Legends cars all across the country, also a part of most CMS pre-race shows.

Charlotte was also the first superspeedway to install lights and stage a night race, The Winston, in 1987, which has become an annual event. In addition, Charlotte hosts two other Winston Cup events, including the World 600 held Memorial Day.

Recent improvements include 10,000 more seats, bringing the total to 157,000; a pedestrian tunnel under turn three; a reconfigured parking area; and a high volume access road from the I-85 freeway to make getting in and out of the track less of a hassle. Inside there is an office complex that is home to many racing related business, 83 corporate luxury suites, and the Speedway Club, where patrons can experience fine dining with a complete view of the track. It's the most decadent way to enjoy motorsports!

In addition to its three NASCAR races, the speedway hosts a spring and fall Food Lion AutoFair show, a nationally televised short track series for Legends Cars, SCCA road racing events, World Karting Association national events, an AMA Supercross event and many other car shows that all keep this facility busy 280 days a year. It's no wonder that Concord and the surrounding areas are home to more NASCAR teams than any other region in the country.

COLORADO NATIONAL SPEEDWAY
Denver, Colorado

Track Facts
Length: 1/2 mile paved oval
Banking: 8 deg. turns; 6 deg. straights

But Colorado has plenty of serious racing as well. Modifieds are some of the most popular classes that run annually, as are the ProTrucks. Joe Starr photo.

Like many other paved tracks in this country, Colorado National Speedway, near Denver, started life as a dirt oval in 1965. The initial length was 3/8 mile until it was increased to its present 1/2-mile length in 1973. In 1989, the dirt oval was paved.

Denver car dealer Marshall Chesrown purchased the oval in 1992 and has since transformed the facility into one of the nation's best stock car short tracks.

Six classes of stock cars run at this track, with the premier class being the Late Model Division, which runs with the NASCAR Winston Racing Series. The NASCAR Featherlite Tour stops by for an event twice a year.

The ProTruck Series class has become very popular, with V8-powered, plastic-bodied replicas of full-size pick-ups drawing full fields and crowds every week. Much of the racing truck interest comes from the recent visits by the NASCAR Craftsman Truck Series. Other types of stock cars that compete at this track include the Grand American Modifieds and the Super Stock classes.

Finally, there are the wild-and-crazy Figure 8 cars and the popular "Train" racing

These three cars are hooked together in what is known as a "trains." It's just one of the promtional events at the Colorado National Speedway that keeps fans coming back for more. Joe Starr photo.

Columbus Motor Speedway is almost a perfect oval, and hosts some great Pavement Late Model races, including one named after the founder, John Nuckles, who built the track in 1945. Earl Isaacs photo.

where three cars are hooked together with drivers in the front and rear cars. This is a wild and exciting off-shoot of the stock car racing sport.

Unlike the coastal areas of the U.S., where people, towns and racing activities are much closer together, this part of the country is spread out and offers more countryside than race tracks. With their NASCAR connection and the quality shows they offer, CNS is a sort of beacon for hard-core racers and fans in the area. This is one reason why the track is receiving national interest on a regular

basis.

COLUMBUS MOTOR SPEEDWAY

1845 Williams Road
Columbus, Ohio 43207

Track Facts
Length: 1/3 mile paved oval
Banking: 10 degrees

Columbus Motor Speedway was built in 1945 by the late John Nuckles. Originally, the track was carved out of dirt as a one-third "true" oval, built strictly for racing motorcycles. The track is still the same basic shape today, although it was paved in 1957.

In the late 1940s, the Roadsters discussed in Chapter 2 were run at the Ohio capital city track. Then in 1950, lights were installed and the track held its first stock car race. Most popular were the Friday night features, which was a class that permitted coupes and sedans built from 1937 to 1949. Although John Nuckles passed away in 1971, the track is still run by his family.

Perhaps one of the more significant things that occurred during a Columbus race was when Jim Cushman installed a crude wing on top of his Modified. A much improved version of the same wing is run on today's Super Modifieds and sprint cars.

For many years, the track was the site of the first ASA race of the season, but no longer. Today, the track hosts two very successful Pavement Late Model races, the first of which is the John Nuckles Memorial, held annually near the end of each season. The final race of the season is also the last race of the Main Event Series sanctioning body. Both races attract many top Pavement Late Model drivers from a number of neighboring states.

In 1989, Columbus Motor Speedway officially became a track in the Winston Racing Series. That membership allows local drivers from the Columbus area to participate for points at the national level.

They don't call Darlington the "Lady in Black" for nothing. Here, Darrell Waltrip (#17) earns some "Darlington stripes" the hard way. Darlington held its first race in 1950, ushering in the superspeedway era. Joe Pestel photo.

DARLINGTON RACEWAY

P.O. Box 500
Darlington, South Carolina 29540-0500

Track Facts
Length: 1.366 Miles
Banking: 25 degrees

Winston Cup Records as of 1998
Lap Record: Ward Burton, 173.797 mph/28.295 seconds, March 22, 1996
Race Average Speed: Dale Earnhardt, 139.958 mph, March 28, 1993

Legend has it that Harold Brasington, a Darlington, South Carolina farmer, had taken a trip to the Indianapolis Motor Speedway and liked what he saw. The difference was that Brasington was a stock car fan and he thought stock cars should have their own showcase for 500 miles of racing too. So he went home, got on his earth-moving equipment and began to carve out his own track. He had designed a perfect oval a little more than a mile in size, and had already carved out most of the track, when he saw he was getting a little too close to his favorite fishing pond, so he abruptly cut back, making the infamous and extremely tight Turn Four (at the time). That turn would test the skills of hundreds of drivers for thousands of laps at the paved track commonly known as the "Lady in Black."

Darlington Raceway held its first race September 4, 1950, launching the superspeedway era of stock car racing. The track has since developed a treacherous reputation, and you really haven't made it in stock car racing until you get your "Darlington Stripes." The term came from the best way to exit turn four and get a good head of steam down the front straight. Drivers in the mid to late 60s would drift up turn four towards the wall and actually brush up against it with their right rear fender. The contact lap after lap would actually rub the paint off the rear half of the quarter panel, thus making a line or stripe. It was a delicate maneuver where being off a few degrees or

To make room for more grandstands, Darlington had to be reconfigured. The start/finish line, shown above in its new place in 1998, was relocated to what was once the backstretch. Turn 4, shown above, was once the old Turn 2. The track is uniquely shaped, much like an egg, unlike any other track on the circuit. Whether or not the story about Brasington cutting back to avoid plowing under his fishing pond is true is still a matter of debate. Bob Fairman photo.

so would either bank shot the car wildly down the straightaway or just lose lap speed and track position.

The track was purchased by the International Speedway Corporation in 1982, and it continues to host the Southern 500, a stock car racing tradition. In the early years, greats like Nelson Stacy and Buck Baker had great success at the track, but perhaps no one had Darlington figured out more than David Pearson, who won there an amazing 11 times during his career. To honor his mastery of Darlington, NASCAR erected the Pearson Tower just outside Turn 4, a state-of-the-art facility that holds 12,000 fans. In more recent years, Darlington is best known for the being the race where the Winston Million was won, once by Bill Elliott in 1985 and by Jeff Gordon in 1997.

As with other NASCAR tracks, the growth of the sport in the 1990s has created the need for expansion. In order to make room for more grandstands, track officials moved the start/finish line to what was once the back stretch. The old Turn 1 is now Turn 3, and Turn 2 is now Turn 4.

Whether or not the story about Brasington is true, there's little argument that the shape of the track is certainly unique to stock car racing. Viewed from the air, it is egg-shaped, with the current Turns 1 and 2 being extremely tight. Then, the backstretch angles outward causing Turns 3 and 4 to be longer and more sweeping. With all of the other numerous improvements to facilities, parking and suites, Darlington is ready to carry on stock car tradition well into the next century.

The old Daytona Beach course ran northbound on the sand, then exited onto Highway AIA and headed south. Racing was very popular on the beach for more than 22 years. Racing ended in 1959 when the Bill France Sr. opened the new Daytona International Raceway. Courtesy Daytona Racing Archives.

DAYTONA BEACH COURSE
Route AIA South
Daytona Beach, Florida

If we weren't going in alphabetical order, this track would have to be near the front of this chapter. That's because it was on the sands of Daytona Beach where professional stock car racing truly began. Where tens of thousands of tourists now play on the beach and get sunburned, there was once some of the best and wildest racing in all motorsports. During the 1940s and '50s, there were a number of great drivers that made their mark on the sand, such as Junior Johnson, Lee Petty, Tim Flock, Curtis Turner, and Marshall Teague.

Racing flourished on the beach for over 22 years. The location of the track would move further south as the town of Daytona grew.

The sand would get rutted, and cars would flip easily. Joe Epton, the NASCAR Chief Scorer during those days, recalls, "We tried to make the track as smooth as possible. We added a clay base material to the turns to stabilize them," he explained.

Actually, almost half of the course was run on a public road, Route AIA, from north-to-south. This was one straight of the oval. The turns and oceanside beach straight were completely on the sand.

Longtime stock car racer Dick Dunlevy Sr. remembers what it was like to run on the strange two-surface course. "You didn't hurt the tires on the sand, but that pavement was like sandpaper and it really cut up the rubber in a hurry. That sand was banked in the turns, and if you had any sense, you'd aim at that bank coming off the blacktop. It was better than using the brakes. But if you weren't really on the gas, that sand could

Daytona International Speedway is NASCAR's crown jewel. It is essentially a tri-oval, 2.5 miles in length. Corner banking is a steep 31 degrees. Speeds used to be very fast, until the restrictor plate was mandated. The Daytona 500 and Speedweek start off each season. Daytona now has lights for night racing too, which are used for the July race it hosts each year. Bob Fairman photo.

Wall-to-wall people, and a media circus with the whole world watching: That just about sums up the Daytona 500 and Speedweek, which rivals the Indy 500 as the "greatest spectacle in motorsports." Tony Hammett photo.

really bog you down."

Shut down during World War II, beach racing came back strong when ten thousand fans came out to watch a race from the sand dunes and some tall wooden bleachers on the turns. One interesting constraint on racing on the beach was the tides, with high tide actually bringing the waves onto the course. "There are about six hours between high and low tide so we had about four hours of running time. The usual race length was 160 miles, but there were times we had to shorten the races when the ocean started taking over the northern portion of the race course," Epton explained.

Racing on the sand ended in 1959 when the France family finished the crown jewel in NASCAR's crown: Daytona International Speedway.

DAYTONA INTERNATIONAL SPEEDWAY
P.O. Box 2801
Daytona Beach, Florida 32120

Track Facts
Length: 2.5 Miles
Banking: 31 degrees (corners); 3 degrees (backstretch); 18 degrees (tri-oval)

Winston Cup Records as of 1998
Lap Record: Bill Elliott, 210.364 mph, 42.783 seconds, February 9, 1987
Race Average Speed: Bobby Allison, 173.473 mph, July 4, 1980

There's a good chance that the Daytona International Speedway would not have been built had it not been for the beach course. Basically, Bill France Sr. got tired of having to continually relocate his beach course as the town grew and land developers took over. He finally purchased some vacant land near the Daytona airport, and began construction on NASCAR's main racing

Like other speedways in stock car racing, Daytona continues to expand. Grandstands liike this one are added to accommodate the growing legions of fans. Capacity is now more than 150,000.

facility and headquarters. His goal was to build the biggest, fastest and longest track in the country, the king of the stock car tracks. Four decades later, that dream is very much alive and well.

Daytona is essentially a tri-oval, 2.5 miles in length, the same distance as Indianapolis. However, the banking on the turns is 31 degrees, so the track is much faster. The track record, for example, is held by Bill Elliott at over 210 miles per hour, just slightly slower than his NASCAR record at Talladega, a bigger track by 1/10th of a mile.

Today, Daytona seats well over 150,000 race fans who come to celebrate the kickoff of the season with NASCAR's biggest race, the Daytona 500. There have been many great stories of racing at the famous track, but it's probably best known for the exploits of Richard Petty, who won the Daytona 500 an amazing seven times. Probably the most famous race is the one in 1976, when it came down to a last lap shootout between King Richard and David Pearson. The famous pair touched a few times before crashing hard and spinning down into the grass in the infield. Pearson kept his car running, and managed to coax it across the finish line first for the win.

The 500 is much more than a race weekend, however. It is now a complete "Speedweek," a week-long spectacle of racing that includes the annual ARCA 200, the Bud Shoot-Out (an all star race for Winston Cup pole winners of the previous year), the Gatorade Twin 125s (a pair of 125-mile qualifying races for the Daytona 500), feature races for the Busch Grand National and Goody's Dash cars, and the first International Race of Champions race.

The July 4th weekend is another traditional Daytona date, the Pepsi 400 Winston Cup race. The race has always been infamous for the weather, which is Florida at its worst. The temperatures on the track can be as high as 125 degrees, which has wilted many a great driver. To solve the problem, NASCAR has added a state-of-the-art lighting system for racing at night, when temperatures are cooler.

Daytona serves as the world headquarters for NASCAR, which is only fitting. For many simply saying the word "Daytona" is enough to conjure up images of stock car history. If you're a stock car fan, you be hard pressed to beat the experience of Speedweek and the Daytona 500.

Dixie Speedway has gone from dirt to pavement and back to dirt. The track is wide, which allows for three- and sometimes four-abreast Dirt Late Model racing action. One claim to fame: much of the movie "Six-Pack" starring Kenny Rogers was filmed here. Top photo courtesy Dixie Speedway; bottom photo Tony Hammett.

DIXIE SPEEDWAY
150 Dixie Drive
Woodstock, Georgia 30189

Track Facts:
Length: 3/8 mile dirt
Banking: 20 degrees

Dixie Speedway was built in 1969, as a dirt oval. However, it was paved in 1972, but only for a few years.

As a paved track, it helped launch the careers of a number of future stars, including NASCAR ace Bill Elliott, who won his first feature race there, and short track master Jody Ridley. Other top guns that ran there included Bobby Allison, Pete Hamilton, Neil Bonnett and Richard Petty.

When Mickey Swims purchased the track in 1977, the first thing he did was change it back to dirt. The track immediately flourished and hosted a number of the NDRA Late Model series races. The Southern 100 race at Dixie was the top dirt short track race in the South.

In the 1980s and '90s, the track continued to be a premier facility in dirt racing. Bill Elliott and Dale Earnhardt ran match races there in 1987, 1988, and 1989. The late Davey Allison showed up one night to compete in his first dirt stock car race, and with the help of Red Farmer, finished fifth in the feature.

Country music star Kenny Rogers made his first major motion picture at the track, "Six Pack." The movie exposed the world of dirt track Late Model racing to quite a few people who had never seen it before, which helped boost its popularity.

Recently, Dixie Speedway has hosted the Hav-A-Tampa Series monster Shoot-Out.

ELDORA SPEEDWAY
State Route 118
New Weston, Ohio 45424

Track Facts
Length: 1/2 mile dirt oval
Banking: 28 degrees

This western Ohio track is probably the most popular short track in the country and has played a huge role in the development of stock car racing since the 1950s.

Built in 1955 by Earl Baltes, who still owns the track today, Eldora has hosted a number of major stock car sanctioning bodies and their events, including ARCA and USAC. Eldora is famous as a breeding ground for up-and-coming talent in both stock car and open wheel racing. Drivers like Benny Parsons, Jack Bowsher, and current NASCAR star Ernie Irwin have all run at the famous dirt oval in the past.

In the 1970s, Baltes established two of what are now the most significant Dirt Late Model stock car events in the country. His World 100 event, first run in 1971, is considered a top prize in Dirt Late Model. The first of the big-dollar races, it is still "The Race" to win even though there are other races held today that pay as much if not more. However, it's the prestige that is most sought after. The event always draws the top guns of the sport, and as many as 200 cars show up each year. To date, there have been three triple winners of the event—Larry Moore, Jeff Purvis, and Donnie Moran.

In 1994, Baltes initiated "The Dream" race for Dirt Late Models with the winner pocketing an impressive $100,000—the largest prize in all of dirt stock car racing. Despite its rural location, Eldora draws huge crowds; the World 100 usually counts 20,000 fans in attendance. Rumors are circulating that Baltes is planning at least one more dirt stock car extravaganza that will be the best yet. Given the long tradition and success he's had with Eldora, it won't be much of a surprise when he does.

Eldora is the site of the World 100, one of the top races in all of Dirt Late Model stock car racing. That and the $100,000 annual winner take all race have made Eldora a popular, national-level track. Courtesy Reese Photos.

Flemington Speedway has long been famous for hot Northeast Modified action. However, they also host Late Model and NASCAR Craftsman Truck races as well. Courtesy Flemington Speedway.

mph, Aug. 10, 1996

Flemington Speedway held its first auto race in 1915, and the winner was Ira Vail. Today, Flemington is known for hosting an annual race each year during its annual fair on the Saturday of Labor Day Weekend. Later on, it added a second race on the Monday, Labor Day.

Then, when lights were installed on May 28, 1955, Flemington became a full-time racing facility, hosting weekly races every Saturday night, usually from April through October. The track was a dirt surface until 1991 when it was paved completely. Many legendary Indianapolis stars raced at Flemington in the early days, and more recently, many Winston Cup stars have visited the circuit. Today, Flemington Speedway hosts races with the top Modified, Late Model and Street Stock drivers from all over the Northeastern United States.

FLEMINGTON SPEEDWAY

P.O. Box 293
Flemington, New Jersey 08822

Track Facts
Length: .625 mile
Front straight: 900 feet
Back straight: 845 feet
Banking: Turns 1 & 2: 6 degrees, Turns 3 & 4: 8 degrees, Straights: 4 degrees

Records as of 1998
Lap Record: Bryan Reffner, 116.907 mph/19.246 sec., Aug. 10, 1996 (Modified)
Race Average Speed: Mike Skinner, 84.812

HAGERSTOWN SPEEDWAY

15112 National Pike
Hagerstown, Maryland 21740

Track Facts
Length: 1/2 mile clay oval
Banking: 25 degrees (turns), 5 degrees (Straights)

Ricky Elliott (#1) leads Kenny Brightbill out of one of Hagerstown's banked turns. This is the Octoberfest 250 in 1994. Tony Hammett photo.

Hawkeye Downs is one of the oldest stock car facilities still going strong. It hosted its first stock car race in 1925. Today, it is a top paved short track stop for many sanctioning bodies, including ASA and NASCAR. Courtesy Hawkeye Downs Speedway.

Records as of 1998:

Lap Record: 17.05 seconds, Scott Bloomquist, 1998

The Hagerstown Speedway, with its wide straightaways and long sweeping turns, is especially well suited for dirt stock cars, so some of the best racing in this class can be seen here. It is not uncommon to see finishes with cars three abreast crossing the line, or side-by-side duels throughout the entire race.

The track was built in 1947, and has been going strong ever since. In recent years, the track has been continually renovated with modern amenities, and in 1989, it was voted "the best overall dirt track in the country." The five-decade-old track has recorded a number of stock car milestones, notably running the first dirt track race with a $50,000 winner-take-all purse, which was run in 1983.

Hagerstown Speedway currently races

both STARS and Hav-A-Tampa Dirt Late Models and is surely on the top five list of any national dirt stock car driver.

HAWKEYE DOWNS SPEEDWAY
4400 6th Street SW
Cedar Rapids, Iowa

Track Facts:
Length: 1/4 and 1/2 mile paved ovals
Banking: 1/4 mile, 5 degrees; 1/2 mile, 5 degrees (straights), 9 degrees (turns)

Records as of 1998:
Lap Records: 1/4 mile oval, 15.86 seconds (Street Stocks); 1/2 mile oval, 19.340 seconds (Pavement Late Models)

Hawkeye Downs Speedway, located on the Iowa Fairgrounds in Cedar Rapids, has a rich stock car racing heritage. The first recorded event was on Labor Day, 1925, when Jalopies were the main attraction.

145

Winston Cup drivers and NASCAR and IMS officials pose along the original strip of brick, the start/finish line, prior to the inaugural Brickyard 400 in 1994.

Then, the Great Depression curtailed most of the track activities until 1937, when the first American Automobile Association (AAA) event was held, attracting a crowd of 12,000. Jalopy racing was the major class run at the track until the 1950s, when IMCA stock cars took over. These ran at the Downs for several years, and featured many name drivers such as Ernie Derr, Ramo Stott, and Don White. IMCA stock cars at the time were very similar to those run by ARCA, USAC and NASCAR, and included factory teams with intense competition between the two competing factories at the time, Ford and Chrysler. The present grandstand and track configuration was constructed in 1966 and has a seating capacity of about 8,000. Weekly and regional stock car racing was conducted on the track up until the late 1980s. In 1988, the track was paved.

The new paved surface attracted a number of national sanctioning bodies and made it yet another of the premier paved short tracks in the nation. For example, during the 1997 season, a half-dozen stock car sanctioning bodies made appearances at the track.

Included in that list was the American Speed Association (ASA) which ran two races on national television, and the NASCAR RE-MAX Series, which now makes an annual stop at the track.

Many current Winston Cup stars like Ken Schrader, Dick Trickle, and Johnny Benson Jr. have competed at the Downs earlier in their careers.

With the repaving of both the quarter and half mile tracks that constitute the facility, a bright future is projected for the track that has been named "Iowa's Superspeedway."

INDIANAPOLIS MOTOR SPEEDWAY

P.O. Box 24910
Speedway, Indiana 46224

Track Facts
Length: 2.5 miles
Banking: 9 degrees

Winston Cup Records as of 1998
Lap Record: Ernie Irvan, 177.736 mph/50.637 seconds, July 31, 1997
Race Average Speed: Dale Earnhardt,

Some people thought that it was a sacrilege to have stock cars racing at the famed Brickyard. But the fans sure didn't. Over 350,000 showed up to watch Indian native Jeff Gordon win the first race. Since then, the Brickyard 400 has continued to be the largest Winston Cup event in terms of attendance.

155.206 mph, August 5, 1995

It might be strange to see the Indianapolis Motor Speedway mentioned as one of the prime stock car racing tracks, but that is exactly what the famous Brickyard has become—and only since 1994.

The 2 1/2-mile brick oval was constructed in 1909, originally as an automotive testing and competition facility for the then-thriving Indiana auto industry. Motorcycles and many types of cars ran there but eventually broke up the original stone surface. The track was repaved with 3.2 million bricks, and has been known as "The Brickyard" ever since. Of course, the track has been repaved several times since with traditional asphalt, but there is still one strip of the original brick left in place: the start/finish line.

The first Indy 500 was held in 1911, and has since become the "World's Greatest Race." This used to be the only race held at Indianapolis Motor Speedway, until 1994,

when NASCAR ran the Brickyard 400. The inaugural race saw the largest crowd ever to attend a NASCAR event. More than 350,000 fans showed up to watch Indiana native Jeff Gordon win. With the fragmentation of the Indy Car sport into the warring CART and IRL sanctioning bodies, there are many that feel that the Brickyard 400 event now generates more interest than the traditional Memorial Day Indy Car event. There has also been, not surprisingly, recurring speculation about the possibility of a second yearly stock car event at the track.

Of course, stock cars are considerably slower than the Indycars, but despite the relatively shallow banking of only 9 degrees, speeds are still impressive, and competition very fierce. The track had to complete a number of extensive changes to accommodate the larger, heavier stock cars. The outer and inner crash walls had to be widened and raised to contain the stock cars in the event of a crash. Pit road was redesigned slightly

Dale Earnhardt takes on fuel and tires at Michigan, 1993. MIS is owned by Penske, and is an important stop on the Winston Cup circuit because of its proximity to Detroit.

and the famous scoreboard tower had to grow some to accommodate the stock car field size of 40, instead of Indy's traditional 33.

MARTINSVILLE SPEEDWAY
P.O. Box 3311
Martinsville, Virginia 24115

Track Facts
Length: .526 Mile
Banking: 12 degrees
Front Straight: 800 feet
Back Straight: 800 feet

Winston Cup Records as of 1998
Lap Record: Ted Musgrave, 94.129 mph/20.117 sec., Sept. 23, 1994
Race Average Speed: Jeff Gordon, 82.223 mph, Sept. 22, 1996

When H. Clay Earles built Martinsville in 1947, he had visions of greatness. Red Byron won that first race on the dirt oval, and the following season, Earles's track landed its first NASCAR race.

More than 50 years have gone by, and Earles is still drawing them in. The track was paved in 1955, and now sits on a 300 acre

site that has grown to include seating for 78,000, six corporate suites, 48 luxury suites, and a fully staffed medical center. Martinsville is further distinguished by the fact that it is the only original track from NASCAR's first year that still holds a race. It's as traditional as the sport of stock car racing itself.

There are some who may argue that the level of racing, the speed and size of the cars, has outgrown the .526 mile track, the shortest on the circuit. But despite this, or maybe because of it, Martinsville serves up some of the best short track racing on the planet. Doing 500 laps at the immaculately groomed track is a required learning experience for any rookie driver.

MICHIGAN SPEEDWAY
12626 U.S. 12
Brooklyn, Michigan 49230

Track Facts
Length: 2 Miles
Banking: 18 degrees

Winston Cup Records as of 1998
Lap Record: Jeff Gordon, 38.583 seconds/186.611 mph, June 16, 1995
Race Average Speed: Rusty Wallace, 166.033 mph, June 23, 1996

Michigan International Speedway is owned by Penske Motorsports, and is considered a premier facility on the stock car and Indycar circuits. Groundbreaking on the facility began on Sept. 28, 1967, the brainchild of a local developer named Lawrence H. LoPatin, then president of American Raceways. He turned to the best to design his course, none other than Charles Moneypenny, who designed the oval at Daytona International Speedway. The infield road course was designed by Formula One great Stirling Moss. In 1973, Roger Penske purchased the track, and has continued to improve it ever since.

There's been racing of one kind or another at the Milwaukee Mile since the 1870s, and the first stock car auto race was run there in 1903. Since the '50s, Milwaukee has hosted ASA and more recently, NASCAR Busch Grand National and Craftsman Truck events. Note that residential housing has sprung up all around the track. Courtesy Milwaukee Mile.

Its proximity to Detroit makes Michigan especially significant for the auto manufacturers, who like nothing better than to beat their rivals on their home turf. The two-mile banked tri-oval with its 18 degree banking in the turns is wide and high enough for racing that is three and sometimes four abreast. There's nothing more breathtaking than to see four stock cars heading into a banked turn four abreast at speeds approaching 200 mph. And Michigan is very popular with the fans, because it is possible to see the entire track from just about any grandstand seat.

With the track layout, speeds are approaching those of Daytona, without the carburetor restrictor plate rule. Michigan can be a tough track, as witnessed by Ernie Irvan. Irvan suffered a severe crash while testing at Michigan in 1994 while at the peak of his career. Many thought he'd never be able to walk again, much less race. However, Ernie proved everyone wrong by coming back to win in 1997 at the very same track that almost ended his career.

MIS currently offers Winston Cup, Busch Grand National and ARCA racing for stock cars.

MILWAUKEE MILE

7722 W Greenfield Ave.
West Allis, Wisconsin, 53214

Track Facts
Length: 1 mile
Banking: 2.5 degrees

Since the 1870s, there has been racing on what is now known as the Milwaukee Mile. Only horses ran back then, until the first auto race in 1903, which was won by a 30-horsepower Columbia auto that ran an average speed of 35.9 miles per hour. In 1998, the track celebrated its 95th anniversary of stock car racing, making it the oldest operating major speedway in the world. Interestingly, the old track was also the site of several Green Bay Packer professional football games in the 1930s.

Although the first AAA stock car race was sanctioned in 1948, it wasn't until the track was paved in 1954 that it really gained prominence and began hosting a variety of events, including ASA races. Most of Milwaukee's history since then is based on

"Irvan suffered a severe crash while testing at Michigan in 1994 while at the peak of his career. Many thought he'd never be able to walk again, much less race. However, Ernie proved everyone wrong by coming back to win in 1997 at the very same track that almost ended his career."

Nashville has more than just country music; it also has a first-class speedway. Although it is unable to expand enough to accommodate Winston Cup crowds, there's plenty of ARCA, ASA, Busch Grand National and Craftsman Truck racing going on. Courtesy Nashville Speedway.

USAC stock car racing and Indy Cars. In the 1960s and '70s, names such as A.J. Foyt, Parnelli Jones, Norm Nelson, Jack Bowsher, Roger McCluskey, Bobby Allison, Joe Ruttman, and Don White raced on regular visits to the track.

NASCAR first appeared at the track in 1984 with its Late Model Sportsman Series, now the Busch Grand National Series. After the 1985 NASCAR event, nearly a decade elapsed until NASCAR returned in 1993. The NASCAR Busch Grand National and Truck Series double-header weekend every Fourth of July is the best-attended of all the Mile's events.

Many of the today's NASCAR stars won major races at Milwaukee in USAC and American Speed Association (ASA) competition, including Mark Martin, Rusty Wallace, Dick Trickle, and the late Alan Kulwicki.

NASHVILLE SPEEDWAY

P.O. Box 40304
Nashville, Tennessee 37204

Track Facts
Length: 5/8 mile

Front straight: 750 feet
Back straight: 750 feet
Banking: Corners; 18 degrees, Straights; 5 degrees

The Nashville Speedway hosted their first race at the Tennessee State Fairgrounds in 1904. Races of various types continued to held there for the next 50 years. Then, in 1958, NASCAR arrived to take advantage of the brand new 1/2 mile oval. The first race was dubbed "National Sweepstakes," and featured legendary drivers like Lee Petty, Curtis Turner, Joe Weatherly (who went on to win) and Curtis Turner, to name a few. The track was lengthened in 1973 to its present 5/8th mile.

Over the years, Darrell Waltrip, Jeremy Mayfield and Sterling Marlin are just a few of the many top drivers who got their start there.

The Winston Cup stopped racing at the track in 1984, mainly because the track did not have the space to build additional seating to accommodate the growing number of fans. NASCAR didn't come back until promoter Bob Harmon purchased the track and made some improvements. In 1995, the Busch Grand National returned, followed by a Craftsman Truck race, and Nashville is humming once again with the sound of V8 racing.

There also have been national-level ARCA, ASA and All-Pro races with the All-American 400 being one of the prominent short track stock car races in the country. In the All-American 400, many of the top drivers from both the North and South meet to duel for bragging rights for stock car racing being a Northern or Southern sport. Any fan witnessing these races usually sees the best short track drivers from both sides of the Mason-Dixon line.

With the great music tradition of the city and the long history of racing at the track, one can guess what will happen in the future. Possibly, there could be a new

Nashville Speedway built in another location such as has been done at a number of locations across the country. But for now, this famous old stock car track still lives and that's the way a lot of fans want it to continue for many years to come.

NEW BREMAN SPEEDWAY

(Closed in 1979, located near New Breman, Ohio)

Track Facts

Length: 1/2 mile dirt oval
Banking: 10 degrees

Although this track was officially closed in 1979, it still sits untouched near the northwestern Ohio town of New Breman. After a long history of racing that spanned more than 50 years, the track sits alone, as if it is waiting for cars to reappear to race again.

The track was constructed in 1926 as a dirt oval, and hosted some of the best stock car racing in those days. In 1931, the grandstands were burned down by angry fans during a riot. In 1967, the track was paved, and it remained this way until 1978, when the pavement was removed, and the dirt surface was restored for the track's final season. The track length was known as a "big half" and the track records for the stock cars were in the 19 second range in the early 1970s.

Granted, this track was best known for its open wheel racing, mostly with sprint cars. But during the 1960s and 1970s, the track hosted USAC stock car events along with a number of local stock car events. Many of the best in the nation at the time, including Roger McCluskey, Al Unser, Jack Bowsher, Dick Trickle, A.J. Foyt and Don White, drove their two-ton stock cars at New Breman. Most of this racing was done when the track was paved.

Earl Bates, the owner of the famous Eldora Speedway, was the last owner of New Breman. However, although he put on events that were closely linked with Eldora,

he was unable to work the same magic at New Breman, and it never had the same prestige among racers and fans. He was forced to close the track in 1979.

PENNSBORO SPEEDWAY

Pennsboro, West Virginia
For Information: 8848 Ely Road
Apple Creek, Ohio 44606

Track Facts

Length: 1/2 mile dirt oval
Banking: Nearly flat

There is nothing quite like the famous Pennsboro Speedway in Pennsboro, West Virginia. It is more than 100 years old, and has a racing tradition that is matched by few tracks still running in this country. However, despite the fact the track is so old, car racing didn't really take place at Pennsboro until the 1950s, because it was primarily a horse track. Actual stock cars didn't make it there until a decade later. In those first days of car racing, Pennsboro was notoriously dangerous, with only a single wooden guardrail as a safety barrier. Consequently the track was marred by a number of serious accidents and deaths.

What makes Pennsboro totally unique is

At Pennsboro, bring goggles if you're a driver, and your own chair if you're a fan. Pennsboro is well over 100 years old, and began as horse track. Cars didn't run there until the 1950s, but have become very popular since. Above, the dust flies at the '95 Dirt Track World Championship. Tony Hammett photo.

Spectating at Pennsboro is rather informal, to say the least. It is in marked contrast to the megaplexs built by SMI, ISC and PMI. However, the racing is great, and the fans love the change of pace. There's nothing like a picnic at Pennsboro. John Farquhar photo.

Phoenix is also part of the ISC stable of tracks, and is one of the few tracks in the Southwest with professional stock car racing. Winston Cup cars debuted in 1988, and have sold out ever since. Courtesy Phoenix International Raceway.

that, in an age of mega-tracks with condos and luxury seats, Pennsboro is almost "retro." There are actually several bridges on the track, because a stream flows through the infield. And there are few real seats. The crowds sit on a large hill along the front stretch, sitting on blankets or lawn chairs, with coolers of food and drink as though they were at a picnic. Sometimes, fans shovel out their seats from the steep hillside!

But there's no doubt they've come for the super dirt racing. Since the 1980s, there have been a pair of national level stock car classic races, both sanctioned by the STARS Dirt Late Model organization. In fact, these are the only two races now held at the historic track each year.

First, there is the Hillbilly 100, which is run in early summer. But the racing gem at Pennsboro is the Dirt Track World Championship race held annually in October, which pays $50,000 for first place. Since the season is pretty well over at that time of year for other organizations, the race draws some top racers from all over the country. There is really nothing that approaches the uniqueness and charisma of the Pennsboro Speedway. Here's hoping that it's around for another hundred years.

PHOENIX INTERNATIONAL RACEWAY
P.O. Box 13088
Phoenix, Arizona 85002

Track Facts
Length: 1 mile oval
Banking: Turns 1 & 2, 11 degrees; turns 3 & 4, 9 degrees

Winston Cup Records as of 1998
Lap Record: Bobby Hamilton, 131.579 mph/27.360 sec., October 31, 1996
Race Average Speed: Dale Jarrett, 110.824 mph, November 2, 1997

Phoenix International Raceway is known as "The World's Fastest Mile," and is significant because it was purchased by ISC in 1998. The track is located outside Phoenix in beautiful desert surroundings, framed by the Estrella Mountains. It first opened in 1964 and since then has played host to all of racing's greats. Indycars, stock cars, sports cars—just every form of motorsport has run at Phoenix over the years, making it the most versatile racing facility in the Southwest. This is one reason why it is always sold out for the annual fall Winston Cup race.

Winston Cup cars made their first visit to the track in 1988 and have been on the schedule ever since. During the 1990s, the seating has been greatly increased along with many other improvements.

Besides the Winston Cup cars, there have been many other types of stock cars running at the facility including the NASCAR Craftsman Truck series, the Featherlite Southwest Tour, and various other Late Model stock car classes.

POCONO INTERNATIONAL RACEWAY
P.O. Box 500
Long Pond, Pennsylvania 18334

Track Facts
Length: 2.5 miles
Banking: varies

Winston Cup Records as of 1998
Lap Record: Jeff Gordon, 169.725 mph/ 53.027 sec., June 14, 1996
Race Average Speed: Rusty Wallace, 144.892 mph, July 21, 1996

Although over the years there were a number of different-size tracks in Long Pond, Pennsylvania, none is more famous than the tri-oval built in 1971.

The first NASCAR race was held here in 1974, and it has since been a two-race stop on the Winston Cup circuit. Pocono has long been recognized as one of the most challenging of all tracks on the Winston Cup tour.

The major reason for this is that the tri-oval varies in banking and turn radius, making it difficult to find the proper suspension setup that is suitable for all three turns. Each turn has a different degree of banking; turn one is the highest with a 14 degrees of bank-

ing, followed by turn two with eight and the final turn with only six degrees of banking. These turns are connected with three straights, each a different length. While the track size may indicate Daytona-like speeds, the tight turns and lower banking make it a chassis man's challenge or nightmare depending on how their car is running. It is also a true test of driver skill, and it is little wonder that it is known as "the superspeedway that drives like a road course." Many of the ARCA cars that race the day before the NASCAR events used to utilize a short track chassis to better negotiate the tighter, smaller turns.

The tri-corner configuration results in 200 mph slingshots on the long straights and photo-finish wins, which please the sold-out crowd, many of whom are seated along the long, elevated front straight grandstand which provides a view of the entire track.

The Mattoli family, who own the track, have constantly upgraded its facilities, including an all-new pit and garage area, and continues to be one of the most competitive stops on the NASCAR tour. Pocono is perhaps infamously noted for the career-ending crash sustained by Bobby Allison in 1988. His horrific crash helped bring about

Racing is close at the 1-mile Phoenix track. In this particular race, the Dura-Lube 500 in 1997, Dale Jarrett came from the back of the field to win. Tim Rempe photo.

"Pocono has long been recognized as one of the most challenging of all tracks on the Winston Cup tour."

Under the lights at Richmond, when most of the races are run. The track surface is smooth and wide, and the grandstands are nearly vertical with clear views of the whole track. It all adds up to a favorite track for drivers and fans alike. Joe Pestel photo.

improvements in driver safety that are in effect today. Bobby was eventually able to recover from most of his injuries, but the great NASCAR career he had was ended prematurely.

RICHMOND INTERNATIONAL RACEWAY
P.O. Box 9257
Richmond, Virginia 23227

Track Facts
Length: .750 Miles
Banking: 14 degrees

Winston Cup Records as of 1998
Lap Record: Jeff Gordon, 124.757 mph/21.642 seconds, March 3, 1995
Race Average Speed: Dale Jarrett, 108.707 mph, Sept. 6, 1997

Richmond goes back to the earliest days of stock car racing. The original track was 1/2 mile dirt and ran stock cars in the 1940s. In 1953, Lee Petty won the first NASCAR sanctioned stock car race.

In 1968, the track was paved, and in 1988, it was completely renovated and redesigned to its present 3/4 mile "D" shape, making it one of the most modern tracks on the circuit. The drivers love the track because of the wide and smooth surface, while the fans love it because the grandstands nearly encircle the track, providing unobstructed views of most of the track from any seat.

Most of Richmond's races are run at night under the lights. The track is located within the Virginia State Fairgrounds, and currently hosts NASCAR Winston Cup, Busch Grand National, Craftsman Truck, Featherlite Modified and Late Model Series races.

SOLDIER'S FIELD
Chicago, Illinois

Any avid professional football fan will tell you that Soldier's Field in Chicago is the home of the Chicago Bears NFL football team. But in the late '40s and early '50s, it was one of the largest stock car racing facilities in the country drawing crowds up to 50,000 for a single national race, which was very big in those days. In fact, until Daytona was built, Soldier's Field ranked only second to Indianapolis Motor Speedway in terms of seating capacity for race tracks.

After World War II, a quarter mile paved track was constructed inside the stadium where the football games are held, with the field itself actually inside the track. During the 1950s, weekly "Hardtop" stock car races were held in front of huge crowds with a record crowd of 68,000 for one 1953 race. The interest even attracted a NASCAR Grand National race in 1956. All this happened literally in downtown Chicago, next to Lake Michigan, introducing thousands of city folks to stock car racing.

Andy Granatelli, of STP and Indy 500 fame, promoted his Hurricane Hot Rods, which were roaring roadsters, to great success at Soldier's Field.

Before it closed in 1970, the track would go through two other configurations, one being a half-mile from 1956 to 1967, and the other a three-eighths mile oval during its last three years. Reportedly the track was shuttered because of protesters who complained about using public park funds to underwrite auto racing, and due to numerous complaints from neighbors about the noise.

Soldier's Field was part of the local "racing wars" of the late 1960s, competing for spectators and competitors with O'Hare Stadium, Raceway Park and Santa Fe Speedway. O'Hare, near the airport, and Raceway, on the South Side, were paved. Santa Fe was to the west and was the only dirt track in the area. All tried to outdo the others by offering more classes and promotional events, such as Figure Eight racing, midgets, and motorcycles. Sometimes a ticket costs only two dollars. Today, only Raceway Park and Santa Fe remain, but Soldier's Field proved that there were large numbers of stock car racing fans in the Midwest, well outside of the traditional southern areas.

TALLADEGA SUPERSPEEDWAY

P.O. Box 777
Talladega, Alabama 35161

Track Facts
Length: 2.66 miles
Banking: 33 degrees

Winston Cup Records as of 1998
Lap Record: Bill Elliott, 212.809 mph/44.998 seconds, April 30, 1987
Race Average Speed: Mark Martin, 188.354 mph, May 10, 1997

Talladega Superspeedway is often described a number of ways. But two most often heard are "biggest and fastest." Opened in 1970 by Bill France, the 2.66 mile, high-banked facility has seen both speed and competition records set over the years. It was designed to be a clone of Daytona, with just an extra tenth of a mile and a different flagstand location. But there's no mistaking it has an entirely different character. Speeds exceeding 200 miles per hour are accomplished on the 4,300-foot front straight, banked 18 degrees, and the

4,000-foot backstretch, banked only 2 degrees. Not much of this speed is scrubbed off in the steep, 33-degree banked turns, making Talladega the site of numerous closed course speed records.

Through the years, Bill Elliott has "owned" the place with eight victories to his credit. But maybe even more impressive is his track record of 212.809 miles per hour, set in 1987. This record was set prior to NASCAR's rule mandating carburetor restrictor plates, which makes you wonder how today's cars, which are much more technically superior to Elliott's '87 T-Bird, would do if allowed to run freely. It is highly possible that this record may never be broken.

The track also holds the distinction of hosting the first 200 mile per hour lap, accomplished by Buddy Baker on March 24, 1970, with an exact speed of 200.447 miles per hour in one of the awesome winged Dodge Daytona race cars.

Talladega is also the site of two other significant records, one set in 1974, as A.J. Foyt set a world's closed course Indy car record of 217.654 miles per hour. A year later, Mark Donohue established a world record closed course average lap speed of 221.120 miles per hour in a Porsche 917 Can-Am

A trio of Winston Cup stars run nose-to-tail at the World's Fastest Super-speedway—the one and only Talladega. Few have mastered this track like Bill Elliott, who has eight wins at this track, and the offical NASCAR Winston Cup lap record of 212.809 mph. Because of that speed and a few other "incidents," Winston Cup cars must now use carburetor restrictor plates when they race there. Randy Jones photo.

Texas Motor Speedway is Texas-size, with seating for 150,000 fans, most of them along this 2/3 section on the front straight. It is the second largest sports facility in the U.S. Courtesy Texas Motor Speedway.

Track Facts
Length: 1.5 Miles
Banking: 24 degrees

Winston Cup Records as of 1998
Lap Record: Jeff Gordon, 175.105 mph, April 5, 1997
Race Average Speed: Jeff Burton, 125.105 mph, April 6, 1997

In Texas, things tend to be oversize, and Texas Motor Speedway certainly lives up to that reputation. The track ranks as the second-largest sports facility in the country, and the third-largest in the world.

TMS is the first track built from scratch by Bruton Smith's SMI. Starting with a clean sheet of paper, a $110 million budget, and plenty of room, Smith designed the granddaddy of them all.

The 1.5 mile Texas Motor Speedway was completed in 1997 and immediately hosted a Winston Cup race, the first in Texas since 1981. The track seats 150,000 fans, with 120,000 in a 2/3 mile section that follows along the front straight. There are 194 skybox VIP suites that can seat 13,192 fans, and with 21 elevators to ferry them up and down. Huge television screens keep fans aware of the action on each side of the track.

The new facility was not without some problems. After the first race, drivers complained of water seepage in turn one, the result of some drainage problems. Bruton Smith promised changes before the next race in 1998, and delivered them to the tune of an estimated $2 million. The banking and track width were changed in turns one and four also, because of driver complaints that they were too tight. The seepage was eliminated with better draining and the entire track surface, although only one year old, was entirely repaved with a finer grain of asphalt before the next race.

You can bet that this facility will be a major player in national level stock car rac-

car.

In addition to the pair of annual Winston Cup races run each year, the track also hosts Busch Grand National and ARCA races. Like many other NASCAR tracks in the 1990s, continuous seating increases have been accomplished at the Alabama track with 5,200 tower seats added in 1996 alone. Talladega. It's a high-speed extravaganza that has to be experienced in person!

TEXAS MOTOR SPEEDWAY

P.O. Box 500
Fort Worth, Texas 76101

ing for decades to come. It has already hosted ARCA, Busch Grand National, IRL Indy cars and NASCAR Craftsman Truck races.

THE THREE HILLS SPEEDWAYS

Dayton Speedway
(Closed in the '80s)

Salem Speedway
2811 Waterson Trail
Louisville, Kentucky 40299

Winchester Speedway
State Route 32
Winchester, Indiana 48295

Fred Funk was credited with building the three race tracks that would become known as "The Three Hills" in the 1930's. Named after the cities they resided within—Dayton, Salem and Winchester—the Speedways were, and still are, primarily known for their extremely steep banking. Constructed long before the days of Daytona and other high banked superspeedways, the banked turns of the "Hills" are an incredible 33 degrees high, but the tracks are only a half mile in total track length. The high banking still causes plenty of breath holding for racers and fans alike and yields plenty of hard racing action. With the unique perspective of looking down at the cars from the infield, it often seems more like a slot car or video game rather than real race cars with real drivers. The same holds true for the many years of open wheel racing held at these tracks. Today, only Salem and Winchester still exist, but Dayton is fondly remembered by many fans.

Dayton Speedway—The track was built in 1934 as a D-shaped five-eighths mile flat dirt track. Three years later, the famous banks started to be constructed with dirt from the infield. Reportedly, there were a number of trolley cars buried there as land fill to aid in the build-up process. Both stock cars and open wheel machines ran during

the pre-war years.

Closed during World War II, the track reopened in 1945 as an asphalt oval. During the 1950s, the famous Dayton 500 stock car event was run, and became one of the most famous races in the country at the time. A young NASCAR organization also sanctioned a number of races at the track during this time period.

There were also a number of ARCA (then called MARC) races during the 1950s. During this time period, the likes of Jack Bowsher, Buck Baker, Fonty Flock, Lee Petty and others ran the famous Dayton banks. In the 1960s, famous Eldora Speedway promoter Earl Baltes managed the track and held a number of stock car races at the facility. During the final days of the track, Dayton promoter Don Thompson tried to bring the grand old track back to its old glory, but it was just too late. Thompson even brought back the old Dayton 500 race for a final bow before the track closed for good in the 1980s. Today, the track site is completely covered with a landfill, hardly a fitting end for such a popular and historic

This is what has become of Dayton Speedway, one of the famous Three Hills Speedways, after a long history of fabulous short track racing of all kinds, including the once famous Dayton 500. David Tucker photo.

157

The Late Model Stock Cars run the pace lap at Salem Speedway, a track that was resurrected from near extinction in the 1980s. Today, it hosts both ARCA and ASA series races to packed grandstands.

A very young Jeff Gordon (45) and Mike Cope battle for position at the 1992 ASA All-Pro race at Winchester Speedway. Randy Jones photo.

race track.

Salem Speedway—Salem Speedway's towering high banks resulted in speeds that far exceeded the other tracks most stock car drivers were used to driving. It also resulted in many spectacular accidents, with a number of drivers paying the ultimate price.

The original track was a regular stop on the national ARCA tour during the 1960s and '70s. During the early 1960s, Jack Bowsher "owned" the track with four straight victories from 1963 and 1964. Benny Parsons at the time an ARCA driver, followed Bowsher as the ARCA Salem top gun with seven straight fast times in the late 1960s. The last ARCA race of that era was

in 1979 but ARCA would be pivotal in the rebirth of Salem some years later.

During the 1980s, Salem seemed headed for the same fate as Dayton. The famous high-banked paved track had begun to fall apart from neglect and lack of funds. Many felt that it was just a matter of time before it would be leveled. But local businessman Don Gettelfinger just couldn't stand to see it happen and with help from the community, was able to refurbish the track and breathe new life into it. The track reopened in 1987 with an ARCA Supercar race, and has been there ever since.

The American Speed Association is currently a regular visitor to Salem, hosting its famous Midwest 300 race. The first ASA race there was run in 1972 and featured a young, local driver named Darrell Waltrip who had been a terror on the track.

Winchester Speedway—One of the most historic tracks in the country, the Winchester Speedway has been in continuous operation since 1914. Through the years, many different types of racing machines have competed on this famed oval. Winchester Speedway is best known for its towering paved high banks, which produce amazing speeds. Drivers heading into turn one cannot see turn two until they are well on their way into it. The same goes for turns three and four.

The track was long the site of the famous ASA-promoted Dri-Power 400, later renamed the Winchester 400, which produced huge crowds for such a local short track. The track would later become affiliated with NASCAR when the NASCAR All-Pro series would run at the famous track. The ARCA stock car series also currently runs an annual race at the old track.

In 1984, the super-fast track was the location for a speed record attempt by driver/car builder Randy Sweet. The stock car he ran looked like a Buck Rogers creation, with huge Plexiglas sideboards and spoilers providing a great deal of downforce, resulting in a blistering 14.74 second lap, a time more

Tri-State Speedway opened in 1957, and currently hosts Sprint car and Dirt Late Model racing. Courtesy Tri-State Speedway.

"The stock car he ran looked like a Buck Rogers creation, with huge Plexiglas sideboards and spoilers providing a great deal of downforce, resulting in a blistering 14.74 second lap, a time more likely at quarter-mile short track."

likely seen at a quarter-mile track.

In recent years, the track has also organized one of the largest, local stock car events in the country: the Stock Car Festival. This race brings up to six classes of stock cars together every fall for one huge event.

Although the original trio of the historic "Hills" may not be intact, the two survivors still offer race fans and brave drivers a unique racing experience, with a little history lesson thrown in for free.

TRI-STATE SPEEDWAY

Route 2, Box 15
Haubstadt, Indiana 47639

Track Facts
Length: 1/4 mile dirt oval
Banking: 15 degrees

Records as of 1998
Lap Record: 12.8 seconds, Dirt Late Models

This southern Indiana dirt track opened in 1957, after a long parade of race cars thundered into the track from downtown Evansville, nearly 15 miles away. That first race was won by Curly Famsley in a '32 Ford.

Since then, Tri-State has become one of the nation's best dirt stock car tracks. The track has always been a quarter-mile from the time it was built and but its size still allows for exciting side-by-side racing.

During the mid-1970s, the entry-level stock car classes were very popular with lots of Chevelles and Camaros. Ed Helfrich had been the longtime promoter, but passed it over to his stock car driving son Tom in 1987, who has managed the classy track ever since. A number of top Dirt Late Model organizations have run at the track including Hav-A-Tampa, Northern All-Stars, and UMP. UMP runs one of its prestigious Summer Nationals races at the facility. More recent drivers that have stopped at Tri-State have included Dirt Late Model stars Donnie Moran, Freddy Smith, Johnny Virdan, Rick Aukland, and Bob Pierce.

Many past famous dirt drivers have run at the track through the years, including former NASCAR driver Charlie Glotzbach, Busch Grand National driver Rodney Combs, ARCA driver Larry Moore, and Winston

The "Bud at the Glen," has become a NASCAR tradition since it first ran in 1986. It is one of only two road course races on the Winston Cup tour, but also, it is the Winston Cup race closest to New York City, which is important for fans and sponsors alike. Drivers get a chance to test their road racing skills, which means much more braking and downshifting than they are used to.

Cup drivers Kenny Schrader and Jeff Purvis.

WATKINS GLEN
P.O. Box 500-T
Watkins Glen, New York 14891

Track Facts
Length: 2.45 miles
11 turns, including 7 right hand

Winston Cup Records as of 1998
Lap Record: Dale Earnhardt, 120.733 mph/73.054 seconds, August 9, 1996
Race Average Speed: Mark Martin, 103.030 mph, August 13, 1995

Watkins Glen, an ISC track, is located in upstate New York and is one of only two road courses on the Winston Cup trail. The Glen, as it is known, started as a street circuit that wove in and around the small town of Watkins Glen, hosting its first race in 1948.

Over the years, it has become a permanent circuit located just outside of town with an international reputation as the site of the Formula One U.S. Grand Prix from 1961 to 1980. However, NASCAR held its first race at the Glen in 1957, and because it is a road circuit and located in the Northeast, it has always had special significance for the teams and drivers. Currently, the "Bud at the Glen" has been run since 1986 on the Winston Cup tour. The Glen is very important to the Winston Cup and Busch schedules as it is the track closest to New York City and the tri-state area of New York, Massachusetts and Connecticut. This area has the second largest population in the U.S. and as such, is quite a market for race fans. The Glen is the only track where race fans in the area can get their NASCAR Winston Cup and Busch Grand National racing entertainment.

How's this for an impressive line-up of Dirt Late Model stock cars? West Plains Speedway is one of the nation's top dirt ovals, and was voted "Best All-Around Facility" for three straight years by readers of *Behind the Wheel* magazine. Its most famous race is the "Show Me 100." West Plains Speedway photo.

WEST PLAINS MOTOR SPEEDWAY

P.O. Box 463
Ash Flat, Arkansas 72513-0463

Track Facts
Length: 3/8th mile dirt oval
Banking: 30 degrees

Records as of 1998
Lap Record: 13.6 seconds, Wendell Wallace, 1997.

West Plains Motor Speedway is located six miles south of West Plains, Missouri, nestled in the gentle rolling hills of the Ozarks. Built in 1988 by Bill and Marvin Ball, the track passed into the hands of Bob and Billie Gibson in 1992, and they immediately expanded and renovated the track.

The track is a 3/8th mile clay surface and has a moderate bank. Seating capacity around the track is an impressive 17,000. For the convenience of the fans, a digital display scoreboard records lap times during the special events it runs as well as lead cars and laps. Also in the pit area is a digital display of car weights, clearly visible to the fans in the stands, to make sure the drivers keep their cars legal.

The track has recently hosted a number of prestigious events, including the Hav-A-Tampa series, the World of Outlaw sprint car series, UMP Summer Nationals, the Midwest Late Model Racing Association, Southern United Professional Racing Association, and its weekly IMCA Modified and UDTRA Late Model events.

But the crown jewel is the "Show-Me 100" which was started in 1993. This Dirt Late Model event has hosted the best of the best in its short history. Drivers from California to Pennsylvania have traveled to this mid-American dirt track to compete for one of the most lucrative purses in Dirt Late Model racing. In 1998, the winner took home $32,000, with the last place driver taking home $3,200.

With its huge attention to the needs of the fans and making racing financially worthwhile for the race teams, the track was voted the "Best All-Around Facility" for three straight years by readers of *Behind the Wheel* magazine.

West Virginia Motor Speedway, a five-eighths mile dirt oval, opened in 1984. It has been one of the regular stops for national dirt stock car sanctioning bodies like STARS, UDTRA, and the All Stars. Courtesy West Virginia Motor Speedway.

WEST VIRGINIA MOTOR SPEEDWAY

417 Grand Park Drive, Suite 201
Parkersburg, West Virginia 29101

Track Facts
Length: 5/8th mile, dirt oval
Banking: 22 degrees

The West Virginia Motor Speedway, built in 1984, is one of the newer dirt tracks in the country, but it has quickly become recognized as one of the leading dirt facilities in the nation. Located next to Interstate 77 on an 80-acre site in the rolling hills near Mineral Wells, West Virginia, this $3.5 million facility has been hosting top Dirt Late Model events from its inception.

The five-eighths mile dirt superspeedway features 65-foot-wide straightaways with 85-foot-wide turns banked at 22 degrees. As far as most local dirt tracks go, West Virginia is pretty high tech, with over $200,000 in quality lighting and an electronic scoreboard, as well as seating for 12,000 fans. Taking their cue from Bruton Smith, the track owners have added luxurious VIP suites, along with a special VIP/Media area. Drivers and crew members have their own facilities complete with restrooms and showers, which is not something you see a many local dirt tracks.

An All Star Circuit of Champions "Wedge" Dirt Late Model race was the first race held at the speedway in June 1985. It was won by Charlie Swartz, a dirt track racing legend.

Throughout the rest of the '80s, the top-rated NDRA series also staged events at the track.

The Midwest-based STARS series races regularly at the track, as does the Hav-A-Tampa series. However, the top event hosted by the track each year is the "King of The Mountain" race.

In 1997, the speedway also hosted the national ARCA stock car series race for the first time. It was one of three WVMS stock car events that received national TV coverage, a real accomplishment since most stock car racing that is broadcast occurs on pavement tracks. Perhaps the greatest recognition the track could have received is when it became part of the Winston Racing Series.

Without doubt, the future and potential of the West Virginia Motor Speedway looks very bright indeed and it will continue to be one of dirt stock car racing's shining stars.

ISC, SMI and PMI: The Big Track Owners

Like any other industry, stock car racing has its "big boys." And that not only includes drivers, crew chiefs and car owners but track owners as well. With racing today drawing such high numbers of people and TV audiences not only in North America but literally across the world, having a NASCAR Winston Cup, Busch race or ARCA race IS big business. There's money to be made with not only the obvious tickets, hot dogs and beer, but with selling the TV rights. Every Winston Cup race is on live, national television and radio contracts are negotiated by each track not the sanctioning body. The selling of souvenirs, track tours and other, non-race day track services are other income sources. Stock car driving schools, track rental for practice and testing as well as filming commercials, VIP suites for entertaining, and even having year-round condos are many of the ways tracks make money on the days when the cars and fans aren't jamming the grounds.

Even with the fantastic growth the sport has seen, there needs to be a cap. NASCAR has room on the schedule for only so many races. Sure, years ago there were as high as 60–70 races a season but many of those were one-day short track events booked two or three to a weekend—something that would be virtually impossible nowadays. So when the NASCAR Winston Cup schedule was cut down to about 30 races a year in the early 1970's, that started putting a premium on literally every race date. Now, with a handful of new tracks such as California, Texas, Las Vegas and Homestead on the schedule, things are getting even tighter. And there's always talk of some new track being planned or already under construction.

One of the best examples of just how the sport is changing is the closing of a mainstay of Winston Cup short track racing, North Wilkesboro Speedway in North Carolina. The 5/8 mile track was the

Bruton Smith

scene of many a tough battle in NASCAR. But the track was family owned and could not compete with the bigger tracks in purse money because there were only so many seats around the track to pay for that purse. So when faced with the opportunity to buy part of the track, Bruton Smith, the man who owns Charlotte Motor Speedway, did so and effectively moved one of the two North Wilkesboro "race dates" to his newly built Texas track. The North Wilkesboro family sold the other half of their track to Bob Bahre, the man who had already brought racing to New Hampshire with his new track. He used North Wilkesboro's other race date to give his Loudon track a second race date per season. Thus, a new track and an existing one got the dates from North Wilkesboro. Both Texas and New Hampshire are bigger facilities and the money spent purchasing the smaller track was well invested in the bigger, more profitable tracks that will hold more people and ultimately make more money.

Does that mean that the short tracks are dead and dying? No, because Bruton Smith and his Charlotte, North Carolina-based corporation, Speedway Motorsports Incorporated (SMI), also bought the high banked, one-half mile track in Bristol, Tennessee. But instead of trading the track's two active Winston Cup dates and in effect shutting the track down like North Wilkesboro, the SMI folks went to work adding more seats and other improvements to generate more income, thus revealing a trend in big time stock car racing—moving race dates and building/buying tracks.

The original multi-track owner was International Speedway Corporation (ISC). The Daytona Beach, Florida, parent operation owned by the Bill France family started it all in 1970 when they built a clone to their highly successful

Daytona track in Talladega, Alabama. But no one thought that much of it as they were the same company that was NASCAR and as such, they could do those things. They could also juggle the schedule to give race dates to the new tracks. Not too long after that, in 1982, ISC bought an ailing Darlington Speedway, the original superspeedway built in the 1950s. Later, when there was a void in the New York market that needed to be filled, a joint operation between Corning Glass and ISC got Watkins Glen, New York, on the Winston Cup circuit. Later, ISC would take over sole ownership of the track, again adding to their stable of tracks. Today, along with Daytona, Talladega, Darlington and Watkins Glen, ISC also owns Phoenix International Raceway and is in joint ownership of the California and Homestead facilities. As of 1999, those tracks account for almost one third or nine Winston cup dates out of the schedule's 32-plus official races.

Bruton Smith and his SMI group now own Atlanta, Bristol, Charlotte, Las Vegas, Sears Point (California) and Texas Motor Speedways. Those tracks can also account for nine Winston Cup races going into the 1999 season, or almost one third of the schedule.

On a slightly smaller scale is Roger Penske and his Penske Motorsports, Inc. (PMI). While Roger's true love may be the Indy

Roger Penske and his PMI are one of the moving forces behind the expansion of stock car racing facilities. Courtesy California Speedway.

style cars of the Championship Auto Racing Teams sanctioning body (CART) he helped found, he is well aware of the value of NASCAR racing. He is not only part owner of the #2 Miller Lite Beer Winston Cup team driven by Rusty Wallace but a player in the Winston Cup track wars as well. He started when he bought his Michigan Speedway, built the Nazareth, Pennsylvania, track where a Busch Grand National race takes place, and broke the ground for the California Speedway. Penske now co-owns the West Coast track with ISC. Penske also purchased a major interest in Rockingham Speedway in North Carolina, winning a contentious bidding war against Bruton Smith.

As the calendar turns to the new millennium, the other tracks on schedule are pretty much individually owned. But a close look shows there are stock holdings of many of the tracks with majority and minority stock holders. That means, as with any publicly held business, things could change at any time. The questions, however, remain. Will the big boys buy up more tracks? Will the short tracks ever be phased out of Winston Cup racing completely? Will there be any more new tracks built in new markets? Those questions are as much a part of racing as the most often asked one: Who will win the next race?

STOCK CAR RACING'S PLAYERS 6

There's little argument that the drivers are the stars of stock car racing. Today, many are as famous and adored as Hollywood's movie stars, especially by fans in the Southeast. Many have their own fan clubs and websites. Certainly, stock car drivers are on a par with their peers in basketball, football and baseball, but it wasn't always so.

There has always been a certain mystique, an aura about racing drivers, that is appealing. This might come from the fact that they do something that most of us lack the nerve to do; that they possess a sense of utter fearlessness and abandon that we can't help but admire, even if it seems a little crazy to be slinging a car 200 mph around a track. These guys lay it all on the line, look danger in the eye without even a split second's hesitation, all to cross that finish line first.

Drivers must be mentally motivated to strive to win at all costs, week after week. They get all the credit for victory, even though stock car racing is decidedly a tremendous team effort, but they also shoulder all the blame when they lose or crash.

Ask any successful driver the key to his success, and more than likely, they will answer "my crew," or "my team." A good driver knows that it takes more than skill to win a race; it takes strategy, timing, and the flawless performance of a dozen or so pit crew members to get there. When looking at stock car racing overall, it is only right that all the top players be included, including those who may never have driven in a race, nor even turned a wrench. But these are the people behind the scenes that in many ways have influenced stock car racing as much as any driver.

There are crew chiefs and mechanical wizards. There are drivers who turned out to be better car owners or racing officials. Some are part of famous racing dynasties, such as the Allisons and Pettys. Also part of this behind-the-scenes group are prominent track owners and promoters who do not have any hands-on connection to the cars. Some are household names, while others are only found in books such as this one. Regardless, all of the people in the following pages, and many others, have made a significant contribution to the sport of stock car racing.

Although only 27 at the time this was written, Jeff Gordon had already become "a player," having won three championships through 1998. Although Gordon represents a new generation of stock car driver, he is following a long legacy of drivers, crew chiefs and car owners that have made this sport what it is today. Courtesy Chevrolet.

THE ALLISONS AND THE ALABAMA GANG

Rick Rickard photo.

Bobby Allison

Robert Arthur Allison is the patriarch of the Allisons, one of stock car racing's family dynasties. Known to his many fans as simply "Bobby," he began racing in Florida under an assumed name so his parents wouldn't find out. At that time, racing was not considered to be a "respectable" thing to do. But once his father found out, he told his son that if he was going to do this for a living, he should at least use his real name.

Bobby and his brother, Donnie, moved to the Hueytown, Alabama, to establish a racing business. Once there, two other stock car legends joined forces with them, and the group became known as the "Alabama Gang."

First to join the Allisons was the ageless Red Farmer— ageless because Red never liked to tell anyone his real age. However, one thing that is known and highly documented is Red's amazing record of over 1000 stock car wins, which took place on all types of stock cars and tracks, from 1/4 mile dirt "bull rings," to superspeedways like Talladega.

About the time Bobby and Donnie had completed the transition from local/regional racers to regular NASCAR competitors, Neil Bonnett, another racer from Hueytown, joined the Alabama Gang.

Bobby Allison's Winston Cup career spanned more than 25 years, from 1961 to 1988. He drove cars for the factories, for other private owners, and for himself. He was well known and widely respected for getting the most out of a car without beating it into the ground, and

for never giving up during a race, no matter how far back he might be. The name Allison is frequently entered in the record books. He is tied for third on the overall win list with 84, and fifth for pole wins with 57. He shares a record for most consecutive wins with four (twice in the same year), most consecutive poles (five in 1972), and most short track poles (seven, also in 1972).

The fans loved him, and let him know it. He was voted Most Popular Driver six times in the years of 1971–73 and 1981–83, and his most favorite accomplishment was when he won his third Daytona 500 in 1988 with his son, Davey, a close second. When the two of them took the checker and pulled up alongside to salute each other, there wasn't a dry eye in the house. It was clearly one of the finest moments in motorsports history.

In 1988, Bobby's career was suddenly cut short by a serious accident at Pocono. Although he eventually recovered from those injuries to drive in an occasional race, his days as a Winston Cup driver had come to an end. Unfortunately, this was the first in a series of bad luck events for the Alabama Gang.

Clifford Allison

Cliff, the youngest member of the Alabama Gang and Davey's younger brother, was another Allison with the right genes. Following in his brother's footsteps, he competed in ARCA and regional Late Model racing with

Davey Allison had more than one mentor growning up. Here, he gets advice from Red Farmer (left), a close family friend and racer with over 1000 wins to his credit. Well-liked by fans and fellow competitors, Davey died in 1993 from a helicopter accident, and it was a tragic blow to the stock car racing community.

Although family and friends urged him to retire after two severe head injuries, Bonnett wanted to return for one more season, a tragic decision. He died while practicing for the Daytona 500.

Yates was crew chief and engine builder, and together, the two made a formidable duo, especially a few years later when Yates purchased the team outright. At the season-opening Daytona 500 in 1987, their first year, Davey put his unsponsored, rookie ride on the outside of the front row at 209 mph (of course, this was before restrictor plates). It was a record for a rookie and a signal of the many good things to come. That same rookie year he won two races; another first. Davey proved this was no fluke by winning two more races the following year, despite watching his father suffer life-threatening injuries. He won the Daytona 500 in 1992 and went on to win one race in 1993 before he was killed in a helicopter he was piloting. With Terry Labonte subbing in the last event, Davey posthumously won the 1993 International Race of Champions title. Even though he was the son of Bobby Allison, he definitely proved himself on and off the track, and to his many fans, he will always be remembered as simply "Davey."

Neil Bonnett

Although his name wasn't Allison, Neil Bonnett was quickly welcomed as a solid member of the Alabama Gang because of his Alabama roots and friendship with the Allisons and Red Farmer. Neil won 18 Winston Cup races throughout his career, which is good enough to tie for 31st on the all-time win list. He drove at different periods for a variety of teams, such as the Wood Brothers, Rahmoc Racing, Richard Childress and others. However, he sustained two consecutive major head injuries late in his career, and was forced to give up driving until he recovered. He kept busy by working as a TV commentator, where his distinctive, friendly voice, extensive knowledge and comfortable manner became popular with fans. During this time, he also worked as a test driver for Chevrolet and Richard Childress, keeping his hand in racing until he could someday drive again. Although he was counseled by friends and fellow competitors to retire, Neil wanted to give it one last shot. While practicing for the 1994 Daytona 500, he sustained fatal injuries when his car crashed.

Although the story of the Alabama Gang has a tragic ending, there's no denying the lasting and profound influence this family has had on the sport of stock car racing.

great success. The next logical step was NASCAR and that's where he went, starting out in Busch Grand National. His talents quickly earned him a regular ride on the BGN circuit and things looked good for the "other Allison," until tragedy struck again. While practicing for a BGN race at Michigan Speedway in 1992, Clifford's car crashed heavily inflicting fatal injuries.

Davey Allison

Davey Allison was the older of the two sons of Bobby and Judy Allison. Together they followed their famous father and learned the racing trade. Davey started his racing career at age 12, sweeping the floors in the family race shop and sorting nuts and bolts for 50 cents an hour. With racing stars in his eyes, his schooling suffered, so Bobby and Judy made Davey a deal: get a high school diploma first, then you can go racing. With this incentive, Davey not only improved his grades, but worked harder to graduate early. Soon after, he was competing in Late Model, then ARCA and NASCAR Busch Grand National, where he quickly proved he was an Allison. It wasn't long before he was running the occasional race or two for a variety of Winston Cup cars, including a stint subbing for Neil Bonnett in Junior Johnson's car, but he didn't have a regular ride. However, he did well enough to catch the attention of Harry Ranier, who signed him to drive the number #28 Ford Thunderbird in 1987. Robert

RICHARD CHILDRESS

No race car driver likes to turn over the keys to his car to another driver, but Richard Childress probably doesn't regret doing it all that much. R.C., as he is often called, already had a great career as a top ten Winston Cup driver when he decided to give a chance to a young driver from Kannapolis, North Carolina, named Dale Earnhardt. As it turned out, it was one of the best decisions R.C. ever made.

While growing up in the Winston-Salem area of North Carolina, R.C. watched the races at the local track, the famed Bowman-Gray Stadium. "The race track was my playground," he says. "I couldn't afford the admission, so I would climb the fence to get in. When other kids had heroes like John Wayne, mine were Cotton Owens and Curtis Turner. After getting caught a couple of times jumping the fence, they finally gave me a job selling programs and peanuts. I was in heaven. Here I was getting paid to go to the race track. It was then that racing got into my blood and has been ever since."

R.C. bought his first race car at age 17 when he plunked down $20.00 for a 1947 Plymouth. He eventually moved up to the NASCAR Grand American series and got into what was then named the Grand National (now called Winston Cup) division as a favor from Big Bill France. At the time, R.C. was racing his Grand American class the day before the Grand Nationals at the brand-new Talladega speedway. France called R.C. at his motel after the Saturday race. "He said that the drivers were boycotting the race the next day and he really needed me to race on Sunday. I told him the only car I had was the Grand American car we raced on that day. He said he didn't care what car I drove as long as I was in the field. Mr. France said he would consider it a personal favor. So, I hung up the phone and told the guys we were going to race. The next morning we pulled back into the speedway, unloaded the car and got ready to race. Richard Brickhouse won, but I had a big time. I had just finished my first Grand National race on the fastest track in America."

He drove his own car from 1969 to 1981, racing in over 280 events. Halfway into the 1981 season, he handed the car over to Dale Earnhardt, who had won the Winston Cup title the previous year. From there came an association that holds the second most championship titles in Winston Cup racing. While Dale is tied with the King, Richard Petty, with seven crowns, six of those great titles came with Richard Childress. Along the way the pair has also visited Victory Lane 64 times, including the 1998 Daytona 500.

There's also the truck team and the second Winston Cup team, driven by Mike Skinner, who gave R.C. the initial, 1995 NASCAR Craftsman Truck Championship. That team has won two races in Japan and earned Rookie of the Year honors in 1997.

Richard Childress Racing started life as a five-man operation with one pick-up truck, an open trailer and working out of a backyard. Today, over 130 employees work out of a 30,000 square-foot state-of-the-art facility that sits on 40 acres not far from R.C.'s old Central Automotive garage, where it all began.

CURTIS CRIDER

Throughout the 1950s, '60s, and '70s, Curtis "Crawfish" Crider was without doubt one of the best short track stock car drivers in the country. He picked up his nickname in a race at Danville Speedway, when he inadvertently left the track and splashed into a creek that was real muddy. As he powered through the creek and back onto the track, Crider noticed he'd picked up a few passengers—some crawfish—and so the name stuck.

Crider competed mostly in the Southeast, and during a career that spanned 25 years, he compiled and amazing record of more than 600 feature race wins.

Crider drove whatever and whenever he could, competing in a variety of stock cars and sanctioning bodies. He participated in the final 1958 Daytona Beach NASCAR race, finishing 13th out of 71 starters, along with running the first NASCAR race at the then-brand new Daytona International Speedway. In 1961, in a Mercury, he set a new track record at Darlington Speedway in a car he had constructed himself.

Crider was also the Florida State Dirt Track Champion

schedule. His best year was 1964 when he finished sixth in the points and had 29 top-ten finishes. His best season ever was in 1973 with 52 Late Model wins, including 21 straight in one stretch. In 1974, he was the track champion at Volusia County Speedway in Florida.

When his racing career was over, Crider, authored a book called *The Road to Daytona*. Published in 1987, the book chronicled his racing exploits, which are legendary.

After he retired, he also became known for his magnificent restorations and replicas of the historic 1930s and 1940s race cars that he drove. Since he built the originals of those cars, who better to build accurate reproductions?

With his huge success on the short tracks of the South, it's really hard to understand why Crider didn't catch the attention of some major sponsor to provide him with a ride to the top.

Crider now spends his time restoring cars he once drove or raced against.

for three straight years starting in 1970. For three straight years (1962 through 1964) he ran the complete NASCAR

DALE EARNHARDT

When you talk about the greatest drivers to ever turn the wheel of a stock car, Dale Earnhardt is sure to be near the top of the list. Few drivers have ever dominated stock car racing like he has, and in fact, few professional athletes have ever reigned supreme for so long. Only Richard Petty, "The King," has as many Winston Cup World Championships (they each have seven), and on the all-time win list, Earnhardt is currently sixth, with 71 wins and counting.

Like Richard Petty before him, Dale Earnhardt also had racing in his blood. His father, Ralph, raced in the NASCAR Sportsman series that would end up being the Busch Grand National Series of today. He was the NASCAR Sportsman champion in 1956 and went on to compete in 51 NASCAR Grand National events from 1956 to 1964. During his brief racing career, the senior Earnhardt didn't like to leave his home area so his racing was limited to events close by. When he did race, he was a regular top ten driver. And although he never won a GN race, he finished second a few times, proving he was in the middle of it all.

A rare smile from Earnhardt as he holds the Southern 500 trophy in 1987. Mike Slade photo.

Earnhardt has 7 Winston Cup championships, tied with Richard Petty.

Dale began racing seriously in 1975, and by 1979, he had graduated to Winston Cup, and promptly won his first race and Rookie of the Year. In 1980, he would win his first Winston Cup championship, the first driver ever to win the Winston Cup title in only his second year of trying. Earnhardt would go on to win the title six more times, in '86, '87, '90, '91, '93 and '94.

Earnhardt has always been popular with the fans, but not always so with fellow drivers. He has duly been nicknamed "the Intimidator," and "Ironhead," which amounts to an accurate description of his hard-charging driving style by his fellow competitors. Go to any Winston Cup race, and you're bound to see thousands of fans wearing "Intimidator" hats, jackets, shirts, stickers—you name it. Few drivers have been as popular or as productive in stock car history.

Since 1984, Earnhardt has driven for one man and one team—Richard Childress—in car #3. All but nine of his more than 71 wins have been with Childress, who is a former Winston Cup driver. Together, the two have dominated the circuit throughout the '80s and early '90s.

In addition to his regular race wins, Earnhardt has won the Winston Select all-star race three times, the Busch clash six times, and the Daytona 125-mile qualifying race a record 10 times in a row. He also won the IROC championship in 1990 and 1995.

By the beginning of the 1998 season, Earnhardt had won on virtually every track on the tour, and had won just about every race at least once, except for the biggest—the Daytona 500. Earnhardt competed in the race 19 straight times, and finished a record four times as runner up. There were several occasions where he was leading with but one lap to go, only to have a cut tire, crash or some other last minute mechanical failure snatch what seemed like certain victory. Finally, after 20 years, he won his first Daytona 500 in 1998, which, by his own admission, is his most satisfying win. In 1999, he tried to defend his title, but finished second to winner Jeff Gordon in one of the closest finishes in Daytona history. That makes five second place finishes for Earnhardt.

Racing with Earnhardt is now very much a family affair. What is simply called Dale Earnhardt Incorporated (DEI) is now a multi-team business headquartered in a magnificent building of over 300,000 square feet of work space. The building itself set new standards for all race shops by using architectural details normally not seen in a shop environment, such as granite and marble floors, and indirect lighting.

With wife Teresa as owner of the Busch Grand National car Dale Jr. drove to the title in 1998, the DEI team also operates the NASCAR Craftsman Truck team driven by Ron Hornaday, and two other Winston Cup teams. The first Cup team was the number one car of Steve Parks and Pennzoil. In 1999, a second Cup team was created for Dale Jr. to make his way into the top class of NASCAR with his father. To give "Little E," as Dale Jr. is known, some seat time in Cup action but not endanger his official Rookie of the Year run the next year (2000), the new #8 Budweiser team ran only five races. The number 8 used on his car has great significance: it was the number Grandpa Ralph Earnhardt used on his car.

Dale's other children, Kelly and Kerry, are well on their way to also becoming top drivers and maybe joining their father in Winston Cup racing. Like the Petty name, Earnhardt is one name also rich with stock car tradition.

MIKE EDDY

When compiling a list of top short track stock car racers, Mike Eddy is sure to be near the top. Nicknamed "the Polar Bear," because of his strong, muscular physique, Eddy has spent most of his career driving paved Late Models in the American Speed Association, winning the title an amazing six times. There were two titles in the '70s, two in the '80s, and a final pair in the 1990s. These titles, by the way, occurred against top drivers like Rusty Wallace, Mark Martin, Alan Kulwicki and Ted Musgrave, to name a few. Even when he didn't win the title, he was almost always in the hunt, finishing in the top five of the points standings 11 times, including a pair of runner-up finishes.

Eddy's career has spanned over three decades, and as of this writing, he is still going strong. To date, he has over 50 feature wins in the infamous #88 cars he has driven through the years, and has led an astounding 16,000 laps in ASA competition.

Never much of one to deal with the media in his early career, Mike changed his style in the 1990s and became an excellent spokesman for ASA and stock car racing in the national medium. "I never went to speech class in

school because I never thought I would need it," he admitted. "Little did I know how important speaking skills would be in stock car racing."

BILL ELLIOTT

The fact that Bill "Awesome Bill from Dawsonville" Elliott has only won a single NASCAR championship belies the fact that he is one of the top competitors in NASCAR history. He is also one of the most popular, having been voted "Most Popular Driver" by the fans 13 times in his career, far more than any other driver.

Many of his career victories (as of this writing, there have been 40) came when he drove for the Harry Melling team from 1982 until 1991. He then drove three seasons for legendary owner Junior Johnson before forming what would ultimately become his own team in 1995.

So far, Elliott's highest achievement has been winning the "Winston Million" in 1985, a feat accomplished by winning three of four selected superspeedway races. When Bill won at Darlington for the big prize, fans added "Million Dollar Bill" to "Awesome Bill." This was the first year the Winston Million had been established, but no one would win it until Jeff Gordon did in 1997, which

happened to be the last year for the bonus program.

Another outstanding achievement, is the record he set at Talladega in 1987 for the fastest lap. His one-lap speed of 212.809 mph will undoubtedly stand for many years to come, mainly because NASCAR returned to restrictor plates to prevent those kinds of speeds from occurring.

Like many other Southern stock car drivers, Bill started on the short tracks of Georgia, part of a racing family that included his brothers Dan and Ernie. Ernie has since developed a reputation as one of the top engine builders in NASCAR.

Arriving in NASCAR Winston Cup racing as a virtual unknown, the family team also used Ford equipment, which was the minority brand in the early 1980s. The reason was very clear; their father, George Elliott, had a Ford dealership and used his love of racing to promote it. In fact, it was the Elliott team that had wrung out the small-block Ford in their Georgia Late Model short track days. In those days they were consistent top runners and one of the very few Fords running short tracks in the country,

much less one geographic area. When they applied what they knew with the Ford engines to what they were now learning in Winston Cup racing, they fared very well for themselves. Their strong running Fords caught not only the attention of the Ford racing folks in Detroit, but Harry Melling who bought into the team just as they were working their way to the front of the pack. Elliott's NASCAR career really took off in 1983 when he finished third in the point standings, followed by a second in '84. In '85, he won an amazing 11 races, yet still only managed a second place in the standings. This was followed by a third place in 1986, a fourth in '87 and finally, the championship in 1988.

To this day, the Elliott team is still using Ford equipment for their own team as well as the second team they started in 1998 with NFL football star Dan Marino.

RAY EVERNHAM

Behind every great driver is a great crew, and the crew chief is often the man who dictates the play—strategy, pit stops, tire changes—and when it comes to talking about the best, Ray Evernham comes to mind. As the crew chief for Jeff Gordon, he's been quickly credited as a major factor in the team's success. Through the 1998 season, Gordon, Evernham and their band of "Rainbow Warriors" have captured three Winston Cup championships and one runner-up finish, and are likely to add to that total.

Ray was a full-time Modified driver from 1979 to 1983. Many feel that his experience as a driver, and his understanding of a car from the driver's point-of-view, has played heavily in his success. In 1989, Ray started a Winston Cup team for Australian driver Dick Johnson before joining Jeff Gordon in 1991 on a Busch Grand National team. Then, the start of the legendary performance with Jeff Gordon began in 1992 as they both joined Hendrick Motorsports to establish the Number 24 DuPont team. A year later, the prowess of the dynamic duo was quickly realized as Jeff Gordon won the Rookie of the Year award.

The management and race-savvy skills of Evernham came to light in 1994 when his Rainbow Warriors pit crew won the Unocal World Pit Crew Championship. He also raised eyebrows calling for only two tires late in the

Charlotte 600, giving Jeff track position and his first Winston Cup win. Recognized by competitors for excellence at making the right call, Ray seems to have a sixth sense when directing his team.

The first Winston Cup title came in 1995 as part of a trio of honors, which also included Ray being honored as "The Western Auto Crew Chief of the Year" and winning the UAW-GM "Teamwork of Excellence" Award. Those in the racing business recognize class and talent of this talented man. He has set the standards for the crew chief of the next Millennium, and they are standards that will be nearly impossible to even approach.

TIM FLOCK AND THE FLOCK RACING FAMILY

One of the most famous racing families in NASCAR history is also one of the first. The Flock Family—Bob, Fonty, Ethel and Tim—were all part of what would be one of the most successful racing families to ever race stock cars.

Bob was a top driver in the Southeast before World War II and before NASCAR, driving Jalopies and Roadsters on a variety of fairgrounds and dirt tracks. He would also be one of NASCAR's first stars. Fonty was the champion of the National Championship Stock Car Circuit in 1947, the sanctioning body that became NASCAR the following year. Then, there was sister Ethel Mobley, who, with other early female drivers Sara Christian and Louise Smith, was an extremely competitive NASCAR performer during the late 1940s and early 1950s.

But the Flock who was most successful was the youngest, Tim, who recorded more than 40 NASCAR victories in his illustrious career. His early success came in the potent Hudson Hornet when he took the 1952 NASCAR Grand National title. After a short retirement, brought on by the disappointment of being disqualified after a victory at the Daytona beach course, Tim hooked up with the famous Karl Kiekhaefer and his awesome Chrysler 300 team. The association really came together in 1955 with an amazing string of 18 straight victories

The Flocks were one of the first families of stock car racing. Shown is one of Tim's restored cars. Tim was the most successful of the family, with two Championships and 40 wins. Bob Fairman photo.

and Tim's second Grand National title. Two of those victories occurred just a single day and thousands of miles apart—a Saturday night race at Syracuse, New York followed the next day in San Mateo, California. After competing and winning the New York race, Tim caught a red-eye flight to California and won again.

A serious ulcer abruptly ended his career in 1958, while he was still in his prime. However, he continued to be involved with NASCAR right until his death in 1998. At the time, Darrell Waltrip wanted to race with Tim's number 300 on his car to help raise funds for the ailing Flock. However, NASCAR enforced their two-digit rule and Waltrip had to renumber his car to race.

THE FRANCE FAMILY

Although you can't say that there would never have been stock car racing without the France family, it certainly would not be in the state it is today. William France and his son, Bill Jr., have been described as "true visionaries," who are almost single-handedly responsible for the enormous popularity and growth of stock car racing.

The story begins just after William and Anne France headed south from Washington, D.C., for a warmer climate and opened up a garage in a coastal town called Daytona Beach, Florida. Part of the reason was because France was a stock car driver, and the move would put him closer to the track on the sand at Daytona. Little did anyone know at the time just how historical this move would become.

Although France was a driver at that time, it wasn't long

before he turned his talents to owning a car, then promoting and creating NASCAR. The first step was to take over the Daytona Beach race, but France had visions much greater than that.

That vision consisted of vast superspeedway race tracks filled with thousands of fans who had come to see close competition. France recognized early on that this would be the key to success. No one wanted to come spend an afternoon watching just one or two cars completely dominate a race, as was sometimes the case in other forms of racing such as open wheel. So France established a strict set of rules designed to keep competition close. If one type of car seemed to gain an advantage, he changed the rules to keep the cars even. He also realized that fans loved their cars, and kept them close enough to the factory originals so they could easily identify with their favorite marque.

France also mastered the art of corporate sponsorship.

Over 30 years ago, he approached R.J. Reynolds and offered them an alternative marketing outlet, and the Winston Cup was born. It illustrates one of the most successful relationships between corporate America and sports in the world.

Over 50 years later, France's sons, Bill Jr. and Jim, oversee the vast empire that their father had started. It now includes a separate company, the International Speedway Corporation, that owns, operates and builds race tracks (Daytona and Talladega are the crown jewels). And NASCAR has grown to include many different levels. Once confined to the Southeast, NASCAR races all over the country. In addition to Winston Cup, there's the Winston West Series, the Busch Grand National and Busch North, the Craftsman Truck Series, the Goody's Dash Series, the Winston Racing series, the Featherlite Southwest and Modified series and tour, the RF/MAX NASCAR ARTGO Challenge Series, the Raybestos Brakes Northwest Series, the Slim Jim All Pro Series and Busch All Star Series.

When Big Bill France handed the entire operation to his son, Bill Jr., in 1972, racing could have stayed pretty much where it was. But like the vision his father had for creating NASCAR racing, Bill Jr.'s own vision was ready to take it to the next level. In 1972, only one year after the entrance of Winston as the first, and to this day, only series sponsor, the next level of growth of NASCAR was already in motion. NASCAR racing, at the time, was nothing like it is now. There was no national TV and radio for their events, no "waiting list" of sponsors to put their corporate names on cars or race track events, and teams were still almost exclusively run by the independent owner, and often the driver. There was no "farm system" for up and coming drivers to learn the NASCAR way nor was there anywhere near the newspaper and magazine coverage that would follow shortly.

The NASCAR of today can be directly traced to Bill Jr. He had the vision to "grow" racing from a regional sport to one that reaches fans virtually all over the world. He also gets the credit for raising and maintaining the level of competition to be the best in the world.

Now, the third generation of the France family is learning the trade and is already in place. They are in the middle of taking NASCAR and stock car racing in general, because as NASCAR moves on, the rest of stock car racing usually follows.

TONY GEORGE

Including Tony George in this section might seem a bit odd for he is the grandson of Tony Hulman, the famous owner who single-handedly rescued the Indianapolis Motor Speedway and some say, Indycar racing. But Tony George has long recognized the value, and popularity of stock car racing, and through his efforts, he established a new race, the Brickyard 400, that became the largest, and one of the most celebrated races on the circuit in just a few years. It is sure to be a tradition, on par with the Daytona 500 and others, in the years to come.

George sensed that fans in the Midwest were hungry for a stock car race, and he was right. When the first race was run in 1995, 350,000 fans showed up, setting a new attendance record for a Winston Cup race. Rumors persist about the possible addition of a second Winston Cup race at the Brickyard, which may happen in the future.

JEFF GORDON

Some of the greatest athletes in history were born with a natural gift. Michael Jordan was born to shoot hoops; Mark McGwire was born to crack a bat; and Jeff Gordon was born to drive stock cars. There are few drivers in

stock car racing history—indeed, in all of motorsports—who have had such rapid, amazing success in such a short time, and have dominated their sport so thoroughly. From 1995 through 1998, he has won the championship three times and finished second in a fashion reminiscent of greats like Richard Petty and Dale Earnhardt.

His background, unlike many legends before him, did not begin with stock cars, but rather open wheel dirt trackers. Gordon is quick to credit his stepfather, John Bickford, with getting him started at age four in quarter midgets as one key to his success. By 13, he was racing sprint cars, and went on to drive all kinds in the USAC Silver Crown series. It was at a Buck Baker's driving school where he discovered that his true love was stock car racing. With the potential he showed at the school and on the track, it wasn't long before someone offered him a ride.

Gordon began his stock car racing career in 1991, driving Busch Grand National cars. That first year, he captured Rookie of the Year honors. In 1992, he had three

Busch wins and 11 poles in Bill Davis's Ford, which caught the eye of Rick Hendrick and Chevrolet.

Before the season ended, Rick Hendrick had already secured a sponsor for what would be Gordon's rookie year and arranged for Gordon's first Winston Cup race to take place that same year, at the last race of the season at Atlanta Motor Speedway.

In his first full season, Gordon gave some indication of the future by surprising everyone with a fourth place finish in points and Rookie of the Year honors. In 1994, he won his first Winston Cup race in only his second season, and finished eighth in the points with seven top-ten finishes. But in 1995, he shocked the racing world by taking the Winston Cup championship with seven wins and eight pole positions, and he was only 24 years old! And, he looked likely to repeat in 1996 with 10 wins, but a number of DNFs had him finishing second to teammate Terry Labonte.

In 1997, Jeff took his second Winston Cup title. Even though he had ten wins, it would go down to the last race at Atlanta before he won by a mere 14 points.

In 1998, Jeff and his crew chief, Ray Evernham, and their band of "Rainbow Warriors" literally dominated the season, winning 13 races, including a streak of four in a row. These wins included his second Brickyard 400 and the Winston No Bull Million. He began 1999 by winning the Daytona 500 by scant milliseconds over Earnhardt.

Many feel that Gordon, at the age of 27, is the greatest of all time, or certainly will be. Curiously, Gordon's first-ever Winston Cup race was the very last for the King, Richard Petty, a changing of the guard if there ever was one. Will Jeff Gordon go down as great as King Richard? Many think so, but only time will tell.

Gordon with crew chief Ray Evernham.

RICK HENDRICK

A keen management mind and a uncanny sense for picking the right people for the right jobs has made Rick Hendrick a success in both the board room and on pit road. The founder of Hendrick Management Corporation, which ranks as one of the largest auto retailers in the United States, he also formed Hendrick Motorsports, fielding Winston Cup teams since 1984. Recognized for his knowledge of the racing sport, Rick was the technical consultant for the Tom Cruise racing movie, "Days of Thunder," and supplied all the cars. His expertise managing his racing operation, both in and out of the race cars, has brought unprecedented success, capped with four straight Winston Cup Championships (1995 through 1998). Three of those titles were won by Jeff Gordon with Terry Labonte taking the fourth. Also, the Hendrick team won the 1997 Craftsman Truck series championship with driver Jack Sprague after finishing second the previous year and in 1998.

But ask anybody in the know with Winston Cup racing their impressions of Rick Hendrick and most likely you will hear about Rick's promotion of multi-car teams. And although it's now the key to success in Winston Cup, Rick Hendrick did it consistently long before it was stylish or the thing to do. He first fielded a three-car team in 1987 with drivers Geoff Bodine, Darrell Waltrip and Benny Parsons. Tim Richmond also drove eight races that same year. Ken Schrader joined the team in 1988 and remained through 1996. Ricky Rudd was a member of the team from 1990 through 1993 before striking out on his own like Darrell Waltrip.

From 1993 through the 1998 season, Hendrick Motorsports has consisted of three full-time teams. In addition to the three teams, Hendrick Motorsports also started building their own chassis and supplying engines for other teams. It wasn't long before other teams realized the advantages of having multiple teams in the same operation communicating with each other and trading technology. Rick proved it was the way to win races.

THE JARRETT RACING FAMILY: NED, DALE, GLENN AND JASON

Ned

Ned Jarrett is recognized as one of NASCAR's finest drivers ever, with 50 NASCAR Winston Cup wins to his credit, which is currently good enough for eighth on the all-time win list. This feat is more amazing when you consider he only raced for 13 seasons. His most impressive years were 1964 with 14 wins and the following year with 13. Those were the two years that Ned also won his pair of NASCAR Champion titles.

But fans today know Ned as the father of Dale, and as one of the more popular TV commentators in motorsports. He not only calls all races for ESPN and other networks, but he also hosts his own TV show. His likable, folksy demeanor and impressive stock car knowledge have earned the respect of the racing community and fans alike.

Dale Jarrett with dad Ned discuss their racing exploits.

Dale

Dale began racing in the Limited Sportsman Division at Hickory Motor Speedway where Ned was the promoter. When Dale made the logical move to BGN racing, he recorded 11 Busch Grand National wins, and never finished lower than sixth in the BGN point standings for six seasons.

By 1984, Dale had graduated to Winston Cup and during the mid to late 1990s, developed his skills to become one of stock car racing's shining stars.

Dale has driven for a number of famous owners including Cale Yarborough, Joe Gibbs, the Wood Brothers, and Robert Yates starting in 1995. That ride was initially temporary, to fill in for Ernie Irvan while he recovered from serious injuries. But the ride became permanent in 1996, and Jarrett finished third in points. In 1997, he contended strongly for the title, leading the points chase for a while, but he, along with everyone else, finally succumbed to Jeff Gordon and settled for second in the championship.

The Jarrett family is close knit, and this was illustrated to race fans and a national TV audience when Dale won his first Daytona 500 in 1993. Ned was calling the race down to the final moments while the CBS camera played on Dale and Dale's mother. Dad "talked" his son around the track for the last lap while Mom watched nervously from the motorhome in the infield. After he crossed the finish line, Ned lost his professional detachment and reacted as a proud papa in an emotional moment that had millions of viewers cheering. It was a truly an emotionally uplifting moment in motorsports history.

Glenn

Dale's brother Glenn was also a NASCAR driver, running a number of years in Busch Grand National. However, he is following in the footsteps of his Dad's "other career" and works as a pit reporter for national TV race coverage.

The Jarrett racing tradition is sure to carry on for another generation, as Dale's son Jason has now started his career, running the short tracks of the Southeast.

JUNIOR JOHNSON

Junior Johnson has either seen or done it all in stock car racing. Starting out as a driver, then turning his many talents to owner, the man who admits to running moonshine in the old days reflects just how this sport has changed. Now inactive after selling the last of his multi-car teams in 1995, Junior can look back on a long and full career while enjoying racing as a spectator. He began driving in 1953, and has raced on the beaches and superspeedways of NASCAR. He has accumulated 50 wins, putting him in a tie for eighth on the all-time win list with Ned Jarrett. His 47 poles put him in the same position for all-time pole awards, even though he retired as a driver in 1966. During those years at the wheel, he drove for an important list of car owners, such as Henry Ford, Carl Kiekhaefer, Smokey Yunick, the Wood Brothers, Buck Baker, Ray Nichols, Cotton Owens, Ray Fox and the official Ford factory-sponsored cars campaigned by Holman & Moody.

Junior then turned his racing attentions to becoming an owner, and the list of drivers he has mentored over the years is no less impressive. Stars and champions such as Fred Lorenzen, Cale Yarborough, Bobby Allison, Darrell Waltrip, Bill Elliott, Geoff and Brett Bodine, Terry Labonte, Sterling Marlin, Davey Allison and Hut

Stricklin have all benefited from his experience. When Junior hung up his racing hat and went back home to the mountains of North Carolina, he did so with six Winston Cup championships as a car owner. He can still be seen as some of the races nowadays, but mostly as a spectator. However, there's no denying the impact he's had on the sport.

TERRY and BOBBY LABONTE

Terry

Two-time Winston Cup Champion Terry Labonte started at age 7 when he drove his first open wheel quarter midget, and continued to do so until he reached the age

limit of 16. As a native Texan, his heroes at the time were Lone Star drivers A. J. Foyt and Johnny Rutherford, both of whom were driving Indy Cars, a direction that he too originally wanted to go. But things didn't quite work out that way, and with help from his father, Terry was able to start his stock car career in one of America's classics, a home-built '57 Chevy.

He developed his skills on local stock car tracks, winning frequently. In 1979, he hooked up with NASCAR team owner Billy Hagan, who would take Terry to Winston Cup racing and continue as his owner and later an associate, all throughout the next decade. In their first full year of Winston Cup, Terry ran the entire 31 races and finished an amazing tenth in the season points. Terry halved that in '83 by finishing fifth, and then went all the way in 1984 by winning the title driving Hagan's Piedmont Airlines #44 Chevy. He also earned the nickname "The Iceman," for his cool concentration in the face of intense pressure and stiff competition.

During the 1990s, Terry continued to run up front, and his chances for another title seemed a near certainty when he joined the successful Hendrick Racing Team in 1994 with teammates Jeff Gordon and Ken Schrader. It was a true "dream team," and it did indeed lead to his second

title in 1996, but it wasn't easy by any means. He faced intense pressure all year long from superstar teammate Gordon, who won 10 times. But "The Iceman" wasn't about to be denied, and won with a steady pace of top ten finishes.

Terry collected another nickname, the "Iron Man," by compiling the longest streak of consecutive races in NASCAR history—602 races through 1998. In 1996, he passed the record held by Richard Petty. To celebrate the event, Terry's sponsor at the time, Kellogg's Corn Flakes, came out with a special, silver paint job for both the tying and breaking of the old record. Today, that silver Chevy Monte Carlo proudly sits in the Hendrick's Motorsports museum in Concord, North Carolina.

Bobby

In more recent years, there's been another Labonte on the NASCAR tracks, with younger Bobby coming on strong in the big time after a sparkling career in Busch Grand National. Many feel that Bobby, who has won a few races and consistently run up front driving for former NFL coach Joe Gibbs, is just a few years away from being a title winner himself.

One memorable Labonte moment occurred in 1996 at the last race in Atlanta. Terry's championship wasn't decided until that last race, which was won by Bobby. The two took a victory lap side by side afterward to tens of thousands of screaming, cheering fans. It was definitely a career highlight for both of them.

Courtesy Chevrolet

FRED LORENZEN

During his brief career, Fred Lorenzen was called "The Golden Boy," mainly because of his movie-star good looks and because he was one of the top competitors on the circuit, winning 26 races from 1961 to 1967. Many figured that he would continue well into the 1970s, but he suddenly decided to quit after the 1967 season. A brief comeback ended as quickly as it began in 1972, and Lorenzen settled into a successful real estate career. To those that have interviewed him, he will admit that he has some regrets, believing he quit much too soon.

The fair-haired driver is best remembered for driving the Lafayette Fords for Holman and Moody. The number 28 Ford Fairlane he drove in 1963 was equipped with a 427 engine, which powered Fred to wins at Atlanta, and in the World 600 in Charlotte, and the Volunteer 500 in Bristol, and third in the points championship.

In 1964, Lorenzen won a total of eight races, but the season was marred by the death of his teammate and close friend, Glen "Fireball" Roberts. Fred also was involved in a serious accident at Daytona and suffered a life-threatening injury to a main artery, and although he won four times the following year in 1965, he didn't achieve the same success from then on until his retirement in '67.

Lorenzen was also noted for being one of the first "Yankees" to run with the good 'ol boys down South. His popularity, particularly around his hometown Chicago tracks, helped give stock car racing some Northern exposure. It was one more step up the ladder to expanding stock car racing on a national level.

MARK MARTIN

Mark Martin has been one of the most popular, most consistent drivers in Winston Cup history. He also one of the most competitive. Martin first came to Winston Cup in 1981 as an independent, fielding his own team. Although he had plenty of drive and talent, it was hard to keep the team going financially and Martin had to withdraw after just three seasons.

So Martin returned to the American Speed Association, where he had already won three championships. He won yet another ASA title before hooking up with owner Jack Roush full-time in 1988 for another try at NASCAR. It was Roush's first year in Winston Cup, having achieved great success in drag racing and road racing.

If ever there was a driver befitting the cliché "always a bridesmaid but never the bride," it would have to be Martin. He has been runner-up in the point standings in '90, '94 and '98, and third in "89 and '93. He's had 29 Winston Cup career wins as of this writing, but one of his more notable achievements is winning three straight

International Race of Champions (IROC) titles—he has four overall—racing against the best from all over the world in every type of motorsport.

Martin is undoubtedly one of the hardest-working drivers on the circuit. In addition to a hectic Winston Cup schedule, he frequently drives in the Busch Grand National series when time allows, and wins there quite a bit—he set the record for all-time superspeedway wins in 1997 for that series. He originally set up and owned the team, but after a few successful seasons, Martin turned it over to the Roush operation, which has become an empire that includes over five teams.

Martin is also credited with developing an acute awareness of the connection between physical conditioning and driving a race car. He was one of the first to physically train and has developed a specific program that is available in books and videos. Many drivers today, even those in other forms of motorsports, have been inspired by his conditioning program. Martin firmly believes that being

in such top condition has spared him from serious injury during some of the accidents he's had over the years.

Mark Martin in his ASA days, where he won four championships. David Tucker photo.

BUTCH MILLER

Butch Miller has long been recognized as one of the best short track drivers in the country, and one of the top ASA competitors. He's won the ASA championship three times, and has so far captured 40 feature race wins.

His ASA career actually had two stages, the first peaking in '87 and '88 when he won the championship both years. Then, after running with other late model stock car organizations, he returned to run 12 ASA races in 1993, and a full season in '94, when he won the title for a third time. According to Miller, the third time was the most special, because competition had increased significantly since he'd left.

It was the 1987 title, though, that was the closest, coming down to the final race against Winston Cup regular Dick Trickle. That same year, he also won four Great American Challenge races and was named to the 1987 Auto Racing All-American Team. A well deserved honor indeed. There were six wins in 1987 followed by nine in 1988. He was also in the hunt in 1989 with a second place points finish.

A measure of the success that Butch has enjoyed in his relatively short ASA career is the fact that he rates third in total winnings behind longtime runners Bob Senneker and Mike Eddy, with earnings close to $1 million dollars!

He then moved into NASCAR Busch Grand National racing for a short time before ending up in the NASCAR Craftsman Truck series where, not surprisingly, he has been a top contender.

Earl Isaacs photo.

BUD MOORE

Bud Moore is one of the most significant innovators stock car racing has ever seen. His tuning ability has produced a long line of successful cars in several forms of racing. He fielded his first stock car in 1962, and driver Joe Weatherly brought home his only NASCAR championship. To date, the NASCAR tally for Bud Moore Engineering stands at 63 wins, 43 poles and that one '62 title.

In addition to NASCAR, Moore has also campaigned Trans Am stock cars where his 0range #15 Mustangs were always a threat to win. With Parnelli Jones at the wheel, there was a championship for Moore in 1970 preceded by a second place finish in 1969.

Other drivers running Moore-prepped cars include Darrell Deringer, Dan Gurney, Bobby and Donnie Allison, Curtis Turner, Cale Yarborough, Tiny Lund, Gordon Johncock, Bobby Isaac, Darrell Waltrip, Buddy Baker, Ricky Rudd, and a fellow named Dale Earnhardt, who, Bud warned Ford, might switch to driving a Chevy if they didn't watch out. Chevy had seen the talent the young driver had and began courting Earnhardt by sending him a brand new Corvette. The idea was for Dale to switch to a Chevy team, which he obviously did with historical results.

Moore is better known for being one of the first engine builders to extract maximum horsepower from small-block Ford engines after big blocks were banned. Moore has always campaigned Fords, even when they were clearly not as competitive. These days, Bud Moore Motorsports is still in the racing business. Despite a few setbacks that set the Spartanburg, South Carolina, team back temporarily, they are currently engaged in the hunt for the Winston Cup title.

LARRY MOORE

When you first meet Larry Moore, you would swear that this is the most laid-back guy in the world. But put him into a dirt stock car, and you will see a great change in that pleasant personality.

Moore's stellar career has been mostly on dirt, and mainly in open wheel sprint cars. Larry ran those machines until 1979, when he switched to dirt Late Models. In that first dirt stock car season, he won an amazing 18 times, including the World 100 at Eldora, his hometown track. In the years to follow, Larry would win two more of dirt stock car racing's most prestigious events.

Larry has also competed with great success in NDRA events, and he even added the National Dirt Track Championship race at Pennsboro Speedway to his hundreds of victories.

Although Larry has raced on pavement in ASA and ARCA, he's most comfortable on dirt, and operates several highly successful dirt track driving schools in Florida and West Virginia. There, he's able to share his experience and skills with a whole new generation of drivers, one of whom might be the next Winston Cup star. Who knows?

Tony Hammett photo.

DONNIE MORAN

Donnie Moran is another dirt track star who's in the top three of anyone's "Best Of" list when it comes to short track dirt racing. In the Dirt Late Model world, he's revered as much as Dale Earnhardt or Jeff Gordon by many fans.

Like many successful racers, Donnie got involved with this style of stock car because it was in the family. His father is the longtime owner of Muskingum County Speedway in Zanesville, Ohio, so Donnie grew up in the sport. His racing team through the 1990s was a family affair. His crew consisted of his sister Rhonda and her husband. Together, the three have captured quite a few wins, the biggest being at Eldora Speedway. Moran has won the prestigious World 100 three times, along with the $100,000-to-win Dream race. He also has won championships with the STARS and All Star Dirt Late Model organizations. He also competed in the Hav-A-Tampa series.

Staton photo.

In 1999, Donnie made a surprise move to Busch Grand National racing. He still plans to run a number of big dirt races, but his concentration will be on NASCAR.

The Moran family track, Muskingum, is now the home of Donnie's stock car driving school. Learning from this driver is definitely learning from one of the best in Dirt racing.

BILLY MOYER

Dirt Late Model superstar Billy Moyer started on two wheels, winning 160 motorcycle races when he was still a teenager. In 1977, he added two more wheels and began racing dirt Late Models with just as much success.

Over the years, he has driven cars for a number of different manufacturers. He started with Larry Shaw-built cars, then moved to Rayburn Cars, before finally settling with Masterbilt where he's had huge success.

His resume is seemingly endless with many "Driver of the Year" honors and several "Dream Team" awards. There have been series titles with the NCRA, USAC, and the World of Outlaws. He has also six titles in the UMP Summer and Winter National events.

Then, there are his accomplishments at three of the biggest dirt stock car races. He's won the biggest event, the World 100, three times with a couple of near misses as well. He's also won the Dirt Track World Championship twice, and the prestigious Show-Me 100 three times.

Over the course of this amazing career, there have been over 500 wins in 26 states at 130 different tracks. He's thought about other types of racing, but thinks that he will finish his stock car career that way he started it—on the dirt!

He'd like to be remembered as a clean driver in competition, and one of the best to ever drive these cars. There are few, if any, who will disagree with that.

Tony Hammett photo.

GARY NELSON

Growing up near Riverside International Raceway in Southern California, Gary Nelson was immediately attracted to stock car racing, although the road course was more known for its sports car racing. "I would watch guys like Dan Gurney and Parnelli Jones. Then, there was Lee and Richard Petty and Fireball Roberts. I watched every type of racing they had at Riverside, but the stock cars were always my favorite."

Nelson even raced a little on his own with some friends at the famous Ascot Park before moving to North Carolina to work with the old DiGard team. Initially, he swept floors and cleaned parts, but eventually worked his way up to crew chief, and served in that capacity for 258 Winston Cup races.

The teams that he's commanded as crew chief have won 21 races, 16 with Bobby Allison as driver. In 1982, the DiGard team was the Winston Cup runner-up in points, and took it one step further in 1983 to win the title. Nelson's teams have won a total of more than $5 million. Another highlight was winning the 1986 Daytona 500 with Geoff Bodine at the wheel. Nelson developed a reputation over those years as the consummate crew chief, an innovator and risk taker who would try anything to get an advantage.

But after the 1991 season, however, Nelson did an about face and "went to the other side." He accepted a position as an assistant to Winston Cup Series Competition Director, Dick Beatty. When Beatty announced 1991 would be his final season, the logical replacement was Nelson. With Nelson in tow at all the races, Beatty taught the "new guy" everything he needed to know before retiring at the end of the year.

Nelson has proven to be the perfect man for the job, given his past experience as crew chief and his technical expertise. He knows all the tricks and then some, and since he has taken over, no one has been able to get anything past Nelson and his tech inspectors. Nelson has literally been there and done that, and he's always one step ahead of the other competitors. As NASCAR Winston Cup Series Director, Nelson oversees the entire series and, with Director of Competition Mike Helton, pretty much makes sure the series remains safe, competitive and as cost effective as possible. That sounds like three simple goals but each area has its own sub-topics to keep abreast of. Safety issues can sometimes affect competition and vice versa. Then there's the areas of related issues such as fans, tracks, vendors and everything else found at a track these days. With his insight learned as a racer, he is the well-qualified to steer NASCAR into the next century.

BENNY PARSONS

Many people know Benny Parsons as a TV commentator who has brightened many a race broadcast with his depth of racing knowledge and experience. That is the Benny of today. However, Parsons is also a former champion in both ARCA and Winston Cup, and to this date, is the only driver to have accomplished this feat. Starting out as a Detroit cab driver, Benny dabbled in local racing before moving on to ARCA racing in the mid-60's. His efforts there attracted attention when he won the 1965 Rookie title and went on to win the ARCA driver's championship in 1968 and 1969 with 16 wins and 18 poles overall.

With such success, the next logical step was NASCAR, where he quickly made a name for himself and won the Winston Cup title in 1973 with a battered but still-running Chevrolet in the last race of the season. By the time Benny traded his steering wheel for a microphone, he had won 21 Winston Cup races, 20 pole positions, and was easily qualified as a racing "expert" analyst.

Courtesy ARCA.

DAVID PEARSON

David Pearson was known around the circuit and by fans as "The Silver Fox." The first part of that name came from his premature gray hair that showed when he removed his helmet. The second part of the name came from being very smart about his driving. David was the kind of driver that seemed to pop up at the front for the win, catching many racers and fans by surprise. Many honors and great words have been bestowed on Pearson and his accomplishments in NASCAR, and he deserves them all. His 105 career victories are second only to Richard Petty.

Throughout his 26-year-career, Pearson drove for a number of very prominent teams. Some of the more memorable include the 1966 season for Cotton Owens when he won 14 races, and in 1968, when he drove for Holman and Moody and captured 16 wins. He would win the first two of three NASCAR career titles in those seasons.

Pearson was one of the top drivers during the "aero wars," in the late '60s when the manufacturers were building and racing streamlined cars like the Talladegas and Dodge Daytonas. Pearson was a rocket in the Holman and Moody Ford Talladega, and won his third NASCAR title in 1969. Although it would prove to be his final title, it certainly wasn't the end of his career. In 1972,

Mike Slade photo.

Pearson signed on to drive for the famed Wood Brothers team and up through the 1977 season, they would win an amazing 43 races. Pearson was exceptionally skilled on the superspeedways and in fact, all but one of those victories was on one. This accomplishment is even more noteworthy when you remember that the Wood Brothers often didn't run the entire season. Pearson also holds a few percentage records such as: best winning percentage for a season with 61.1%, single season percentage on superspeedways at 62.5%, and career superspeedway wins at 16.8%.

Pearson will always be remembered by longtime fans for his drive in the 1976 Daytona 500. He and Richard Petty, two of the greatest to ever drive a stock car, were battling the entire race. On the very last lap, coming out of turn four to the checkered flag, the two came together and spun off onto the infield grass. As the many fans watched in awe, Pearson was able to nudge his battered Wood Brothers car across the finish line ahead of The King by using only the starter button.

He was one of NASCAR's best ever, both on and off the track, where he was a fan favorite because of his quiet, shy personality. Pearson was also legendary for smoking cigarettes during a race. He would often light up during long yellow laps, and some swear they caught him smoking during green laps too. Of course, those days are long gone, and in his retirement, he oversees his son Larry's career, who has won two Busch Grand National titles to date. The Pearson racing tradition continues.

THE PETTY CLAN: LEE, RICHARD, KYLE AND ADAM

Lee

The Petty name is so entrenched into the fibers of stock car racing, that even those with no interest in racing have heard of "The King," Richard Petty. But the Petty legacy begins further back, with Richard's father Lee.

Lee Petty was truly one of the founding competitors of stock car racing. He ran races in the very first season, 1948, and until 1964. During that time, he competed officially in 429 NASCAR races, and won 55 of them, putting him seventh on the all-time winner's list. He still holds the record for the most NASCAR dirt track wins with 43. He also won the NASCAR Championship three times: 1954, 1958 and 1959. Like many other top drivers at the time, Lee was also his own crew chief. The fans appreciated his work and voted him the most popular driver in 1953 and 1954.

Lee will permanently be in the record books for winning the very first Daytona 500 in 1959. In 1960, he became the subject of controversy when he protested the winner of the Daytona 500, his son Richard. A check of the scoring sheets revealed that Richard was actually a lap down at the finish, so the win was pulled from him and awarded to the second place finisher, which happened to be Lee Petty!

Richard

Richard had already been driving for two years by that time. As a teenager, he and his brother Maurice were drafted into service to work as Dad's pit crew. This gave both an incredible experience and insight into stock cars and what made them run fast. When Richard was given the go-ahead to try his hand at driving in 1958, he had an already established team to support him. In just two years, he won his first race, not to mention the near-miss at Daytona mentioned above, and he never looked back.

No one in motorsports history has yet to equal the astounding success Richard Petty would enjoy during the next 25 years, and there are many who believe that no one

Petty in his trademark #43 in '91, a year before he retired.

One of his lessor-known records is his position of eighth on the top 200 mph qualifiers for eight times—a record that most likely will not be broken.

Adam

Adam Petty is the first fourth-generation driver in motorsports, a fact Richard Petty points outs proudly. Adam is headed for the same Winston Cup trail as his father, grandfather and great-grandfather. After some ASA and ARCA races in 1997 and '98, Adam, the son of Kyle Petty, took on a full schedule of BGN racing in 1999. There he raced the likes of Dale Earnhardt Jr. and Jason Jarrett. If plans hold true, he will join his father, Kyle, in Winston Cup in the near future. Will he end up in the famous #43 or strike out on his own with #45? Time will tell.

ever will. Richard is firmly entrenched on the top of the all time win list with 200 checkered flags, 158 second place finishes and 126 pole positions. Petty won an amazing 27 races out of 48 in 1967, came close again in 1971 with 21 wins out of 46 and earned a career total of $7.75 million in prize money, back in the days when purses were a fraction of what they are today.

Other Petty records that still stand include: most career superspeedway wins with 55; most short track wins with 139 career and 24 in one season; most consecutive race wins with 10; most wins at one track (15 each at North Wilkesboro and Martinsville); most wins from the pole (61) and 15 in one season; most career starts (1,177). In addition, he was voted Most Popular Driver nine times, and is tied with Dale Earnhardt with seven Winston Cup Championships.

Petty retired as a driver in 1992, but he continues to campaign number 43 as a car owner.

Kyle

The next generation of Petty is Richard's son, Kyle. When Kyle won his first race in 1979, an ARCA event, his future was set. Driving stints for the Wood Brothers, Felix Sabates and his Dad would follow, and he got his first Winston Cup win in 1986. Today, Kyle owns and drives his own team, called PE2 (for Petty Enterprises 2) with Dad as partner. To date, he has 8 Winston Cup wins, tied for 45th overall on the career win list. Always the outspoken one, and often very entertaining with his quick wit, Kyle is as at home on TV as he is behind the wheel.

Kyle Petty was never afraid to speak his mind. The younger Petty had quite a reputation to live up to, and made his own mark.

RICKY RUDD

Ricky Rudd began racing in motocross and go-karts in the late 1960s, and first drove a Winston Cup car in 1975. He paid his dues and came close several times, but he wouldn't win a Winston Cup race until 1983. Then he began an amazing streak of winning at least one race every year through 1997, when he won one of the biggest races of them all, the Brickyard 400. He lists that Indy win as his all-time favorite. The Rudd streak continued in 1998 with a tough win at a hot Martinsville, Virginia. The likable owner/driver Rudd now "owns" the record all by himself at 16 years straight and still counting going into the 1999 season.

Early in his career, Ricky ran cars owned by his dad before driving for notable owners Richard Childress, Bud Moore and Kenny Bernstein. He then drove four years for Rick Hendrick before starting his own team, sponsored by Tide detergent, in 1994. He says that being an owner provides an exciting second life in Winston Cup racing. But he says that the most exciting part of racing is still "going for the green flag."

Ricky Rudd is best known for his skills on the few road courses NASCAR runs. He's won a number of them and is always considered as the man to beat at places like Watkins Glen and Sonoma. Consistency has been the key to his successful career as well, which has resulted in a second in 1991, a fifth in 1994, and a sixth place finished three times in points standings. He is still hunting for that first Winston Cup championship, which may still be just around the corner.

WENDELL SCOTT

Although you may not find Wendell Scott at the top of any NASCAR record books, his accomplishments in the sport deserve special recognition, mainly because he achieved so much with so little, and against so many odds.

Scott started his career in the late 1930s, at a time when racism dictated that blacks have separate facilities. Scott, who is African-American, never had much support and did most all of his own mechanical work. However, early in his career, Scott won an astounding 127 Modified and Sportsman races.

In 1961, he felt that his equipment was good enough to compete with the top drivers in NASCAR, even though he had very little budget. According to Scott, there were a number of drivers that were unhappy with his presence and made things pretty tough for him on and off the track. However, he persevered, and won his first and only race in 1963. He continued to compete, mostly with second-hand cars from the previous year. In 1969, he competed in 51 races and finished in the top 10 eleven times, his best ever season. In all, Scott competed in 495 Grand National and Winston Cup races, an unbelievable feat for such a low-budget operation.

The final year of his driving career was 1973. That year, Scott was driving in a competitive Junior Johnson car, one of his best rides ever, when he was involved in a huge crash at Talladega and suffered serious injuries. He would drive his final Winston Cup race later that year, finishing 12th at Charlotte.

Scott was portrayed in a 1977 movie called "Greased Lightning" by actor/comedian Richard Pryor. At the time, Scott indicated that the movie accurately portrayed how difficult it was to be black in a predominantly white sport. While he will be remembered by many as the first African-American to win a stock car race, those who knew Wendell personally remember him as a determined and skilled racer who excelled at a career he truly loved. He still is a role model for many African-American racers, some of whom display his name on their cars as a form of dedication.

Rick Rickard photo.

BOB SENNEKER

Mention the term "Blue Bird" to any Late Model pavement stock car racing fan and they will tell you it's the name of the distinctive blue #84 cars ASA superstar Bob Senneker has driven over the years.

Senneker has competed against and beaten top-notch Winston Cup drivers such as Mark Martin, Alan Kulwicki, Rusty Wallace, Ted Musgrave, and Johnny Benson when they were climbing the ladder through ASA on the way to Winston Cup. Senneker has proven that he's got the talent, but the lucky breaks just haven't come his way.

Although he has many wins, Senneker has only won the ASA title once (1990), but that certainly isn't indicative of his credible skills. He's come close a number of other times with three seconds, four thirds, three fourths, and four fifths. As you can see, consistency is the cornerstone of his remarkable career.

Bob began his ASA career in 1973, the first year for the series. His best seasons were 1984 with nine wins, 1977 with eight and 1982 with seven. In all, he has won 82 ASA events and is the overall leader in career ASA earnings.

BRUTON SMITH

Bruton Smith has but one simple goal: To provide the fans with the finest racing experience possible. Smith has done more to revolutionize the sport from the fans' perspective than any other owner/promoter, and has set trends that other track owners are forced to follow.

His flagship racing track is Charlotte Motor Speedway, which is one of the most luxurious facilities on the circuit. But he has been in an acquisition mode, adding Atlanta, Bristol, Sears Point, Las Vegas and Texas Motor Speedway to his stable of tracks. Once part of the Speedway Motorsports group, they receive extensive upgrading often with condominiums for sale where people live year round. The first condos he built at Charlotte were looked upon with some amusement by skeptics. Who would want to live at a race track? But now, when Smith announces condos will be built at one of his new tracks, they are usually sold out before construction even starts.

Smith was the first to include office and year round entertainment facilities, such as restaurants and clubs, at the tracks and they, too, have been very successful. When driving by Charlotte and its Speedway Club building, it's

hard not to think that it is downtown Charlotte.

Smith's dream of making his own track from scratch was realized as Texas Motor Speedway where he said he wanted a track that would still be around 100 years from now. No expense was spared and after a little tweaking, the facility did surface as one of the best in all of racing.

There was a time when there were rumors he would make his own stock car circuit. Bruton continues to amaze race fans and those inside the sport on a regular basis with new standards for race tracks. There is usually no exposed concrete, with virtually everything freshly painted or clad with fan-friendly materials. There's always something to see at a Speedway Motorsports track and vendors are not at all far away from just about any seat.

Part of those ever-raising standards come from promotion. At Charlotte, the promoter is Humpy Wheeler. Cut from the P. T. Barnum mold, Humpy has elevated pre-show entertainment to a new art form. Stunts, military fly-bys and operations are but a few of the items Humpy uses to get more people out to the track. As far as the actu-

al racing goes, Charlotte is the home of the longest stock car race, the Coca-Cola World 600, was the first super-speedway to run under the lights, and hosts The Winston, one of NASCAR's few all star style events. Bruton Smith and his people also ran the first nighttime Indycar race.

Realizing that not everyone has the money to fund a Winston Cup operation, Smith and his SMI group came up with the idea of a national league of smaller, less expensive racers called Legends. These economical cars are now racing nationally with great success.

DICK TRICKLE

Although younger fans probably tell you that Dick Trickle's career has revolved around NASCAR competition, veteran fans will tell you that NASCAR was the final leg of a great racing career that included over 500 wins in various stock car racing series. One can wonder what Dick would have done had he gotten his chance at the big time during his younger days.

But even though his NASCAR career was contested while Dick was in his 50s, the skills groomed with the American Speed Association and other short track organizations are still in place. Since 1989, Dick has been a fixture on the Winston Cup trail running with a number of different teams. That first full season saw him show six top five and nine top ten finishes. For that effort, he was the Winston Cup Rookie of the Year running for the Stavola Brothers.

It was for the ASA running in the 1970s and '80s, though, that many remember Dick Trickle. He won the ASA title twice and is near the top in all ASA categories.

The title years are 1984 and 1985. In just over 200 ASA starts, Trickle won 32 races against many competitors who were on their way to Winston Cup. He also got the pole position 45 times, and led an amazing 6,662 laps.

His driving skill is possibly exceeded only by his capability to set up, repair and maintain his cars. There was none better mechanically than Dick Trickle. He was definitely a driver from the old school and would most likely have had more success in Winston Cup had he raced 25 years earlier.

Trickle accepts the trophy for one of his 7 consecutive ARTGO wins, in 1979. He had 5 of those wins in one 24-hour period! ARTGO photo.

CURTIS TURNER

He was tough, sported handsome good looks, came from hard times in his youth, but most of all could really drive the wheels off a stock car. He was loved by the fans and put on a great show. Unfortunately, his competitive, combative nature sometimes clashed with Bill France Sr.—sometimes in a big way.

In 1961, as an already an established star, Turner tried to unionize the top NASCAR drivers, which infuriated France. During the union confrontation, Turner also had plans for building a superspeedway of his own just north of Charlotte, North Carolina, which didn't work out. France had had enough, and suspended him from NASCAR racing. He wouldn't relent until 1967, when Turner returned in the famous gold and black number 13 Chevelle built by Smokey Yunick. Showing he hadn't lost his touch, he put the highly controversial car on the pole for the Daytona 500. While he didn't win the 1967 race, he did attract a great deal of attention, which was Turner's style.

Off the track, he enjoyed a reputation as a hard partier. On the track, though, Turner was a tough competitor, and was called "Pops" by the other drivers—not because of his age, but because of his tendency to "pop" other drivers off the track when they got in his way. But the fans still adored him, and voted him "Most Popular Driver" in 1956.

He ran his first NASCAR race at the old Langhorne Speedway in Pennsylvania. Many other wins would quickly follow. During 1956-1959, Turner was one of the stars in the highly popular NASCAR Convertible Division. In the first season, he roared to an amazing 22 wins. The convertibles were popular with fans, because they could get a clear view of their favorite drivers sawing at the wheel as they powered through the turns. Nine more victories came the following year in 1957, including four straight and three straight on two occasions. By the time the ragtop series had ended, Turner had recorded 38 wins. In the Grand National Division, Curtis scored 18 wins and 18 poles, most in Fords, and despite the six-year ban imposed by France. One has to wonder what he might have been able to do if he'd raced those six prime years.

Like many of today's top drivers, Curtis owned and flew a private plane. Ironically, even though he'd survived many crashes in his day as a driver, he would die at the wheel of his small plane when it crashed into a Pennsylvania hillside in 1970.

DARRELL WALTRIP

Darrell Waltrip got his first taste of speed in a go-kart at age 12. Four years later, he sat in his first stock car, and he's been in that mode of racing ever since. His first race car was a '36 Chevy Coupe that he ran at the local dirt track near his Owensboro, Kentucky, hometown.

He quickly proved himself to be one of the nation's top short track drivers, efforts which paid off quickly when he jumped to Winston Cup in 1972, making his debut at Talladega for a semi-permanent ride. His first race car at that race was the same one that won the 1967 Daytona 500 with Mario Andretti driving. The Holman and Moody car was refitted with Mercury sheetmetal for this first race, even though it was five years old. Taking occasional rides for others and driving his own car when he could, he wouldn't land a full-time Winston Cup ride until 1975, when he promptly set about making history.

Waltrip's accomplishments during the 1970s and 1980s were the result of both innate driving excellence and consistency. During these two decades, he won three championships (1981, 1982, and 1985), was second three times (1979, 1983, and 1986), finished third in 1978, fourth in 1977, 1987, and 1989, and fifth in 1980 and 1984.

Much of Waltrip's success came when he was teamed with legendary car owner Junior Johnson. For six seasons the pair roared to 43 of his 84 career victories (third on the all-time win list, with 37 on superspeedways) before Waltrip moved on to the Rick Hendrick stable. With the Hendrick/Tide ride, he accomplished one of his long-term goals. In 1989, Darrell made his 17th trip to the Daytona 500, driving car number 17, and finally won the great American race. In Victory Lane, he celebrated with a dance and slam-dunked his helmet into the ground for the jubilant crowd.

At the time this was written, Waltrip was still an active

driver, although as a substitute only. He sold his team in 1998, and is scheduled to retire at the end of the 2000 season. Waltrip will always be remembered as one of the finest to ever turn a wheel on a stock car track.

WOOD BROTHERS

Few teams in NASCAR history raced as long and as hard as the one owned by Glen and Leonard Wood (Leonard is in the photo at right), known simply as "The Wood Brothers." Hailing from the sleepy Civil War town of Stuart, Virginia, this family operation has been NASCAR racing since 1953, when they campaigned the first of a long series of #21 Ford and Mercury race cars. The drivers that have driven for them is a "who's who" list of NASCAR's finest. Glen Wood, with his brother Leonard as crew chief, fielded cars for Junior Johnson, Speedy Thompson, Curtis Turner, Marvin Panch, Freddie Lorenzen, Dan Gurney, A. J. Foyt, Cale Yarborough and Parnelli Jones in the early days. In the modern era (recognized as '72 on) the list is no less impressive, with Donnie Allison, David Pearson, Neil Bonnett, Buddy Baker, Kyle Petty, Dale Jarrett and Morgan Shepard taking their turns at the wheel. David Pearson was at the wheel during some of their most successful seasons.

Together, the trio won an amazing 43 races in the red and white, Purolator-sponsored Fords and Mercurys, a feat even more astounding considering that the Wood Bros. never ran more than 22 races a season.

The Wood Bros. also were well-known for hiring a ringer or two, in particular, Dan Gurney, who was primarily a road course driver, to race at Riverside Raceway in California. Gurney won so many times that others started calling it "the Dan Gurney race." But the Woods could build a car to win on anything. Their record of 12 wins at Daytona (including both Daytona 500 and Pepsi 400 events) is still unbeaten as of this writing.

The Wood Brothers were also one of the first to realize just how important pit stops were to winning, and drilled their crew until they excelled over all the others. They developed new, faster air wrenches and quicker-lifting hydraulic jacks. It wasn't long before other teams took note, and adopted the Wood Bros.'s techniques. In fact, even Indycar teams brought them in for consultation at the Indy 500.

The Wood Brothers team is one of the most successful in history. The tally as of this writing is 96 wins and 116 pole positions, including Michael Waltrip's win at the '96 Winston all-star race. Wood Brothers Racing is now run by the next generation, their sons, Eddie and Len Wood. With success in their genes, watch for another span of wins from the #21 team from Virginia.

CALE YARBOROUGH

If you had to sum up Cale Yarborough with just one word, it would have to be "tough." Perhaps his greatest, most significant achievement is that, to date, he is the only driver to win three consecutive Winston Cup championships. He did it driving for Junior Johnson in 1976, 1977 and 1978. Yarborough is fifth on the all-time win list with 83 and holds the record as the only NASCAR driver to pass the magic 200 mph mark or better 15 times. That statistic shows why Yarborough is also known for being tied at third on the all-time superspeedway win list with 47, and second on the superspeedway pole winners list with 46. Even when Yarborough's poles are tallied for all types of tracks, he is still third on the list with 70. In addition, he is tied for most consecutive wins (4, with Darrell Waltrip, Dale Earnhardt, Harry Gant, Bill Elliott, Mark Martin, Jeff Gordon), has the most wins in a short track season (7, in 1976) and most poles in a season (14 in 1980). Some of his years were seasons with a limited schedule as he wanted to cut back before actually retiring.

Yarborough began driving his own car, and got his first Winston Cup win, in 1965. He jumped into the factory wars, dueling Petty and Pearson, while driving for the Wood Bros. in the late '60s, racking up 13 wins for them. He joined Junior Johnson's operation in 1973 and drove for him until 1980. During that time, he won an amazing 55 races in car #11, including those three consecutive championships already noted. Consistency was the key to those three titles as the team ran all 90 scheduled races in three years and only failed to finish seven times. After leaving Junior, he drove the #28 for Harry Ranier in what would be the first NASCAR modern day qualifying lap of over 200 mph at the Daytona 500 in 1984. But on the very next lap, the car took off like an airplane. Yarborough was not hurt in this spectacular crash, but he only continued to drive until 1988, when he retired. However, he turned his considerable talents to owning and managing a team, where it didn't take long for him to be competitive once again.

ROBERT YATES

Robert Yates has a little known secret. Though he is long associated with Ford race cars, his many fans are unaware that the man they think is devoted to Ford is partially responsible for the return of archrival Chevrolet to NASCAR racing in the early 1970s.

Robert was working at the Ford arm of NASCAR, Holman & Moody, when he was approached to build some engines for the new Chevy Monte Carlos that were ordered by the promoter of Charlotte Motor Speedway. The idea was to draw long-suffering Chevy fans to the track. Robert asked permission and was cleared for the night job at Junior Johnson's. Little did anyone know the stunt would end up with Chevy not only returning in earnest but winning big for the next 25-plus years. Those Chevys that started out as a gimmick would be the very cars Robert would have to square off against race after race.

After Holman & Moody dissolved, the Charlotte-born Yates went to work at Junior Johnson's shop, heading up the teams' first engine department. His Chevy engines scored an impressive 24 top-three finishes for Junior's Chevy, now driven by Bobby Allison. It would be the beginning of a long relationship with the Allison family.

Robert joined the DiGard team for Darrell Waltrip's first full season where the team grabbed 10 top ten finishes, three poles and ended up eighth in points for 1976. He stayed with DiGard for another four years when the team became a powerhouse in NASCAR with a total of 24 wins with Waltrip in the driver's seat. Bobby Allison then joined on and in 1983, the DiGard team won the title over Waltrip—Allison's and Yates's only championship to date. One factor that allowed the team to clinch the title was found in Robert's motors—consistency. For the schedule of 30 races, the red and white Miller Beer car nabbed an amazing 25 top ten finishes with six of them wins. The next year, 1984, Robert built DiGard engines for the last two wins of the King, Richard Petty, numbers 199 at Dover, Delaware, and number 200 at the historic July Daytona race.

In 1986, he joined Ranier/Lundy racing, the #28 car with Cale Yarborough driving. The 11,000 square foot shop they used near downtown Charlotte was the basis for the one he uses today. After numerous additions, the current shop is five times its original size.

The very next year is when the team not only hired Davey Allison, but put the rookie on the Daytona front row at 209 mph, a two-way record for a rookie. It was the first of five poles for Davey and Robert and was capped off with two rookie year wins, another first. In 1987, Robert was serving as engine builder and crew chief and had the opportunity to purchase the team and did just that.

The rest, as they say, is history, as Allison and Yates set a number of records and had over four years together

before Davey was killed in his helicopter accident. At the time of death, Davey was ranked ninth in winnings with over $6 million dollars earned with Yates.

Since then, working with drivers such as Ernie Irvan, Dale Jarrett and now Kenny Irwin, Yates has proven himself as a man who can spot talent. Irwin joined the team and despite having to wring out the brand-new Ford Taurus race car, placed the car on the front row and finished in the top ten. This feat is reminiscent of Davey Allison and rates Irwin as the only active driver to complete such a feat. Time and time again Robert Yates Racing (RYR) is always a threat to win any time they show up at the track. The first year as a two-car team, the team nabbed the Daytona 500, the Coca-Cola World 600 at Charlotte and the Brickyard 400 at Indy. The man who always seems to be smiling is one of the most loved and respected in the NASCAR garage.

SMOKEY YUNICK

Smokey Yunick never drove his own distinctive gold and black cars. He didn't have to. Drivers just about lined up to get into them as everyone knew the #13 cars from Daytona Beach's "Best Damn Garage in Town" were sure to be the fastest thing on the track. Known for his innovated, rules-bending technology, Smokey's cars were usually found at the front of the pack.

During the height of the 1967 factory wars between Ford and Mopar, Smokey brought a totally home-built Chevy Chevelle to Daytona and handed the keys to Curtis Turner. Having driven for Smokey in the past, Turner knew exactly what to do and promptly put the Chevy on the pole for the Daytona 500. The car remains controversial to this day despite the fact it was completely destroyed a few weeks later attempting to qualify for an Atlanta race. The technology Smokey used in this car was a forerunner of today's Winston Cup car. It was a transition period, when race cars were becoming much more purpose-built for racing from the ground up, rather than modified street cars. Smokey didn't quit tinkering when he stopped owning cars as he was heavily involved with the GM/Buick V6's used in Busch Grand National racing.

One of the best stories about Smokey and the #13 Chevelle is, as Smokey says, "a great story but just not true." It took place a year after Curtis Turner put the car on the pole in 1967. For the 1968 Daytona 500, Smokey had brought in another sleek looking #13 Chevelle. As the fictional story goes, Smokey's car was going through NASCAR inspection. It had gotten to the part where the fuel cell/gas tank was removed from the car, to check it for holding the correct amount of fuel. Smokey was given a list of items wrong with the car that had to be corrected before they would let the car out for practice. The story goes that Smokey got fed up with the 12 things NASCAR had thought wrong with the car and said, "Well, make it 13." With that statement, he threw the gas tank, still empty and disconnected, into the back seat of the car, climbed in and fired it up and drove it away—much to the amazement of the officials and others in the garage!

The car was never allowed to race and Smokey later sold it. Twenty years later, in 1988, Smokey found the car, bought it and restored it. When he brought the finished car to Daytona to photograph it, they still didn't want the car on the track. Shortly after the restoration, the car was auctioned off for $100,000.

NASCAR STATS & RECORDS

Note: The following information is current through the end of the 1998 season. It is subject to change from that point on. After all, records were made to be broken.

NASCAR GRAND NATIONAL & WINSTON CUP CHAMPIONS
BUSCH GRAND NATIONAL CHAMPIONS

Winston Cup Champions 1949-1998

1949–Red Byron, Olds 88
1950–Bill Rexford, Olds 88
1951–Herb Thomas, Hudson
1952–Tim Flock, Hudson
1953–Herb Thomas, Hudson
1954–Lee Petty, Chrysler
1955–Tim Flock, Chrysler
1956–Buck Baker, Chrysler
1957–Buck Baker, Chevy
1958–Lee Petty, Olds
1959–Lee Petty, Plymouth
1960–Rex White, Chevy
1961–Ned Jarrett, Chevy
1962–Joe Weatherly, Pontiac
1963–Joe Weatherly, Mercury
1964–Richard Petty, Plymouth
1965–Ned Jarrett, Ford
1966–David Pearson, Dodge
1967–Richard Petty, Plymouth
1968–David Pearson, Ford
1969–David Pearson, Ford
1970–Bobby Isaac, Dodge
1971–Richard Petty, Plymouth
1972–Richard Petty, Dodge
1973–Benny Parsons, Chevy
1974–Richard Petty, Dodge
1975–Richard Petty, Dodge
1976–Cale Yarborough, Chevy
1977–Cale Yarborough, Chevy
1978–Cale Yarborough, Olds
1979–Richard Petty, Chevy
1980–Dale Earnhardt, Chevy
1981–Darrell Waltrip, Buick
1982–Darrell Waltrip, Buick

1983–Bobby Allison, Buick
1984–Terry Labonte, Chevy
1985–Darrell Waltrip, Chevy
1986–Dale Earnhardt, Chevy
1987–Dale Earnhardt, Chevy
1988–Bill Elliott, Ford
1989–Rusty Wallace, Pontiac
1990–Dale Earnhardt, Chevy
1991–Dale Earnhardt, Chevy
1992–Alan Kulwicki, Ford
1993–Dale Earnhardt, Chevy
1994–Dale Earnhardt, Chevy
1995–Jeff Gordon, Chevy
1996–Terry Labonte, Chevy
1997–Jeff Gordon, Chevy
1998–Jeff Gordon, Chevy

Busch Grand National Champions 1982–1998

1982–Jack Ingrim
1983–Sam Ard
1984–Sam Ard
1985–Jack Ingrim
1986–Larry Pearson
1987–Larry Pearson
1988–Tommy Ellis
1989–Rob Moroso
1990–Chuck Bown
1991–Bobby Labonte
1992–Joe Nemecheck
1993–Steve Grissom
1994–David Green
1995–Johnny Benson Jr.
1996–Randy LaJoie
1997–Randy LaJoie
1998–Dale Earnhardt Jr.

All-Time Winston Cup Race Winners (1949-1998)

1. Richard Petty	200	Ricky Rudd	19
2. David Pearson	105	Buddy Baker	19
3. Bobby Allison	84	Davey Allison	19
Darrell Waltrip	84	Fonty Flock	19
4. Cale Yarborough	83	20. Geoff Bodine	18
5. Dale Earnhardt	71	Harry Gant	18
6. Lee Petty	55	Neil Bonnett	18
7. Ned Jarrett	50	21. Marvin Panch	17
Junior Johnson	50	Curtis Turner	17
8. Herb Thomas	48	22. Dale Jarrett	15
Rusty Wallace	48	Ernie Irvan	15
9. Buck Baker	46	23. Dick Hutcherson	14
10. Jeff Gordon	43	Lee Roy Yarbrough	14
11. Bill Elliott	40	24. Tim Richmond	13
Tim Flock	40	Dick Rathman	13
12. Bobby Isaac	37	25. Donnie Allison	10
13. Fireball Roberts	32	26. Cotton Owens	9
14. Mark Martin	29	Paul Goldsmith	9
15. Fred Lorenzen	26	27. Kyle Petty	8
Rex White	26	28. Jim Reed	7
16. Jim Paschel	24	AJ Foyt	7
Joe Weatherly	24	Bob Welborn	7
17. Benny Parsons	21	Marshall Teague	7
Jack Smith	21	Darrell Dieringer	7
18. Speedy Thompson	20		
19. Terry Labonte	19		

All-Time Winston Cup Pole Winners (1949-1998)

1. Richard Petty	55	11. Davey Allison	14
2. David Pearson	49	Ricky Rudd	14
3. Bobby Allison	47	12. Harry Gant	13
Cale Yarborough	47	Mark Martin	13
4. Dale Earnhardt	43	13. Fred Lorenzen	12
5. Bill Elliott	37	Benny Parsons	12
6. Darrell Waltrip	32	14. Fireball Roberts	10
7. Jeff Gordon	21	Lee Roy Yarbrough	10
8. Rusty Wallace	20	15. Terry Labonte	9
9. Buddy Baker	17	Donnie Allison	9
10. Neil Bonnett	15		

Alberta Northwest Late Models
403-963-9606
Site 2, Box 38, RR1, Carvel, Alberta T0E 0H0 Canada
Sanction: Canadian Late Model Stock Cars

Allied Auto Racing Association
314-928-1716
3929 Summertime Drive, St Charles, MO 63303
Sanction: Modifieds, Late Models, and Street Stocks

American Motor Racing Assoc.
614-622-7316
P.O. Box 1136, Coshocton, OH 43812
Sanction: Modifieds and Stock Cars

American Speed Assoc. (ASA)
765-778-8088
550 North Pendleton Avenue, Pendleton, IN 46064
Sanction: Pavement Late Models

American Racing Club of America (ARCA)
313-847-6726
P.O. Box 5217, Toledo, OH 43611
Sanction: Pavement Late Models, Race Trucks

Busch All-Star Series
904-253-0611
P.O. Box 2875, Daytona Beach, FL 32120
Sanction: Dirt Late Models

Canadian Association for Stock Car Auto Racing (CASCAR)
519-641-1214
9763 Glendon Drive, Komoka,

ON M0L 1R0 Canada
Sanction: Pavement Late Models

Dirt Motorsports, Inc. (DIRT)
315-834-6606
1 Speedway Drive, P.O. Box 240, Weedsport, NY 13166
Sanction: Modifieds

Dwarf Cars, USA
602-495-9869
P.O. Box 25794, Tempe, AZ 85285
Sanction: Dwarf Cars

Florida Pro Series
904-755-9302
Route 3, Box 175-K, Lake City, FL 32024
Sanction: Pavement Late Models

Gold Star Series
612-440-1994
13442 Zarthan Avenue South, Savage, MN 55378
Sanction: Pavement Late Models

IMCA Deery Brothers Series,
319-472-2201
P.O. Box 921, Vinton, IA 52349
Sanction: Dirt Late Models

Iceman Super Car Series(ISCS)
419-729-1634
5639 Benore Road, Toledo, OH 43612
Sanction: Pavement Late Models

Inex Corporation(INEX)
704-455-3896
5245 NC 49 South, Harrisburg, NC 28075
Sanction: Legend Cars

International Championship Auto Racing
219-747-3427
P.O. Box 9126, Fort Wayne, IN 46899
Sanction: Modifieds

International Motor Contest Associates—Canada
403-779-2218
Box 68, Youngstown AB T0J 3P0 Canada
Sanction: Modifieds, Stock cars, Late Models

Internation Motor Contest Association (IMCA)
319-472-2201
P.O. Box 921, Vinton, IA 52349
Sanction: Modifieds, Late Models, Stock Cars

International Race of Champions (IROC)
908-542-4762
45 Park Road, Tinton Falls, NJ 07724
Sanction: IROC Stock Cars

Keystone Legends Assn. of Stock Car Auto Racers
610-395-5303
P.O. Box 75, Orefield, PA 18069
Sanction: Legend Cars

Main Event Racing Series
740-922-4851
121 North Water Street, Uhrichsville, OH 44683
Sanction: Pavement Late Models

Maritime Assn. of Stock Car Auto Racing (MASCAR)
506-849-3686

11 Donald Road, Wells, NB E2S 1A7 Canada
Sanction: Canadian Late Models

Michigan Modified Assoc.
517-834-5796
P.O. Box 1, Owosso, MI 48866
Sanction: Modifieds

Mid-American Stock Car Series
414-849-7036
P.O. Box 227, Chilton, WI 53014
Sanction: Stock Cars

Mid-Atlantic Championship Series
412-349-7978
P.O. Box 13, Creekside, PA 15732
Sanction: Dirt Late Models

Mid-Atlantic Modified Tour
804-744-7943
P.O. Box 13234, Richmond, VA 23225
Sanction: Modifieds

Mid-State Vintage Stock Car Club(MVSCC)
315-782-7216
P.O. Box 62, Calcium, NY 13616
Sanction: Vintage Modifieds

Midwest Allstar Racing Series
920-849-4551
Sanction: Pavement Late Models

Midwest Classic Racers
313-839-1233
P.O. Box 1796, Troy MI 48099
Sanction: Dwarf Cars

Midwest Independent Superlate Series
517-787-7212
P.O. Box 6390, Jackson, MI 49201
Sanction: Pavement Late Models

Midwest Late Model Racing Assn. (MLRA)
816-650-5063
324 South Buckner Tarsney Rd., Buckner, MO 64016
Sanction: Dirt Late Models

Modified Stock Racing Assoc.
714-498-2823
2731 Via Santo Tomas, San Clemente, CA 92672
Sanction: Four-Cylinder Late Models

National Association for Stock Car Auto Racing (NASCAR)
904-253-0611
P.O. Box 2875, Daytona Beach, FL 32120
Sanction: Winston Cup, Busch Grand National, Trucks, Goody's Dash, along with a number of regional series

National Championship Racing Association
918-836-4242
1211 South 101 East Avenue, Tulsa, OK 74128
Sanction: Late Model Stock

National Late Model Sportsman
334-653--8921
Sanction: Dirt Late Models

Northeast Pro Stock Association
207-873-4022
P.O. Box 98, East Vassalboro, ME 04935

Sanction: Pavement Late Models

Northern Allstars Late Model Series, Inc.
812-689-4899
641 Columbia Avenue, Osgood, IN 47037
Sanction: Dirt Late Models

Ontario Stock Car Assn. of Asphalt Racers
519-343-3949
P.O. Box 239, Palmerston, ON N0G 2P0 Canada
Sanction: Pavement Late Models

Professional Racing Organization
603-433-8448
P.O. Box 4327, Portsmouth, NH 03802
Sanction: Race Trucks

Rally Race Trucks
614-622-7316
P.O. Box 1136, Coshocton, OH 43812
Sanction: Race trucks

Short Track Auto Racing (STARS)
330-682-3053
8848 Ely Rod, Apple Creek, OH 44606
Sanction: Dirt Late Models

Short Track Super Trucks
414-849-7036
Box 3227, Chilton, WI 53014
Sanction: Race Trucks

Six-Pack Series
305-821-6644
Sanction: Pavement Late Models

Southern All-Star Racing (Pavement)
205-539-4484
1300 Meridian St, Huntsville, AL 35801
Sanction: Late Models, Modifieds

Southern All-Star Racing (Dirt)
205-539-4484
1300 Meridian St, Huntsville, AL 35801
Sanction: Dirt Late Models

Southern Auto Racing Assn.
813-847-2747
7030 Osteen Road, New Port Richey, FL 34653
Sanction: Modifieds

Southern United Professional Racing
504-275-5060
12561 South Choctaw, Baton Rouge, LA 70815
Sanction: Dirt Late Models

Sunoco American Late Model
937-338-3815
13929 State Route 118, New Weston, OH 45348
Sanction: Dirt Late Models

Texas Int. Drivers Assn. (TIDI)
210-655-3222
3222 Leyte, San Antonio, TX 78217
Sanction: Dirt Late Models

United Dirt Track Racing Association (UDTRA)
770-516-6717
P.O. Box 2300, Woodstock, GA 30188
Sanction: Dirt Late Models

United Midwest Promoters (UMP)
812-473-4412
5010 Winding Way, Evansville, IN 47711
Sanction: Dirt Late Models

United Speed Alliance Racing
770-719-0204
125 Commerce Drive, Suite D, Fayetteville, GA 30214
Sanction: Hooters and Pro Cup Stock Cars and Modifieds

United States Racing Assoc.
319-373-7771
P.O. Box 1368, Cedar Rapids, IA 53406
Sanction: Modifieds

USA Demolition Derby & Fig. 8
313-483-0574
6440 Denton Road, Belleville, MI 48111
Sanction: Demo Cars and Fig. 8

West Coast Auto Racing (WCAR)
310-374-1133
323 Ardmore Ave, Hermosa Beach, CA 90254
Sanction: Stock Cars and Dwarf Cars

Western All-Star Late Model Series
800/908-6800
Sanction: Dirt Late Model

WSSOTA Promoters Assoc.
612-428-3600
21601 John Deere Lane, Rogers, MN 55374
Sanction: Dirt Late Models, Modifieds

INDEX